Virginia Woolf

The Marriage of Heaven and Hell

Peter Dally

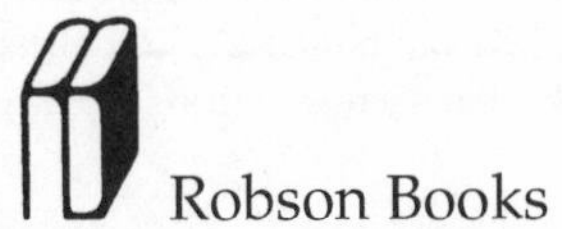
Robson Books

First published in Great Britain in 1999 by Robson Books, 10 Blenheim Court, Brewery Road, London N7 9NT

British Library Cataloguing in Publication Data
A catalogue record for this book is available from the British Library

ISBN 1 86105 219 7

Typeset by Pitfold Design, Hindhead, Surrey.
Printed and bound in Great Britain by
WBC Book Manufacturers, Bridgend, Mid Glamorgan.

Contents

Acknowledgements

I am grateful to the Librarian, University of Sussex Library for permission to quote from the Leonard Woolf papers; the Society of Authors as the Literary Representative of the Estate of Virginia Woolf to quote from 'On Being Ill', *Three Guineas, The Voyage Out, Mrs Dalloway, The Waves, To The Lighthouse*, 'Professions for Women' all published by the Hogarth Press; the Executors of the Estate of Virginia Woolf for extracts from *The Diary of Virginia Woolf*, edited by Anne Olivier Bell (the Hogarth Press), *The Letters of Virginia Woolf*, edited by Nigel Nicolson (the Hogarth Press), *Moments of Being*, edited and introduced by Jeanne Schulkind (the Hogarth Press), *A Passionate Apprentice: the Early Journals of Virginia Woolf*, edited by Mitchell A. Leaska (the Hogarth Press), *A Very Close Conspiracy* by Jane Dunn (Jonathan Cape); Quentin Bell's *Biography of Virginia Woolf*, vols 1 and 2 (the Hogarth Press), *The Autobiography of Leonard Woolf*, vols. 1 and 2 (the Hogarth Press), *The Letters of Vita Sackville-West to Virginia Woolf*, edited by Louise DeSalvo and Mitchell A. Leaska (Hutchinson), *Lytton Strachey: the New Biography*, by Michael Holroyd (Chatto & Windus); *Deceived with Kindness; A Bloomsbury Childhood*, by Angelica Garnett (Chatto & Windus); Oxford University Press for allowing extracts of *The Prose and Poetry Writings of William Cowper*, vol. 1, edited by James King and Charles Ryskamp, Leslie Stephen's *The Mausoleum Book*, introduced by Alan Bell (Clarendon Press); *Anny Thackeray Ritchie* by Winifred Gerin, and *Tennyson* by Robert

Bernard Martin; John Lehmann's *Virginia Woolf and Her World* (Thames & Hudson); Orion Publishing for allowing extracts from *The Letters of Leonard Woolf*, edited by Frederic Spotts (Weidenfeld & Nicolson), *Vita and Harold: the Letters to Vita Sackville-West and Harold Nicolson*, edited by Nigel Nicolson (Weidenfeld & Nicolson), *Leslie Stephen: the Godless Victorian*, by Noel Annan (Weidenfeld & Nicolson), *Vita: the Life of Vita Sackville-West* by Victoria Glendenning (Weidenfeld & Nicolson), and *Vanessa Bell*, by Frances Spalding (Weidenfeld & Nicolson); David Higham Associates for quotes from *Virginia Woolf*, by James King, Leonard Woolf's *The Wise Virgins* (Arnold), *Elders and Betters*, by Quentin Bell (John Murray) and *An Unquiet Mind*, by Kay R. Jamieson (Alfred A. Knopf): Professor Pat Jalland at Melbourne University for extracts from *Octavia Wilberforce* (Cassell) and the *Selected Letters of Vanessa Bell*, edited by Regina Marler (Bloomsbury).

Preface

Books on Virginia Woolf continue to flood the market, but an extraordinary gap exists regarding the illness from which she suffered: manic depression. Her diaries – surely the fullest year-by-year record ever of the effect of the disease on a creative life, work and relationships and, less reliably, her letters and her husband's autobiography, are wonderfully revealing to the trained eye. Yet each new book, even when written by the medically qualified, fails to reveal the effects of Virginia Woolf's mood swings, and the biological and environmental interactions responsible for them.

The four children of Leslie and Julia Stephen were all talented, and from her earliest years Virginia stood out as the story-teller, the writer, the one who would continue the Stephen literary tradition. For most of the year the family lived in London, but summers were spent in St Ives in Cornwall and were the happiest times of Virginia's childhood, their memory kept, squirrel-like, in her creative store. She was highly strung and imaginative, and often difficult, jealously demanding her 'rights'. But in no way unusual; Virginia seemed a thoroughly normal child.

The death of her mother at puberty, followed by that of her half-sister, was devastating, yet she weathered the shock and eventually emerged more or less intact. But during the emotional upheaval, chemicals in the brain that had previously been quiescent stirred into activity and 'switched on' the mental disease that was to influence Virginia's life so profoundly over the next forty years.

Manic depression exists in every known society. It was well described by early Greek physicians, but only during the last century has it been defined and separated from other mental illnesses.

The condition showed itself in a yearly cycle of mood changes: depression in late winter and early spring, and then again in September; elation in the summer, sometimes in November. By the time she was 19 Virginia had come to recognise the pattern and told her cousin, 'My Spring Melancholia is developing into Summer Madness.'[1]

Virginia's fluctuations of mood between depression and high spirits are known as cyclothymia. At first the mood changes were comparatively mild but, when she was 22, after her father's death, she became mad and for almost a year was disabled by manic depression. She recovered but in 1913, following her marriage to Leonard Woolf, she had a second, more violent and prolonged attack of madness.

The distinction between cyclothymia and manic depression is one of degree. Any marked shift of mood results in changed feelings and perception. When Virginia was depressed she saw herself as a failure; a failed writer, a failed woman, dwarfed by her sister, Vanessa. She believed she was old and ugly and impotent. She felt people laughed at and ridiculed her. She became afraid of strangers and filled with anxiety. When 'high' or hypomanic, Virginia felt 'a great mastery over the world',[2] and she 'scarcely wanted children'; she had 'an insatiable desire to write', to show herself off, to socialise, gripped by the 'Spirit of Delight'.[3]

The deeper the mood swing, the more exaggerated the distortions, and eventually fantasy came to replace reality. In severe depression, when this occurs the cyclothyme becomes insane, or mad, and is diagnosed as having manic depression. The depression which Virginia developed without fail between January and March was potentially the most dangerous. Depression at other times was unpleasant, often incapacitating for many weeks, but never led on to hallucinations. All Virginia's breakdowns into insanity had their origin in the New Year period.

Patterns of illness vary individually, but Virginia Woolf had the classic form of the disease: alternating swings of mood occurring with the seasons. Treatment today has improved since her day, but for long-term stability there still remains the need for a trusted understanding partner who can assume temporary command of the patient's life at critical times; a need all too often misunderstood by Virginia Woolf's biographers.

Virginia Woolf

Chapter One

Julia Stephen

Virginia's mother, Julia Stephen, came from a large family renowned for beauty rather than intellect, and although Julia was often gloomy, even melancholic, she was never seriously depressed, and none of her relatives was remotely insane. It is true that Julia's maternal grandfather was a drunk and extravagantly wicked,[1] and that her aunt Julia Margaret Cameron, the renowned Victorian photographer, was a notorious eccentric, but not a manic depressive. Virginia's genetic inheritance for cyclothymia came wholly through her father. Nonetheless, Julia contributed a great deal to Virginia's temperamental instability and indirectly therefore to her mood swings.

Julia was adored by her husband and children, friends, and the many lame dogs, sick and deprived, whom she nursed and supported. She appeared to one and all the essence of goodness and beauty, a true angel both in and outside the house, always prepared to give of her time to those in need.

She was the 'darling of darlings' to her mother, who would have only Julia as attendant during her frequent illnesses. Leslie Stephen, her husband, wanted her continually at his beck and call, to mother and encourage him and lift his self-esteem. When the children fell ill Julia insisted on nursing them herself. Her presence filled the home with light and warmth. Virginia could never have enough of her mother, but she had to be ill or noticeably upset to receive Julia's full attention. No sooner was Virginia better than her mother was off on some other mission of mercy. Had she been challenged she would have responded with, 'To serve is the highest expression of your nature'.[2]

There was a disconcerting contradiction in Julia. She gave her time and attention wholly to those in need, yet she gave little of *herself* and withdrew once her task was done. She was intensely private and it seemed she could not come close to anyone when outside her caring role. Her husband sensed this absence of deep involvement and worried that she did not love him as she had loved her first husband. Julia would never openly admit to loving Leslie after their marriage. He called her a heartless woman and it was only half in jest. Virginia too, fretted: 'I can never remember being alone with her for more than a few minutes.'[3]

Julia never let herself go emotionally. She kept herself and her world under tight control. No one was allowed to take liberties: friends who stepped over the boundary were dropped, an awkward child was despatched to bed and ignored. Her difficult, autistic stepdaughter Laura was sent away to an institution. It was noticeable how much harder Julia was with daughters than with sons.

Beneath Julia's warm and caring exterior was a rigid anxious woman, fearful of exposing her deeper feelings. She never confided. She rarely expressed anger – icy disapproval was her usual reaction – but when it flared up the shock was the greater for being unexpected. It took Leslie by surprise and shook Virginia. 'She would suddenly say something so unexpected, from that Madonna face, one thought it *vicious*.'[4]

In company Julia could be gay, the life and soul of any party. When she was absent Hyde Park Gate became dark and dull for Virginia, despite the merriment of siblings. Leslie's gloomy mood and the resulting stultifying atmosphere were alleviated by her presence. Julia had a gift for drawing out people of all classes and listening to their troubles. She soothed unhappy children to sleep with her stories. She listened patiently to her husband and gave him the encouragement and assurance he wanted. She laughed and chatted in society. But when not engaged, sitting with a book or sewing, signs of melancholia emerged. Virginia used to watch her and came to recognise her sadness, the gloom and silence within. She did not enjoy her existence. She had no wish to end her life but she believed death would be the greatest boon. Her melancholia distressed Leslie; it was somehow deeper, all-embracing and different from Leslie's histrionic depressions. When he chided her for being 'less happy than I could wish', she answered that her contact with 'sufferers' and the 'terrible havoc made by death' outweighed peace and happiness.[5]

It was a woman's duty, Julia declared, to care for her kith and kin, to devote herself to the happiness of her husband and children, and give any time left to others. Women should never put themselves first. Julia was a powerful personality and she stamped herself and her views firmly on her daughters. Not until she was in her mid-forties, writing *To the Lighthouse*, did Virginia begin to loosen the ties with her mother.

Julia's mother, Maria (Mia) Jackson née Pattle, was born in India, the middle of seven sisters, all but one of them renowned for their beauty. Nervous and delicate, she grew up feeling closer to Sara, her next oldest sister, than to her mother. When that sister became engaged, Mia was thrown off balance and lunged headlong into marriage when barely 17 years old.

Her husband was a good-looking Calcutta physician, Dr John Jackson, 14 years her senior. Trained at Westminster Hospital Medical School, he joined the medical services of the Bengal Presidency. He was well regarded professionally, by not only Europeans but 'Indian Ranees and Natives of the highest classes', and lectured at the Medical School of Calcutta.[6] Mia was looking for a prop and perhaps he provided one at first, but before long he began to bore her; she thought him dull, his interests narrow. Like her sister, Mia's main interest lay in the arts, but Dr Jackson was lukewarm. His granddaughter Virginia looked on him in later life as 'a commonplace, prosaic old man',[7] but that was probably pure hearsay, picked up from her parents, for she was only five when he died.

Perhaps another reason for choosing John Jackson as husband was Mia's lifelong valetudinarianism. Nothing pleased her so much as discussing her ailments with a sympathetic, or helpless, listener. Her emotional needs, trivial or otherwise, were transplanted in to bodily discomfort: headaches, indigestion, rheumatic pains, abdominal complaints. Pain was Mia's chief means of communicating boredom, dissatisfactions, and disappointments. Dr Jackson either failed to recognise his wife's signals or, one suspects, turned a blind eye to them. At any rate, the Jacksons' relationship slowly deteriorated.

Mia Jackson produced two daughters and then, after a six-year interval, Julia was born in 1846. Mia at once made Julia the centre of her life to the virtual exclusion of her husband. It is more than likely that Julia's health and, no doubt, her own was the excuse for quitting India when Julia was two and returning to London. Leslie claimed that Julia believed she was her mother's least-loved daughter, although the evidence points to the fact that Mia worshipped Julia.

Dr Jackson stayed on in Calcutta for another seven years after his wife's departure. When he gave up his practice and returned to London, shortly before the Indian Mutiny, he was a stranger in every sense to the nine-year-old Julia. She felt no affection and seems to have been indifferent to his presence, much as her mother was. He set up in medical practice for a time but he had few or no outside interests, and no influence with any of his family. Leslie Stephen observed that 'he did not seem to count as fathers generally count in their families'.[8]

Mia Jackson quickly found her feet in London with the help of her sister Sara and husband Thoby Prinsep. The Prinseps were living in an old converted farmhouse, Little Holland House, in what is now West Kensington. Holland House itself had been the centre of the Whig aristocracy at the beginning of the century and in the 1860s Little Holland House became an 'Aristocracy of Intellect', the 'Temple of the Arts'.[9] Sara Prinsep – known as the 'Principessa' – was the driving force, and the power of her personality, together with the deep interest and involvement she and her husband had in all the arts, attracted painters and writers, and even politicians of the time, to the Sunday afternoon gatherings. Cultural snobs the Prinseps may have been but their home provided a stimulating, Bohemian atmosphere for Mia Jackson and her daughters.

Tall, elegant and handsome, Mia attracted much attention. Thomas Woolner, the pre-Raphaelite sculptor, was loud in his praises for 'the beautiful Mrs Jackson and her three beautiful daughters'. But it was on Julia, as she grew into adolescence, that the painters' eyes became fixed. Burne-Jones took her for his model in *The Annunciation.* G. F. Watts played with her. Holman Hunt and Thomas Woolner each wanted to marry her. Aunt Sara and Uncle Thoby were proud of her. Her mother was delighted, for looks came a close second to illness in Mia Jackson's book.

Julia's beauty was remote, cold and, from the beginning, touched with melancholia. Men put her on a pedestal and admired her from a distance. Part of her reserve came from shyness and a sense of intellectual inferiority – although she spoke French well and knew enough Latin and History to instruct her children in those subjects – but some of it, perhaps, hid boredom. At a party or a picnic on the river she might be seen standing alone and unattended, her mind apparently elsewhere.

Yet Julia, particularly before her second marriage, possessed a warmth that would emerge when she was at ease and enjoying herself. Then her gaiety was infectious and could spread like fire through a room. Even in later life it would be felt by her children.

It was Julia who created 'that crowded merry world which spun so gaily in the centre' of Virginia's childhood and which for Virginia vanished on her death.[10] Many people saw her as 'stern and judgemental'. There was certainly no mistaking her disapproval: 'If she had looked at me as I have seen her look at some people, I would sink into the earth,' Leslie Stephen told his children.[11]

Julia's interest in nursing and 'good works' developed early through her experiences with her mother. Discussion of her mother's symptoms, and those of family and friends, occupied a good slice of the day and when Mia Jackson was particularly troubled Julia would rarely be long away from her side. Not that Mia's ills were entirely psychosomatic for, in her late thirties, when Julia was nine or ten, she developed the first attack of what sounds to have been rheumatoid arthritis. That lasted several months and Julia was closely concerned with looking after her. Although, characteristically, the disease remitted, there were further attacks and in old age she was badly crippled and restricted to spending most of her days in a chair.

Julia's satisfaction was to fetch and carry for her mother, pour out this or that of the numerous medicines – which included morphia and chloral – discuss her condition and make her comfortable. In her mother's eyes, Julia was perfect and indispensable.

Nursing came to be an important way for Julia to express her feelings and be valued. It was always difficult for Julia to show or admit to open affection; she seemed to be afraid of giving too much of herself away. She told her daughters, 'Be sympathetic; be tender; flatter; deceive; use all the arts and wiles of our sex. Never let anyone guess that you have a mind of your own.'[12] Through nursing she was able to do good and be looked upon as angelic, all the while remaining detached and in control. She occupied the centre of her stage, and yet her real self remained hidden. She kept her thoughts to herself. Years later, she wrote revealingly that 'the relations between the sick and the well are far easier and pleasanter than between the well and the well.'[13]

Mia Jackson occasionally worried that Julia, her 'lamb', was too solemn and secretive for her own good. She had few friends in childhood and none with whom she was intimate. She was not close to either of her sisters, although she was fond of the eldest Adeline and, despite the ten-year gap between them, became the confidante of Adeline's unhappy marital experiences.

Her uncle Thoby Prinsep probably understood Julia better than anyone. She worshipped him and early on in life came to look on him as a father-figure. He was nearly 60 when Julia and her mother arrived in England. A dynamic, extroverted man, he had held high office in the East India Company until retirement some ten years before. Like his wife, he was very involved in the arts and literature and one of his hobbies was to translate Persian poetry. He seems to have taken a close interest in Julia and she responded with a 'simple, uncritical, enthusiastic' hero-worship.[14] Little Holland House was her home of education, where she learnt social ways and acquired many of her attitudes and interests. She spent much of her youth there and was, no doubt, spoilt and allowed to feel important. She became knowledgeable in the arts, learnt 'to listen devoutly' to distinguished men: 'to accept the fact that Watts was a great painter, Tennyson a great poet; and to dance with the Prince of Wales'.[15] Julia became, in other words, a well educated and cultured upper-class young lady. Sometimes she accompanied the Prinseps on their tours abroad, usually, but not always, with her ailing mother. She was invariably extremely anxious at any separation, worrying about her mother's health and comfort and generally fearing the worst. Telegrams and letters of reassurance went backwards and forwards in a steady stream between mother and daughter whenever they were parted.

Separation anxiety can be catching and readily passed on to the next generation. Virginia was similarly affected and, from the age of seven or eight, was intensely anxious when separated for long from her mother and later mother-substitutes. When Julia was late home, even by a few minutes, Virginia would work herself up into a lather of anxiety.

It was during a visit to Venice with her mother and the Prinseps that Julia met Herbert Duckworth and immediately fell in love. Mia Jackson may not have been much surprised but she probably had very mixed feelings over the prospect of losing her lamb. But Uncle Thoby approved, despite Herbert being more hearty than aesthetically minded, and helped to persuade his sister-in-law to agree to the marriage. Julia was married soon after her twenty-first birthday in 1867.

Herbert Duckworth was 13 years older, a barrister with plentiful private means. His family were minor county gentry and, despite their money having come originally from commerce, he was clearly a good catch.

Julia was, she claimed, immensely happy in her marriage to Herbert. Although she never spoke of him to the Stephen children, Virginia came to believe, from what she learnt from her half-sister Stella, that Julia idealised Herbert, 'the perfect man: heroic, handsome, magnanimous, "the great Achilles whom we knew"'.[16] He was certainly different in every way from the intellectual Leslie Stephen, her second husband.

Marriage did not change her controlling nature and from the start she mothered Herbert and fussed over his health. She was fearful she might lose him and was on tenterhooks whenever he was away from home for long. Once, he missed his train home and, when he failed to arrive at the usual time, Julia panicked and nearly collapsed.

Her apprehension turned out to be justified when, after only four years together, Herbert suddenly died of a brain haemorrhage. Julia was inconsolable: a world of pure love and beauty had been taken away. Her anger and despair were immense, but she could not express her feelings. She refused to share her grief and her anger grew. Who could she direct it against other than herself? She could not rage directly against Herbert for leaving her, nor her mother hovering in the background. They were sacrosanct. Instead she made God the target of her anger. From henceforth, she declared, she was an atheist. She would no longer believe in a Christian God who permitted such suffering.

Through her action Julia not only released anger but hurt her mother deeply, for Mia Jackson was a devout Anglican who pleaded and prayed for her daughter to return to the Faith. Julia was stony-hearted. So far as she was concerned, God was dead. Perhaps for the first time in her life she refused to give in to her mother.

Whatever unsaid satisfaction Julia may have derived from this psychological twist, it did little to relieve her grief. Her anger persisted and melancholia became part of her nature, colouring her views of the world and life. For a while she wanted to die but she was now responsible for three children and, in any event, she lacked the self-destructive streak of her youngest daughter. She followed Samuel Johnson's advice and filled every waking moment with humanitarian activity: caring for the children, helping her mother and doing good works outside the home. She often exhausted herself and melancholy was never far away, but her visits to the sick and needy helped her to keep up appearances: 'Cheerfulness is a habit to be acquired', she firmly declared. 'no one venturing to attend the sick should wear a gloomy face.'[17] So she passed the next nine years until she married Leslie Stephen in 1878.

Chapter Two

Leslie Stephen

Leslie was born in 1832, three years after his brother Fitzjames. He was considered by his parents from infancy to be delicate and highly strung. As a result he was over-protected and spoilt by his mother, who continued for many years to treat him as a sickly child. Leslie took full advantage of his position and came to expect his mother and devoted young sister to satisfy his every wish and need. They usually did and when they failed to come up to expectation a paroxysm of rage ensued. He adored his mother and confided his fears to her, but in the presence of his father Sir James Stephen, the great colonial administrator, he became a changed being, inhibited and shy, incapable of talking freely about himself or his feelings. He feared his father – for no specific reason – and found him unapproachable. In turn, his father complained how 'very inarticulate and very reserved' his son was.[1]

In 1847 Sir James became deeply depressed and had to retire from the civil service. He was never an easy man to manage and over the next year or two the patience of his wife must have been strained to the limit in looking after him. Significantly, Leslie collapsed in depression the following year and spent much of that summer in bed. At the time he was being tutored for Cambridge and living at home with virtually no friends. His brother was already at Trinity Hall, Cambridge, 'successful and competent'. Although Leslie thought of himself as inadequate by comparison with Fitzjames, he was reasonably confident of getting into Trinity and was not unduly worried by the impending exams. It may be that Leslie's depression was, partially at least, an unconscious attempt to draw his mother's attention from her husband on to him. It was certainly a pattern that was to recur more than once during Leslie's marriage to Julia whenever he felt neglected.

All his life Leslie worshipped his womenfolk – mother, wives and substitutes – and painted them in angelic colours but, in return, he expected them to be perfect in every respect: always ready to come running, however inconvenient, to pander to his needs. Woe betide them if they disappointed him: the air was filled with recriminations. During his marriage Leslie's behaviour exhausted Julia and caused immense difficulties between him and his children. Virginia firmly believed that 'it would have been better for our relationship if she [Julia] had left him to fend for himself'.[2]

Leslie went up to Trinity Hall when still 17. The new life there, away from home, transformed him. He grew in self-confidence, made friends and, at the end of the first year, won a scholarship. He also 'toughened up'. He became an enthusiastic oarsman and, eventually, a renowned rowing coach, a formidable walker covering 30 or 40 miles a day, and a climber whose exploits in the Alps are still recalled. Mountaineering was a pleasure he delighted in and, until Julia's death, he spent many of his holidays in the Swiss Alps. As he climbed, always in silence, his anxieties evaporated. But it was the conquest of the mountain rather than a search for tranquillity, a need to prove to himself, as much as to the world, that he was not the weak, mollycoddled youth of pre-Cambridge days that really motivated him. Yet however great his successes on the mountains or in the intellectual world, fear of being thought a failure was never far removed. Whenever he became depressed self-doubts immediately began to plague him.

Leslie was elected a Fellow and Tutor of Trinity Hall in 1854. The fellowship required him to take Holy Orders and he was ordained the following year. He was expected to take priest's orders within a short period but an inexplicable delay of four years ensued. Sir James, a staunch Evangelist, was disturbed and tried again and again to persuade his son to act, but not until his father was dying did Leslie move and enter the priesthood.

Two years later Leslie faced a crisis of identity: was he to continue his enjoyable but narrow life at Cambridge and end up as a don in an ivory tower, or follow his brother's example and seek to establish himself in the wider world of London? His father believed that Leslie's delicate nervous system rendered him unfit for the competitive work market, and particularly the field of journalism where Fitzjames had already made a name. Leslie should not leave the protective environs of Cambridge, Sir James had counselled, but if he did he must return home and live with his mother and sister.

Leslie's solution to the dilemma was to lose his faith and become an atheist. He had never been a heartfelt Christian and religious controversy and doubt were widespread in academia at that period, (Darwin's *The Origin of Species by Natural Selection* had been published in 1859), and Leslie now came to see that many of the biblical stories on which his Christian faith rested were unsustainable. The literal truth of Noah's Ark, when viewed in the light of reason, vanished into thin air. He abandoned the priesthood. In so doing he had to give up the fellowship and so effectively ended a Cambridge career.

Leslie's loss of faith was surely linked to the death of his father and represented a rejection of his authority; for it was not a passive process, a simple loss of belief, but an aggressive rejection of Christianity. Leslie now became a militant agnostic, renowned for his writings and the logic of his arguments. His influence in persuading doubters was considerable and, in fact, Julia Duckworth's interest in him was first aroused after reading one of his articles and finding intellectual justification for her own atheism.

If Leslie had been motivated to free himself from his father by rejecting Christianity, he was only partially successful. A parent is far more difficult than God to kill and the phantom lives on long after death, as Virginia was to discover. Leslie's conversion to atheism, by forcing him to leave Cambridge, certainly freed him to enter a wider, more satisfying world wherein he prospered and became a respected figure. At heart, however, he continued to feel a sham and a failure, never really deserving of good opinion.

In 1867, when he was 35, Leslie married the younger of William Thackeray's daughters, Minny, then aged 27, a whimsical woman 'with beautiful eyes'. Watt's portrait of her shows a 'sweet', to use Leslie's description, 'rather dreamy face'. Leslie was attracted and thought her 'pure minded and free of any taint of coarseness or conceit or self-consciousness'.[3] His sister Caroline Stephen, a fair eccentric herself, saw her as 'quaintly picturesque'.[4] It is difficult to see what the two had in common apart from a mutual admiration for Minny's father and his works. She was also inclined to be vague and spent much time rescuing flies from drowning in the garden after rain, and feeding stray cats. Nonetheless, she proved to be a capable housekeeper and caterer.

Minny's mother had schizophrenia (the illness had begun at Minny's birth), and needed constant care although she lived on to the age of 76, and Minny's aunt was 'so queer as to be almost on the borders of sanity'.[5] Possibly Minny herself, had she not died in pregnancy, would have broken down and become mentally ill.

The pressure of being Leslie's wife was not inconsiderable but Minny was protected from Leslie's more extravagant demands and bullying by her older sister Anny, who lived with the couple and was able to control Leslie through a mixture of humour and ridicule. The sisters had always been close and became more so after their father's death in 1863. 'I shall never be separated from

Anny except during my wedding tour,' Minny had told Leslie before their marriage.[6]

Anny was warm-hearted and enthusiastic with a lively sense of fun. She was very sociable, rather scatterbrained, extravagant and a compulsive talker. She was also fond of Leslie. Her chief complaint against him was the 'cold bath effect' he had on their enthusiasms.[7] She could reduce Leslie to silent rage by her chattering and caused furious scenes when she ran up debts and was unable to pay her share of the household expenses. But Leslie's outbursts mostly went over the Thackeray girls' heads and Anny was more amused than chastened. Leslie was almost always brought to heel and a scene would end with Leslie lending Anny money to pay her debts which, to her credit, she invariably repaid in the new quarter.

It was all in marked contrast to the scenes that would occur in Leslie's second marriage. Julia Stephen, lacking Anny's sense of the absurd, was unable to deflect Leslie's wrath and laugh at him. She pandered to his whims and by doing so, as Virginia complained, perpetuated his bullying egocentric habits.

Minny's first pregnancy miscarried but, in December 1870, Laura was born. The child was autistic but the parents failed to remark on her strangeness and she was treated as normal while Minny lived. Five years later Minny again became pregnant; she felt unwell from the beginning and, in the last month, developed eclampsia and died after a series of fits. The child was stillborn.

Leslie's grief was deep but not unmixed with self-pity and resentment. For a while he withdrew from friends and continued to work, editing *Cornhill Magazine* and writing his ambitious project *The History of English Thought in the Eighteenth Century*. He came to rely on Anny, who stayed on and looked after him and Laura for eighteen months until her unexpected and, to Leslie, unwelcome marriage. Anny, nearing her forties, had fallen in love with her cousin Richmond Ritchie, 16 years younger and an undergraduate at Trinity. His frequent visits to the house had already begun to concern Leslie when, on coming into the drawing-room one afternoon, he found Anny and Richmond kissing. Incensed, he told her she must 'make up her mind one way or other' to marry or to give up Richmond.[8] He assumed his ultimatum would at once bring Anny to her senses. Richmond had no money and the age gap was, Leslie thought, indecent. To his astonishment she chose marriage and Leslie became distraught; that Anny could desert him was almost more than he could conceive. The prospect of being abandoned and left on his own aroused intense anxiety and he was reduced for a time to helpless indecision.

He was rescued from his plight by a neighbour, Julia Duckworth. She had been a friend of the Thackeray sisters for many years and frequently visited Anny. She had looked on Leslie with awe and trepidation and kept her distance for fear of irritating or boring him, but she now saw him daily. She listened patiently to his repetitive denunciations of Anny's marriage and then, suddenly, throwing caution to the winds, told him he was jealous and angry only because he was losing Anny. She stood up for Anny and in so doing lost her fear of Leslie. Leslie in turn was impressed by her firmness and from then on came increasingly to depend on Julia. When Richmond asked Leslie for an interview in order to arrange the terms of marriage, Leslie insisted that Julia be present for moral support.

At Anny's wedding he and Julia made a peculiar-looking pair. Leslie 'looked very deplorable', silent and gloomy, while Julia 'wore the thickest black velvet dress and heavy black veil [it was a hot day in August, 1877] and gave the gloomiest, most tragic aspect.'[9] It was a foretaste of what lay ahead for this unusual couple who complemented so well each other's needs.

Leslie soon asked Julia to marry him, but at first she was hesitant. She liked Leslie but she had 'no courage for life'. Her ambivalence was patently clear. What she offered Leslie with one hand she took back with the other: 'I do love you with all my heart', she wrote to him, 'only it seems such a poor, dead heart'.[10] She felt no passion within her love for Leslie. She was attracted to his mind and, above all, to his overwhelming need for her, his pathetic helplessness.

She discussed the question of marriage with her mother who, not surprisingly, advised against it. Mia Jackson feared for Julia's happiness and, what was no doubt unsaid, her own position if Julia should adopt a new life. But Uncle Thoby, although terminally ill at Freshwater in the Isle of Wight, gave the marriage his approval. Julia returned from seeing him and told Leslie she meant 'to be as good a wife as she could'. On 26 March 1878 the 'tall, grave and thin couple' were married.[11]

Chapter Three

The Stephen Marriage

Leslie and Laura moved into Julia's house at 22 Hyde Park Gate. The three Duckworth children accepted their stepfather with remarkable equanimity. George, the eldest, was ten. He possessed his father's good looks and easygoing temperament and was the apple of his mother's eye. He, in turn, adored Julia who was always 'his own darling Mother'.[1] Stella, a year younger, was just as devoted to her mother and already beginning to shape up to Julia's notion of a 'perfect' daughter. Gerald was born after his father's death and, as the centre point of Julia's grief and attention, became the 'delicate child' of the family, pampered and difficult.

Julia was a strict disciplinarian and all her children were well brought up, good mannered and polite. The contrast between the courteous, conventional Duckworth children and the eight-year-old Laura was extreme. Leslie described her at this time as a 'normal, though obviously backward, child',[2] but, in fact. she was seriously autistic, possibly from Asperger's Syndrome. This condition is characterised by inappropriate social interaction, repetitive behaviour, bizarre intonation and body language, and poor motor co-ordination. Intelligence is usually in the low–normal range. The child's inability to communicate and the chilling way he or she ignores and looks through anyone else present can be very disturbing.

Autistic behaviour develops during the first three years of life and is always strongly influenced by how the child is treated. While Laura's mother was alive and when warm-hearted Anny cared for her, Laura's eccentric behaviour could be and was readily overlooked, but with Anny's departure she deteriorated and regressed. When she went to live with the Duckworth children, where she was expected to behave as a normal child, the effect was catastrophic. Leslie repeatedly lost his temper over her strange behaviour, her inarticulate ways of thinking and speaking. His unsuccessful attempts to teach Laura to speak, read and write terrified the girl and served only to increase her regression. Eventually he was forced to accept defeat and hand over Laura's management to Julia.

Julia was convinced that Laura's behaviour was entirely due to her having been brought up badly and she was sure the remedy lay in firm discipline and strict training. When she discovered she was wrong she became more and more punitive and eventually, after four years and when pregnant with Virginia, banished Laura to the top of the house in the care of a 'governess', after which she was only seen at family meals. Five years later she was sent away to a 'home', and later still to an asylum. Julia washed her from her mind as a hopeless lunatic, but Leslie continued to feel responsible and to visit his daughter until his death. Laura lived to be 76.

Julia Stephen quickly became pregnant. Vanessa was born in May 1879 and Thoby followed 15 months later. Julia wanted another boy but it was Virginia who arrived on 25 January 1882. Her last child, Adrian, was conceived at the beginning of the next year.

Julia's reactions to her pregnancies throw a light on her personal difficulties and the tensions and problems Virginia encountered in early life.

Some women are profoundly affected by the sex of their child. Julia was cheered when her infant proved to be male, and depressed when it turned out to be female. Julia perhaps visualised each of her children *in utero* as male – certainly when pregnant with Virginia she imagined a boy and referred to him as Chad – and was disappointed when a girl was born. Julia took the line that males are superior to females, but that throughout their lives they need to be protected and mothered. She believed a women's primary role in life was to care for her men: husband first, then sons. For Julia the birth of a son, full of promise, was the start of a natural loving process. A daughter was no better than a formless lump of clay at birth which had to be pummelled and moulded into a 'perfect' woman.

Julia's sons were admired and loved, her daughters criticised and made to conform. Julia could always make Leslie jealous by speaking of George with 'so evident a thrill of maternal love and pride'.[3] She fussed over Gerald and pampered Adrian. Only with Thoby, who was disconcertingly self-contained and distant, was she more reserved and less at ease. She was a strict disciplinarian with her daughters, particularly the eldest, Stella, whom she treated with 'the severity with which she should have treated her own failings'. When Leslie protested on more than one occasion, shocked by her harshness, she justified herself on the grounds that she 'felt Stella part of myself'.[4]

Leslie quickly adapted to the marriage. His pattern of life, in fact, continued much as before: he continued to go on walking holidays on his own, his work satisfied him and his comforts were ably provided by a protective Julia. She gave him 'an infinity of care'. His one complaint and wish was that she would become more happy. Her melancholic looks when she was with him – not a single photograph shows Julia smiling, although she was capable of being merry in the right company – must sometimes have irritated and upset Leslie, as well as arousing his anxiety over the depth of her love. Time after time he asked her to say she loved him and she always avoided giving him a direct answer. He enjoyed their sexual life although how much was duty and how much was pleasure to Julia – given her self-confessed 'deadness' – is an open question. There were no apparent difficulties on that score, although Leslie once warned that, 'by abstaining so much', he became even more obstreperous, or as he called it, 'tantarous'.[5]

Julia was ill for some months after Vanessa's birth and no sooner did she begin to improve when her mother's rheumatoid arthritis flared up. At the time Mia Jackson was staying at Eastnor Castle, the home of her younger sister Lady Somers, and Julia was at once summoned. She nursed her there for several weeks and then brought her to London, where she stayed before moving on to the Brighton home of her second daughter Mary Fisher to convalesce.

Mia was left partially crippled after this relapse and consequently decided to move permanently to Brighton to be near her daughters. For some years she went the rounds of the spas and hydros and underwent the current fashionable treatments without lasting benefit. In her latter years she was confined to a wheelchair. Much of her later disability was genuine but it can never have been easy for the Stephens to distinguish real physical distress from manipulative behaviour. She made frequent demands on Julia, and Leslie was more than once angered and driven to protest at what he considered unreasonable calls. He was not being altogether unfair when he said his mother-in-law needed 'managing' rather than 'nursing'. Leslie tolerated much from her and put up with Julia's absences from home with, for the most part, little more than a rumble of protest. Not that he was ever physically inconvenienced. Julia always ensured his comforts were catered for and his favourite food prepared, and by the time Virginia was a few years old, Stella was able to deputise efficiently for her mother.

Julia warned Leslie before marriage that she would continue to nurse her mother and respond to her calls, as well as visit the sick and the dying, and might sometimes be away from him for days and even weeks. He had agreed readily at the time but as the years passed, and the demands on Julia from her mother and other relatives continued, his protests slowly became louder. In the first four years of marriage, until he undertook to edit *The Dictionary of National Biography*, he was generously supportive of his wife. He accompanied Julia when she went to nurse her mother in 1879 and later travelled with her to Brighton to settle Dr and Mrs Jackson into their new home. It was during those trying months that Julia again became pregnant.

Thoby was born in September 1880. The birth and early weeks were uneventful but she had no time to recover her full strength before her eldest sister Adeline Vaughan fell critically ill with heart disease and Julia at once went to her assistance. Friends criticised her for leaving her young children but Leslie stoutly defended her. Adeline's death added to Julia's melancholia but did not prevent her becoming pregnant again, this time with Virginia (christened Adeline Virginia after her aunt).

Virginia always claimed that she and her younger brother Adrian were unwanted children, but there is no evidence for this and it is much more likely that Julia wanted to become pregnant. Melancholic women frequently compensate for their unhappiness by conceiving and, once pregnant, Julia was convinced she had another male child to love and protect. One can only presume her disappointment when 'Chad' turned into Virginia, but Julia was a determined woman and, despite Leslie pronouncing Chad to be the last child, a fourth pregnancy followed. Adrian became her 'Benjamin', her 'Joy' and she spoilt and pampered him and treated him in baby fashion until her death. Virginia was jealous of the attention Adrian received, and was disparaging and often very cutting of him late into their lives.

Whatever hopes for happiness in the marriage Julia may have had, they soon faded, although she never ceased to be the good wife. There was no possibility of Leslie taking over Herbert Duckworth's role and becoming another 'great Achilles', for he was the antithesis of Herbert in character and interests, but he was capable of being sympathetic and understanding, as he had demonstrated during their courtship. Had he developed that side and paid more attention to Julia's needs and less to his own, Julia's melancholia might have lifted. But Leslie was too fixed in his ways to change. He left all family responsibilities to his wife, although he continually criticised and interfered with her decisions. Whatever the problems at home, however tired or unwell Julia might be, Leslie went off on his climbing holidays to the Alps or on long country walks with the Sunday Tramps, an 'athletic fraternity . . . which he founded after his second marriage'.[6] The couple never travelled abroad together. Leslie rarely saw a play or went to a concert or picture gallery, which Julia would have enjoyed. They shared almost nothing outside the home and family.

He went on a hiking tour in the last trimester before Virginia's birth, when Julia was unwell. Remembering Minny's death in pregnancy, Julia might have expected him to curtail his holidays, but he merely sent her a note warning her to rest, for if any disaster occurred *he* would suffer dreadfully: 'life would indeed be bleak'.[7]

Yet Leslie loved his wife. 'Good God! how that man adores her,' Henry James, a family friend, observed, but for once the great novelist failed to paint the full picture.[8] Leslie's devotion to Julia led him to expect total devotion from her and this allowed him to behave with extraordinary selfishness in his marriage. He expected to be mothered; every complaint listened to and understood, every pain kissed away. He wanted Julia to be instantly available, willing to abandon whatever she was doing to please him. It irked him terribly that Julia would never say she loved him but he never wondered why, never looked below the surface and allowed himself to glimpse resentment over his behaviour. His anxiety only served to increase the self-pitying scenes which led Julia having to hold him as though he was a small child. His tantrums, which sometimes disturbed the house, were often contrived 'in order to extort [from Julia] some of her delicious compliments'.[9]

Julia was trapped, for the more she petted and mothered Leslie, the more greedy and infantile he became. Yet had she ignored him he would have become 'tantarous'. She would not have tolerated such behaviour in the children – although George and particularly Adrian had special dispensation – but her compulsive need to mother Leslie immediately took over when he appealed to her. Virginia, watching critically, condemned her mother for making a fetish of Leslie's health and comfort that, in the end, disrupted the household and, Virginia believed, hastened Julia's death.

Why did Julia indulge Leslie? From her earliest years at Little Holland House she had been adored by men of ability and fame. They had praised her beauty, painted her, sought her in marriage, in short, had valued her and placed her on a pedestal; she had been made to feel a goddess. By the time of her first marriage she had become conditioned to attracting male adoration. With the passage of years the quality of adoring men had dropped and one of Leslie's attractions for Julia had been the breadth of his learning and renown in the literary world. Julia's pleasure in being the object of Leslie's adoration was immense, and although she was exhausted by much of his behaviour she was trapped in her own addictive needs.

Time after time Leslie would wring his hands and lament that he was a failure as a writer and bewail his inability to be the genius he should be. Julia would listen and take his hand and comfort him, assuring him he really was the great man she knew him to be, respected and sought after by everyone. She repeated praise she had read or overheard; he was famous, admired, quoted and known everywhere. Gradually he allowed her to calm his agitation until, soothed, a contented child, he sat back and adored her in turn.

Until 1882, the year of Virginia's birth, Leslie's mental stability was good and his neurotic behaviour, by and large, restricted to reasonable limits. Thereafter he deteriorated steadily and became an increasing burden on his wife and family.

In 1882 *The Science of Ethics*, on which Leslie had worked for the past five years, was published. It was not the success he anticipated and he was upset by the lack of enthusiasm. At the same time he learnt that the *Cornhill Magazine* he had edited for nine years was running at a loss, its circulation having halved during his editorship.

He at once resigned but almost the next day he was invited 'to edit a vast new project' thought up by the publisher George Smith: *The Dictionary of National Biography*.[10] It was a daunting challenge involving choosing who to include and exclude, and then finding suitable contributors. He had to keep a tight rein on the length and quality of the articles, watch for plagiarism and ensure promised contributions were delivered on time. Over and above all that, Leslie was himself a major contributor and 'wrote the lives of most of the major poets and writers'.[11] The '*DNB*' that was to be the great achivement of his life was well within his intellectual capacity, but the demands it made on his emotional life were too much for him and it slowly crushed him.

The first volume appeared in 1884 after little more than two years and thereafter a new volume appeared quarterly without fail. The pressure on Leslie was unremitting, despite his having an exceptionally able assistant in Sidney Lee. Fear of failure haunted him and he was never free of anxiety. The work came to obsess him and he thought and talked of little else.

Almost from the time of the *DNB's* inception Leslie began to break down. His sleep, normally sound, became broken. Waking with 'the horrors', convinced he was capable only of third-rate work, he would rouse Julia and, in Ancient Mariner style, pour out his fears. Eventually, exhausted and pacified, he drifted back to sleep, leaving his wife wide-awake and worried. The strain on Julia was immense. Watching the effect of the *DNB* on her husband made her loathe the work. She struggled to persuade him to give it up and in 1885 warned George Smith that she feared for Leslie's state of mind. But Leslie's pride was almost too great for him to admit defeat, although he agreed to make some concessions. Thinking to spare himself, he gave over to Julia the handling of the household finances. All that achieved was increased friction between husband and wife, for Leslie was incapable of giving Julia a free hand and continually criticised her. The weekly inspection of expenses invariably ended in noisy shouts about extravagance, and the banging of doors. The more depressed he became, the more outrageous was Leslie's behaviour; exhausted by the broken nights Julia's patience, hanging by a thread, started to give.

Although by the beginning of 1887 Leslie was on the edge of a breakdown, he continued to cling to the editorship. All Julia's pleading for him to resign was ignored. In desperation she appealed to the family doctor who, recognising the crisis, ordered Leslie to take a holiday of at least three weeks in the Alps. He obeyed reluctantly and when, after walking twenty miles a day for a week, he felt better, he began badgering Julia with daily letters demanding his early return. He assured her that she was the best cure for his nerves and the longer he stayed away the worse he would be. Julia, however, was at the end of her strength and would brook no compromise. Leslie threatened 'tantarums' but she not only stood her ground but suggested he stay away an extra week.

Leslie's satisfaction on returning home was short-lived, for after a few weeks Julia was summoned to Brighton to nurse her dying 83-year-old father. Stella ran the household efficiently in her absence but whatever she did compared badly to Julia in Leslie's eyes. At first he tolerated Julia's absence but his letters soon became angry and self-pitying. Julia was neglecting him, for *his* needs were surely as great as the dying man's. When Dr Jackson died after ten days, Leslie expected Julia to return home immediately after the funeral, and when she stayed on, saying her mother needed her, he became irate. He suggested his mother-in-law should return with Julia and stay with them until she felt better. When he heard that Mia Jackson wanted Julia to remain at Brighton for a second week to sort through her father's papers he was incensed. Julia, he wrote, was allowing herself to be manipulated by her mother, whose nerves were perpetually weak. Indignant letters flowed between them, until finally, Julia cast off pretence and admitted she was exhausted and needed time away from him and the family.

Leslie was astonished and disturbed. It had never occurred to him that Julia could be run down. Puzzled, he travelled down to see her and thrash out the matter. He returned, only partially mollified and without Julia, who stayed on for a further two weeks.

Leslie's mental health continued to deteriorate and household tensions were high. There were always broken nights and histrionic scenes; Armageddon was at hand; he was threatened with financial and professional ruin; Juila's extravagance would end in their bankruptcy. Leslie had giddy fits, which were diagnosed as 'stomachic vertigo' by the family doctor but were probably manifestations of panic attacks. Yet, remarkably, he continued to produce good work and it was not until 1891, after 26 volumes, that he handed over the editorship of the *DNB* to Sidney Lee. He continued to contribute biographies to the *Dictionary* until shortly before his death.

The strain on Julia persisted despite Leslie having given up the *Dictionary*. She had to spend long hours reassuring him he was still the country's leading man of letters. She encouraged him to begin the book on the English Utilitarians he had been planning for some years, which he might write at his own pace and without pressure. But nothing could hold back the tide of depression and he continued to worry about his reputation and the future until the end.

Inevitably the children suffered, especially Virginia and Adrian; 'the *DNB* crushed [Adrian's] life out before he was born', wrote Virginia. 'It gave me a twist of the head too. I shouldn't have been so clever but I should have been more stable without [it].'[12] Her anxiety was heightened by the noisy scenes, her mother's increasingly obvious exhaustion and her father's distress. She sat reading *DNB* articles, confused as to where her loyalties lay.

In 1892 Mrs Jackson died. Julia's grief went deep, for the relationship between mother and daughter had been intense and complex. Her death brought out Julia's guilt; she could have done more for her mother, she had not been a good daughter. As ever, she was unable to share her misery with anyone, and certainly not her daughters. Leslie was sympathetic, within his limitations, although in his heart he was probably glad to see the last of his rival for Julia's affection.

Julia, in her unhappiness, immersed herself in good works and before long:

> she had expanded so far, into such remote recesses, alleys in St Ives, London slums, and many other more prosperous but no less exacting quarters that retrenchment was beyond her power.

She drained herself. Leslie, at night, would look up from his book, press her hand and protest, 'There must be an end of this, Julia,' but he was powerless to halt the decline.[13]

In March 1895 Julia was taken ill with influenza. Recovery was slow and at the end of April signs of heart disease developed. On 5 May, in Leslie's words, she sank 'quietly into the arms of death'.[14]

Chapter Four

Virginia's Early Life and Temperament

Virginia was a robust infant despite Julia having stopped breastfeeding at ten weeks (with Leslie's somewhat reluctant agreement), too tired to continue. During her nursery years she was a lively, imaginative child; playful, affectionate and disputative, in no way unusual. By the time she was five she was highly strung, an inventive story-teller and already a bookworm.

The turning point in Virginia's character formation came, according to Quentin Bell, when all the children went down with whooping cough – a dangerous disease then – and were sent to Bath to convalesce. When she returned she was thinner, more introspective, and prone to anxiety at night. It is an age when children are struggling to establish an identity and to assimilate those aspects of a parent they most admire. Virginia surprised her sister at this time by asking her which parent she preferred. Vanessa unhesitatingly chose her mother and was astonished by Virginia's choice of their remote father.

Yet Virginia adored her mother and always strove to have more of her. She admired her beauty, craved her company, sought her praise, anxiously wanted to know her whereabouts. Virginia's delight was to be soothed by her voice and touch, to listen for the rustle of her dress as she came upstairs into the night-nursery, to smell her fragrance as she bent to give a goodnight kiss. When her mother was absent Virginia's world shrank.

Julia could be warm-hearted, but the demands made on her by eight children, one of them autistic, a husband whose sanity sometimes seemed in doubt, a demanding mother, and a trail of invalids left her little emotion to spare for Virginia. She was a disciplined, if driven, woman and she had, of necessity, to economise on her time and energy. Not only did she have a large house to run and six or seven servants to organise, but when the children were young she and Leslie taught them the three 'R's and the rudiments of History, English and French.

Neither she nor Leslie were good teachers. Both were impatient with slowness or any hint of stupidity. Leslie was liable to lose his temper and thump the table when not understood. Julia never lost self-control but she was more punitive and harsher in her reactions than Leslie. Leslie was basically kinder and, once an outburst was over, he would regret the scene and attempt to mend fences. Julia never backtracked. She said hurtful things which she meant.

Virginia was only five when Julia banished Laura from Hyde Park Gate to a 'Home', although the girl continued to join the family at St Ives in the summer for two more years. Virginia loathed her and looked on her as a 'vacant-eyed girl', an idiot who stammered and grimaced and was a figure of fun, who sometimes howled and broke things or threw them into the fire.[1] What really disturbed her, however, was her mother's cold harshness to Laura, her shocking rejection of the girl when it became obvious that Laura would never conform.

The effect of these scenes on Virginia made a lasting impression. Throughout her life she shrank from any passing idiot or imbecile. When an 'idiot boy sprang up with his hand outstretched, mewing, slit-eyed, red-rimmed' during a walk in Kensington Gardens, she was too upset to mention the incident even to Vanessa.[2] And years later when, walking with Leonard, they encountered a long line of 'miserable, ineffective, shuffling, idiotic creatures, with no forehead or no chin, and an imbecilic grin', she declared 'they should certainly be killed'.[3] The intensity of her reaction is indicative of the horror and anxiety Laura aroused in Virginia, a horror that came both from her own dislike of Laura and the sight of her mother's rejection of the girl, which set Virginia's vivid imagination to work, making herself the disobedient child.

Julia was 'the very centre of that great cathedral space which was childhood', and Virginia's emotional security rested on her mother.[4] But as she grew up she increasingly found herself at odds with her mother's views on womanhood and the contrasting roles of men and women. Julia fervently believed a woman's duty lay with husband and family, and she gave short shrift to any feminist views; along with Octavia Hill and Beatrice Webb she signed Mrs Humphrey Ward's *Manifesto Against Female Suffrage* in 1889. Her rules were uncomplicated. Women ran the home and men had charge of all important matters outside the home. Julia maintained they were mentally superior to women, although at home they depended on their womenfolk and had to be looked after. Virginia could not accept such a doctrine of male superiority. She bitterly resented her brothers going to school while she and Vanessa were educated at home, taught to dance and sing and prepare themselves for the marriage market. She wanted to be independent, to become a writer like her father.

Leslie believed 'Ginny' would 'become an author in time'.[5] He gave her the run of his library, recommended books to read and made her feel 'special'. She absorbed his ways and literary habits but, although she admired him enormously, she was never emotionally close to him. She emulated him but could not love him, in the way she did her mother. Julia did nothing to dampen Virginia's literary enthusiasm – she herself wrote rather depressing children's stories recounting the misfortunes that befell rebellious children, and a book on nursing – but one suspects she looked on Virginia's scribblings and 'blue stocking' ways as a passing phase to her future life as wife and mother.

Virginia's need for her mother and, later on, mother substitutes to openly *demonstrate* their love came very early on. She was extraordinarily greedy for affection. Even in her fifties she would still 'demand her rights' from Vanessa, 'a kiss on the nape of the neck, or on the eyelid, or a whole flutter of kisses from the inner wrist to the elbow.'[6] It embarrassed everyone but until Virginia received a 'sign of love' she would persist.

Virginia's anxiety, observed by both parents, increased steadily through childhood. Some of it was probably constitutional and inherited from her father, although the effect of cyclothymic genes is not usually seen until after puberty; cyclothymes, as a group, are not characteristically anxious children. There was plenty of anxiety in the Stephen household in the 1880s, mostly generated by Leslie, which would have affected Virginia, but the core of her anxiety lay in the conflict of loyalties to mother and father, and resulting confusion. She could not survive without her mother's love. She could not accept a life outside her father's world.

She felt safe with her father in his library. She was his favourite child. He made her feel they were in league together. She in turn, a cherubic child when small, charmed him. 'I never saw such a little rogue', Leslie chuckled as the two-year-old squeezed up to him and demanded a kiss, or sat on his lap and picked crumbs from his beard.[7] She never feared him, even when witness to one of his fearful rages. She might feel anger and contempt but her bond with him was untouched.

Virginia's love for her mother was more complicated and on a deeper level, and rarely returned to Virginia's satisfaction. No sooner did she have Julia's attention than her mother was away. There was always a sense of absence and, although Virginia knew she was loved, anxious doubts kept arising. Had she offended? Was she the least-loved child? Separation anxiety grew. When Julia was away from home Virginia was restless and apprehensive.

This was most apparent in London, where Julia travelled everywhere on horse-drawn buses, and street accidents were common; Virginia always recorded the accidents she saw in the streets in her diary. When Julia was late home Virginia would hover near the front door, peering out of the window, unable to settle until the familiar figure came in sight.

During the three summer months that the family spent at St Ives Virginia was far less anxious. She saw more of her mother. Julia visited the local sick but they were few compared to London, and within walking distance, and Julia's mother was too distant for her daughter to respond to every call. Instead, Mrs Jackson sometimes came to stay with the Stephens at Talland House, along with old family friends. Julia was able to relax and tensions noticeably dropped. Virginia looked on those summer holidays as the happiest time of her childhood, and Cornwall and St Ives always retained a magical quality for her; Talland House on the hill above the town, and the sea, 'more congenial to me than any human being'.[8] Virginia felt united with her mother in a way that was impossible in London. The sense of unity, no more than momentary, gave way to rapture, the memory of which was indelible.

That sense of unity returned when her mother died and, with George and Vanessa, she went to meet Thoby at Paddington Station, summoned back from school. The glass dome of the station was ablaze with light from the setting sun and as she walked along the platform she became lost in rapture, her fears dissipated, at peace and united within herself; 'It was surprising – as if something were becoming visible without effort.'[9]

In striking contrast was the unreality which could possess Virginia at moments of high anxiety, when her surroundings changed in quality and feeling and became unfamiliar, and time and space were distorted. At its height a threatening sense of isolation set off panic which almost paralysed her.

Virginia's first experience of this was at St Ives when she overheard her parents discussing the suicide of a neighbour. Later that evening, walking in the moonlit garden, she came across an old apple tree that seemed to contain the horror of the suicide, the man's despair. She stood staring at the tree, the furrows on its bark forming strange patterns in the moonlight, unable to move, panic rising.

Again, in Kensington Gardens, she went to cross a rain puddle on the pathway when 'for no reason I could discover everything suddenly became unreal. I was suspended. I could not step across the puddle. I tried to touch something . . . the world became unreal.'[10]

These experiences led her to believe that 'something terrible' lay in wait for her, some malign fate. She became conscious of her own 'powerlessness' to ward it off and she felt 'dumb horror' and depression.[11] Forty years later Virginia reproduced the incident of the puddle in *The Waves*:

> There is the puddle,' said Rhoda, 'and I cannot cross it. I hear the rush of the great grindstone within an inch of my head . . . All palpable forms of life have failed me. Unless I can stretch and touch something hard, I shall be blown down the eternal corridors for ever.'[12]

Virginia sought a philosophy which might provide a sense of unity. The seed had been planted at St Ives when she was nine or ten. Looking at a flower she had a revelation; the ring of earth surrounding the plant was part of it, and with the flower made up a whole. Like many revelations the observation itself was banal, but the emotion was intense. It set in train a line of thought which in time evolved into the idea of there being a pattern behind everything, within every event. If she could discover that pattern, the event – good or bad – would become whole and comprehensible. The 'sledgehammer blows' of fate might be understood and even utilised.[13]

On the surface Virginia's ideas appear commonplace, for most people try to make sense out of chaos, but she gradually introduced a mystical element into her thinking:

> the whole world is a work of art . . . we are parts of the work of art. *Hamlet* or a Beethoven quartet is the truth about this vast mass that we call the world. But there is no Shakespeare, there is no Beethoven; certainly and emphatically there is no God; we are the words.[14]

It was through words that Virginia tried to make order out of chaos. She discerned:

> some real thing behind appearances; and I make it real by putting it into

words. It is only by putting it into words that I make it whole; this wholeness means that it has lost its power to hurt me, it gives me, perhaps because by doing so I take away the pain, a great delight to put the severed parts together. Perhaps this is the strongest pleasure known to me. It is the rapture I get when, in writing, I seem to be discovering what belongs to what.[15]

That rapture always visited Virginia in the early stages of her novels: she galloped ahead without pause, free of anxiety, in control of events, powerful and self-contained.

Stella Duckworth came naturally to be a second mother to Virginia and Adrian. She had been devoted to Julia – a 'beautiful attendant handmaid, feeding her mother's vivid flame, rejoicing in the service and making it the central duty of her life' – and looked on her mother as 'a person of divine power and divine intelligence'.[16] The umbilical cord was never cut and mother and daughter developed a telepathic understanding of each other. Stella had almost no independent life and apparently no desire for one. She could not bear to be parted from her mother and even a short separation distressed her. When she was rarely persuaded to go away for a holiday she was 'white as a ghost' for days before taking a tearful leave, which the watchful Virginia always noticed.[17]

She attracted men but invariably refused their proposals. Since Julia believed that 'an unmarried woman has missed the best of life',[18] she would have pushed Stella into marriage before long, had she not died. While the family was at St Ives in the summer of 1894, Stella turned down for a second time her most persistent suitor, Jack Hills, and afterwards a fascinated Virginia listening intently through the bedroom wall, heard the sound of her crying.

The twelve-year-old Virginia's ideas of marriage reflected her age: gathered mostly from books and passing remarks and regarded with a mixture of fear and excitement. The subject was never discussed in any real terms at home and Virginia, although puzzled by Stella's resistance to marriage, may have intuitively understood why. Twelve years later, when Vanessa began to hint at marriage, Virginia was to echo Stella's tearful cry, 'What can it matter where we are so long as we are all together?'[19]

Men could sometimes seem alarming. Virginia's huge, handsome, cyclothymic cousin Jim Stephen was attracted to Stella and liable, when hypomanic, to burst into Hyde Park Gate and demand kisses.[20] It was both thrilling and frightening, made more so when Virginia and Vanessa were told to pretend that Stella had gone away.

When Virginia was five or six years old, her half-brother Gerald stood her upon a table and explored her 'private parts', an act she recalled years later with a 'shiver of shame'.[21] The effect on her psycho-sexual development was probably minor but her dislike of Gerald was enduring. Her attitude to George, her other half-brother, was much warmer although he is held to be a sexual monster by Virginia's feminist admirers. In her childhood he was a father-figure and Virginia looked on him then with affection. When he died in 1934 she was distressed, and her last conversation about him with her doctor, shortly before she killed herself, showed she 'evidently adored him'.[22]

After Julia died, George continued to live at Hyde Park Gate 'in complete chastity' until he was 36 when, soon after Leslie's death, he achieved his ambition of marrying into the aristocracy.[23] Before then he undertook to bring out his half-sisters in society, and for several seasons Virginia endured the ordeal of dances and dinner parties that, although they provided interesting material for future writing, left her cold with embarrassment and boredom. According to Virginia, when she was half-asleep in bed, George would creep in and throw himself on top of her crying, 'Don't be frightened . . . and don't turn on the light. Oh, beloved. Beloved!'[24]

George invariably behaved like an affectionate puppy with his half-sisters, embracing them in public and kissing them exuberantly. He may well have lain on Virginia's bed and kissed her and uttered endearments – it was quite in keeping – but it is unlikely that he went further. She gave a witty account of these encounters to the Memoir Club which reduced everyone to tears of mirth. George was, she declaimed in hypomanic style, 'not only father and mother, brother and sister to those poor Stephen girls, he was their lover also.'[25]

In July 1911 when hypomanic and prone to fantasise, she revealed 'all George's malefactions' to her old Greek tutor and friend Janet Case, who was so shocked 'she dropped her lace, and gasped like a benevolent gudgeon. By bedtime she said she was feeling quite sick, and did go to the W.C., which, needless to say, had no water in it.'[26] Virginia pulled no punches when high! A year earlier in the summer, she had fabricated an absurdly funny but malicious story about Vanessa that had so outraged their humourless friend Saxon Sydney Turner that Vanessa had to protest angrily.

The account of George's lovemaking probably contains a core of truth but there is no evidence that Virginia was distressed by it. On the contrary, she may have been amused and enjoyed the fondling. Petting with parental substitutes (and George was still one in 1902) always gave her satisfaction. It may also have reassured her that male sexuality was harmless.

Chapter Five

Deaths – The First Major Breakdown, 1904

Julia died on 5 May. Leslie was distraught; he had once again been abandoned. The 13-year-old Virginia was confused. She frightened her half-sister Stella by telling her, 'When I see Mother, I see a man sitting with her.'[1] Perhaps in Virginia's imagination Julia had left the Stephens to rejoin Herbert Duckworth.

It was impossible to grieve and mourn at Hyde Park Gate. The sound of Leslie groaning and repeating his wish to die tolled like a knell through the darkened house, and a steady stream of visitors repeated platitudes and shed tears. Virginia could speak to no one of her loss and fears, her sense of abandonment, the desperate need for affection. The children clung together but none of them spoke of their mother or her death.

Stella, at first too shocked even to speak Julia's name, hid her feelings in public. When Virginia surprised her alone and in tears, she sprang up, wiped her eyes and protested that nothing was wrong. Still, in the end, it was Stella who rescued Virginia from 'this great interval of nothingness'.

Pulling herself together, Stella took charge of the family; there was no one else. She looked after her stepfather and attended to his comforts, listening patiently to his self-pitying stories. The more she gave, the more he demanded and, as time passed, Stella, trying her best to emulate Julia, grew thin and pale with exhaustion. Julia's death had taught Leslie nothing. His tyrannical egotism and need for sympathy blinded him to Stella's distress.

> She was [he told a friend] my great support; she is very like her mother in some ways – very sweet and noble and affectionate. I am sometimes worried by thinking that she ought to be a wife and mother and that she may find reasons for leaving me.[2]

When she did marry, two years later, his world turned topsy-turvy.

Virginia was seriously ill for many months after Julia's death but she did not become insane. She retreated to her room, her refuge and hiding-place, and became almost housebound. The outside world was threatening and she feared meeting people. Depression and anxiety almost paralysed her; she slept badly and lost weight. She could no longer write or even read for a time. But she did not go mad; she remained, trembling, in touch with her surroundings.

Stella came to her rescue. Her half-sister became the mother-figure she needed. She looked after Virginia with great understanding and affection, far more so than Julia had done, and gradually Virginia responded and began to feel more secure. Stella insisted on Virginia leading an ordered life, drinking supplementary milk, taking her medicines and following Dr Seton's prescribed routine. She had to go out several times a day; usually to walk with Leslie in Kensington Gardens, meet Vanessa after her Art class, and to shop or make social calls with Stella. As she improved she began to devour books at such a rate that Leslie was concerned. But he liked his daughter's bookish voracity, and he discussed books with her and advised her on what to read. Virginia thrived and her admiration for her father grew.

Fifteen months after Julia's death Virginia's anxiety returned when Stella became engaged to Jack Hills. There was 'excitement and emotion and gloom' in the family. Adrian cried. Leslie was upset but said, unselfishly for once, 'We must all be happy because Stella is happy' – a command which, poor man, he could not himself obey.[3] Virginia was as distressed as her father, angry and appalled at the prospect of losing her second mother. That October she had panic attacks and Dr Seton reimposed restrictions on her reading and mental activity.

Stella's marriage did not take place until April 1897, due to Leslie's delaying tactics, but the wait was beneficial to Virginia. Stella went to great lengths to include her half-sister in the wedding preparations, and to reassure her she was not being abandoned. She repeatedly emphasised she was leaving home only to move into the house across the street, and she would continue to see and watch over Virginia as before.

Virginia's jealousy of Jack, mild in comparison to Leslie's, slowly diminished. She made an effort to get to know him and she came to picture his love for Stella in idealised terms. It was her 'first vision then of love between man and woman' and she envied their closeness.[4] Jack was passionately and demonstratively in love and Stella responded by growing in confidence and looks. As Virginia saw their happiness her anxiety abated and by the beginning of 1897 she was well enough to start a diary.

However, as the marriage date neared, her fears re-emerged. She delayed until the very last moment, going to church to hear the banns read, although that may have been more a protest against attending church than the marriage itself, and she refused to kneel. She bought a wedding present, a lamp, just two days before the wedding and the strain was so great she almost fainted and had to be brought home by cab.[5] She and Vanessa were bridesmaids; 'Goodness knows how we got through it all – certainly it was half a dream, or a nightmare', Virginia recorded.[6]

Stella returned home from the honeymoon at the end of April feeling ill, with 'a bad chill on her innards', eventually diagnosed as appendicitis complicated by peritonitis.[7] Three months of intermittent illness followed, during which time Virginia's state of mind mirrored Stella's condition. At first she could not sleep alone and moved into Vanessa's bedroom. She haunted Stella's bedside. Her relief when Stella improved was enormous; 'Now that Old Cow [Julia's nickname for Stella] is most ridiculously well and cheerful

. . . thank goodness'.[8] But Stella's improvement was short-lived, and Dr Seton stopped Virginia's lessons in Greek and Latin and ordered extra milk and medicines. A week before Stella's death Virginia collapsed with 'rheumatism' and 'fidgets', and was put to bed.

Stella died on 19 July, after a mistimed operation. Had Dr Seton been in attendance (he was incapacitated by sciatica) he might have opposed the surgeons and perhaps saved Stella's life – and altered the course of Virginia's. Her lifelong distrust of doctors had a firm foundation.

Stella's death, coming so soon after her mother's, was shattering. 'But this is impossible,' Virginia kept repeating to herself, 'things aren't, can't be, like this.'[9] Her diary tailed off and ended with the year, not to be resumed for 20 months. However, the ending was not entirely without hope: 'Courage and plod on – They [the years] must bring something worth the having.'[10] This time Virginia could grieve, for she was able to talk and share her feelings with Vanessa and Jack.

Before Stella died it was known she was pregnant; Virginia may have connected her death in some way with sex. There was gossip at the time that Jack 'had in some way injured' his wife through his rapacious sexual demands and roughness.[11] According to her friend Violet Dickinson – who later became another maternal substitute for Virginia – Stella had found intercourse painful.

Problems built up between Virginia and Vanessa over the following two years, which were not unlike the complications that were to follow Vanessa's marriage to Clive Bell ten years later. Jack Hills continued to haunt the Stephen family, visiting Hyde Park Gate every evening and spending weekends with them at holiday time. Vanessa and Virginia took turns to comfort him, listened to him sympathetically and held his hand. At Painswick, where the Stephens stayed after Stella's death, one or other of the sisters walked in the garden with him after dinner, and that September they stayed with him at his parents' home, Corby Castle.

Virginia, with her novelist's instinct and curiosity, persuaded Jack to talk about his feelings for Stella, and his sexual desire and frustrations. 'We were [mentally] "intimate" for years', she wrote, but she was not physically attracted to him.[12] She liked him but his main interest for her lay in what he revealed of himself and men's sexual lives and, above all, because he had been Stella's husband.

Vanessa, on the other hand, who had regarded Stella more as a friend and sister rather than a mother, was physically drawn to Jack and he in turn to her. Virginia increasingly felt left out of the relationship and became jealous, suddenly afraid of losing her last remaining prop.

It was all very theatrical: three lonely unhappy people, seeking comfort from one another. The affair petered out but only after George had intervened to point out that it was illegal for in-laws to marry. To Virginia's short-lived delight, he asked her to persuade Vanessa to see sense. There was a scene between the sisters, which ended in Virginia asking for forgiveness, and mutual embraces.

As the only women in a household of demanding men, Virginia and Vanessa drew together and closed ranks, forming, in Virginia's words, 'a close conspiracy'.[13] Vanessa became responsible for the household affairs from 1897 to Leslie's death in 1904. Virginia called this time 'the seven unhappy years', but they were valuable years for her. She read prodigiously, guided by her father. She studied Latin and Greek. She kept a journal and experimented with differing styles of writing, composed essays and wrote some perceptive sketches of people. She discovered a love of music and went to concerts, and began to make friends and to move tentatively outside the family circle.

Minor cyclothymic swings had begun around the age of 17 but she was, for most of this time, comparatively stable and well. Her weight was steady, menstruation regular and there were no panic attacks or outbursts of unreasonable temper.[14] Life was mostly a dull, undemanding routine, without undue stress.

The unhappiness of these seven years came from conflicting feelings towards her father. He was, she thought, a split personality: the good, literary, humane man she adored and the bullying, brutal, egocentric tyrant she hated. Her ambivalence was not of course new, but it became magnified through his cavalier treatment of Vanessa.

Every Wednesday after lunch, Vanessa presented the household accounts for her father's inspection. After a moment's silence he invariably accused her of extravagance and became heated and abusive: 'I am ruined. Have you no pity for me? There you stand like a block of stone . . .'[15] He would roar and hammer on the table but Vanessa never responded. She stood mute, looking into the distance until at last, with a heavy sigh, Leslie signed the cheque and she immediately left the room.

Virginia was outraged by the brutality of these scenes, feeling 'unbounded contempt' for her father 'and pity for Vanessa'.[16] His melodramatic behaviour was reserved entirely for women. Virginia was certain her father would have restrained himself had a man been present. He looked on his womenfolk as part saint, part slave, there to satisfy his infantile needs. Julia and Stella had stuck to the rules of his game but Vanessa refused to play. When Stella died he assumed Vanessa would put on the mantle of the Angel in the House and he was astonished and upset to discover he was wrong, unable to adapt his ways. Angry though these scenes made her, Virginia did not follow Vanessa from the room. She sat on in silence hoping perhaps for some sign from her father that might redeem him in her eyes. After a time he would abandon his self-pity and look at Virginia and say, half contritely, 'You must think me . . . foolish.'[17]

Leslie treated Virginia more like a man potentially his equal than one of his women. She was like him in many ways, and she was easily his favourite child, the one destined to become a writer, to follow the Stephen tradition.

Virginia had immense admiration for the good literary father, his honesty and unworldliness and sincerity, and she criticised her mother for not having checked his unpleasant egocentric side. But like her, she believed the *DNB* to have been responsible for much of his later deterioration. The loved and hated father continued to obsess her long after his death, and she argued and raged against him and told him what she had dared not say to him in life.

She craved Leslie's love and respect, but that could only come, she believed, through literary success. She never argued with him in life or challenged his opinion, even to herself. An unenthusiastic comment from him about her work would have been a terrible rejection and she never showed him any of her writing. The idea for her first novel, *The Voyage Out*, came to her at Manorbier in South Wales, after Leslie's death. Some years later, while writing the first draft, she had a dream where she showed him the manuscript and 'he snorted, and dropped it on the table, and I was very melancholy'.[18] Recalling him when she was famous, Virginia confessed that had he lived on to be 100, she could not have become a writer: 'no writing, no books'.[19] Any criticism from him would have destroyed her.

It was a truth that her husband Leonard came to understand intuitively. He always read the manuscript of each novel and Virginia waited on tenterhooks until he pronounced it to be 'Your best'. Only then was Virginia's mind put at rest. It mattered not that she thought, 'Has he not *got* to think so?' The approving words were crucial.

Virginia and Vanessa had few secrets from one another during those seven years. Each industriously pursued her own interest. Vanessa went to Cope's School of Art three days a week until 1901, when she entered the Painting School of the Royal Academy. Virginia had lessons in Greek twice a week, and read widely and developed her descriptive powers. They supported each other, confided, ridiculed and laughed about the family and friends, especially their half-brother George who was forever wanting to turn them into elegant young ladies. Vanessa alone at that time gave Virginia the warmth and care she needed, and encouraged her fantasies and sense of the absurd. Their nicknames from nursery days lived on: Virginia, Billy (goat); the *singes,* the Apes; Vanessa, the Dolphin.

Virginia listened sympathetically when Vanessa railed against their father but there were times when she would have liked to talk of his good side, his understanding and sensibility, but Vanessa gave her no opportunity. Any suggestion that Leslie had good qualities would be met by sulky silence and a wall of rejection, which Virginia had to avoid at all cost.

Leslie became ill in 1902 with cancer of the bowel. He continued to work and summer holiday with his children until his death, but the old fiery spirit was gone. During this time the twenty-year-old Virginia desperately needed a sympathetic ear, to unburden herself of guilt and love, to speak of the agony of losing her father. Vanessa could not help. It was then that Virginia found what she most needed: a maternal 'aunt'.

Violet Dickinson was 37, a tall, gawky spinster, well read, musical, cultivated, with a natural charm. She had been a close friend of Stella's and Virginia had always liked her, although previously she had not known her well. Perhaps Violet Dickinson recognised Virginia's plight and made a deliberate effort to be sympathetic. Whatever it was, Virginia responded and threw herself, literally and metaphorically, into Violet's arms. Violet reciprocated. Virginia's mind had always interested her and she was prepared to mother her and meet her emotional demands.

Virginia discussed every detail of her father's terminal illness with Violet and brought out her anxieties and admiration: 'He is such an attractive creature, and we get on so well when we're alone.'[20] She clung to Violet gratefully: 'You are the only sympathetic person in the world. That's why everyone comes to you with their troubles.'[21] Within a short time Violet had come, together with Leslie, to occupy the centre of her thoughts. She wove childish fantasies of herself and Violet. Violet was a kangaroo whose pouch was a 'haven for small kangaroos'. Virginia became 'Sparroy', derived from Sparrow and Monkey. It is noteworthy that, with Vanessa, Violet, Leonard, and Vita, Virginia became in make-believe some species of monkey. In childhood Virginia had enjoyed visiting the

London Zoo, watching the small monkeys cling to their mothers, perhaps identifying with them.

The pleasure of embracing Violet Dickinson aroused 'hot volcanic depths' in Virginia.[22] 'I wish no more. My food is affection.'[23] Some of her letters to Violet, like those to Vanessa, read like love letters but it is wrong to see the relationship in terms of adult sexuality. Virginia craved intimate mother-love, not the erotic.

Violet Dickinson must have been both surprised and gratified by Virginia's passion; she was not alarmed and continued to provide the affection Virginia needed. Whether or not she had a lesbian side is entirely conjectural and rather beside the point. Virginia was neither looking nor ready for such a relationship.

Inevitably there were moments when Virginia's emotional demands became too much, and Violet told her so. Virginia was only momentarily nonplussed: 'a blessed hell-cat and an angel in one', she declared, using her father's imagery.[24] But Virginia was by no means always all child in the relationship. She liked Violet as a person, and took a close interest in Violet's life, talked over her difficulties, discussed books and the theatre and acquaintances in common. But it was as a mother-figure that she was most important to Virginia, and when this role ended so did their intimacy.

Leslie died on 22 February 1904. After the funeral the Stephens, with George Duckworth, went to Manorbier on the Pembrokeshire coast, which was not unlike St Ives, for a month. Virginia felt the loss acutely. She dreamt of her father and could not accept he was dead. She was tormented; she should have done more for him, told him of her devotion, demonstrated her love.

The group walked along the cliffs, and went on 'queer little expeditions' organised by George 'to help pass the time'.[25] Virginia clung to her family, for, when they were all together, Leslie, and

Julia as well, seemed near. Outwardly they all got on but Virginia felt increasingly cut off and isolated. She could not speak to any of them about her grief. Thoby was too reserved, while Adrian, who had disliked and feared his father, was far from unhappy at his death. Vanessa, too, felt released and was enthusiastically organising everyone, planning to leave Hyde Park Gate and its past and take up new lives. It was, Virginia told Violet Dickinson, hard to listen and speak to them about her father: 'You can't think what a relief it is to have someone – that is you, because there isn't anyone else to talk to.'[26]

Virginia's depression was not incapacitating and there were days when she came alive and no longer felt 'like a cow with her nose in the grass'. She read and wrote, and one day, 'walking the down on the edge of the sea', suddenly saw the outline of the novel she wanted to write.[27] It was like a brilliant flash of light, illuminating the gloom and, with hindsight, perhaps a sign of lurking trouble, for Leslie's death had coincided with springtime cyclothymic depression.

Virginia's resentment was building up against Vanessa. Her sister's dismissal of Leslie, her wish to forget their past, her gaiety and plans for the future upset her. She minded leaving Hyde Park Gate with all its associations and memories. She wanted everything preserved, and she kept thinking she would find Leslie at home on her return. Her sense of loss was becoming overwhelming: 'I wonder how we go on as we do, as merry as grigs all day long,' she complained.[28]

Virginia's resentment was increased by Vanessa's scolding for picking at food or going to bed too late, but at the same time she desperately wanted her sister's affection; not even Violet Dickinson could replace her for long as mother-substitute.

From South Wales the Stephens travelled to Italy, reaching Venice on Easter Sunday. Virginia, who had not been further than Boulogne before, was excited and her spirits momentarily rose. Venice seemed an amusing and beautiful place, and she liked the people. But the respite was short-lived. Depression returned and she began to feel trapped and anxious, 'like a Bird in a Cage'.[29] They moved to Florence, where they were joined by Violet Dickinson. Virginia had been looking forward to the reunion, but her spirits failed to lift. She behaved badly, was dull and 'tempersome', and the atmosphere grew increasingly uneasy.

Virginia angrily watched Vanessa enjoying herself, exploring churches and palaces and enthusing over frescoes and pictures. Her resentment bubbled over in outbursts of temper. More alarmingly, towards the end of their stay in Florence, signs of paranoia began to appear:

> Germans are brutes – there is a strange race that haunts hotels – gnome-like women who are creatures that come out in the dark. An hotel is a sort of black cave.[30]

Black humour perhaps, but it was inappropriate. Virginia was trapped in her own black cave. Travelling back to England they spent a few days in Paris, and joined a 'real Bohemian café party', which included Clive Bell and the painter Gerald Kelly, where they talked of 'Art, sculpture and music until 11.30'.[31] Vanessa was in her element. Virginia was over-stimulated and pushed one step nearer the abyss.

Virginia became manic two days after she returned home; wildly excited, three nurses were needed to control her. Anger against Vanessa poured out in torrents of abuse and violence, and her sister was forced to withdraw. Violet Dickinson came to the rescue and Virginia was taken from Hyde Park Gate to Violet's country home, Welwyn, at Burnham Wood.

Virginia was difficult to control for about three months. She was deluded, and heard voices tempting her to 'all kinds of wild things'.[32] Birds sang to her in Greek. She believed Edward VII – who had been crowned in 1902, shortly before her father's death – lurked beneath the bedroom window among the azaleas, shouting smutty words. Once she jumped from the first-floor bedroom window, landing harmlessly in the bushes, perhaps in response to 'voices' or while experiencing a panic attack. It was probably not a deliberate attempt on her life, although she had moments of intense despair.

Mania was succeeded by depression but by September Virginia was sufficiently in control of herself to join the family on holiday. As she recalled the angry scenes with Vanessa she became anxious, and clung to her sister, wanting to be told she was still loved. She wrote to Violet Dickinson, 'I really think she is happy with me now.' She pleaded to be allowed to return home for good and promised Vanessa there would be 'no more disgusting scenes over food'.[33] Vanessa was in the midst of moving to 46 Gordon Square and had just begun at the Slade School of Art, and she was not convinced of Virginia's full recovery. Not until 6 January 1905, when Dr Savage pronounced her 'cured', was Virginia finally accepted back into the family.

Chapter Six

Vanessa's Marriage – Virginia's Instability

The Stephen children were at last on their own. Gerald had set himself up in a flat and, in the autumn of 1904, George married Lady Margaret Herbert.

Virginia's breakdown had made Vanessa very aware of her sister's vulnerability and the burden of responsibility that was now hers. She insisted Virginia follow Dr Savage's advice to the letter: plenty of food and sleep, rest and quiet, hot chocolate and, if needed, mulled wine at bedtime. Combining the roles of loving sister and worried mother was not easy with someone like Virginia who, while demanding to be Vanessa's child, simultaneously sought to dominate the relationship.

Vanessa did not mind playing mother to Virginia for, exasperating as it could be, her maternal instincts were strong. Virginia became 'my own baby', her 'own beloved monkey', rewarded with petting and grooming if 'he' behaved well. Virginia revelled in the baby talk and sensual play but protested when Vanessa insisted she lead a healthy lifestyle. She objected to the life of a semi-invalid but the memory of a mad Virginia screaming abuse at Vanessa was still frighteningly vivid to both.

Virginia began to have work published. Two articles had come out in November, and she now reviewed regularly and wrote articles for several publications, including the *Times Literary Supplement*. Already Virginia worked in a highly disciplined fashion, always reserving the mornings for work.

Early in 1905 she was persuaded to lecture on History and English Literature to working-class adults at Morley College; once a week, until the end of 1907, she taught a small group, mostly of women, with a mix of enthusiasm and amusement. The experience added a sense of achievement and increased her confidence, although it hardly broadened her social horizon: 'One has to be so cheerful with the lower classes', she wrote, 'or they think one diseased'.[1]

Vanessa and Virginia led a full social life, with concerts and plays and the occasional party and dance, but for Virginia the most interesting event of the week was the Thursday evening 'At Home', started by Thoby to keep in touch with his old Cambridge friends. At these gatherings Virginia met young men of a type and class she had not encountered before, intellectuals for the most part who discussed art and literature, religion and love, far into the night. They were altogether different from the men of the conventional social world Virginia had met in the ballrooms of Belgravia.

She and Vanessa had been briefly introduced to some of Thoby's friends during visits, carefully chaperoned, to his rooms at Cambridge. Now, in the freer air of Gordon Square, Virginia studied them and began to join in their discussions, her confidence increasing when she found she was listened to with respect. There was Clive Bell, Thoby's closest friend. He was 'an astonishing fellow . . . a sort of mixture between Shelley and a sporting country squire'. And Lytton Strachey, 'the essence of culture . . . Exotic, extreme in every way . . . so long, so thin that his thigh bone was no thicker than Thoby's arm . . . a prodigy of wit'. While Saxon Sydney Turner was 'an absolute prodigy of learning . . . very silent and thin and odd . . . the most brilliant talker because he always spoke the truth'.[2] Only Leonard Woolf among Thoby's close friends was absent:

> a Jew who trembled perpetually all over . . . so violent, so savage; he so despised the human race. One night he dreamt he was throttling a man and he dreamt with such violence that when he woke up, he had pulled his thumb out of joint.[3]

Woolf was absent because he was in Ceylon. The Stephen sisters had met him in Cambridge in 1902, and he had dined with them at Gordon Square, at Thoby's invitation, shortly before sailing for Colombo in October 1904, but he was a dim memory to them. Virginia, still scarcely back to normal in 1904, had barely noticed him.

Thoby influenced both his sisters. He was a handsome, genial giant of well over six feet, and gave out an attractive sense of gentle strength and warmth. Friendly in manner, he was also unusually reserved and invariably hid his deeper feelings. Virginia remarked that sex seemed a taboo subject to him: she had no idea of his sexual preferences, and not once after they left the nursery did he kiss her or Vanessa. In their early childhood Thoby and Vanessa were very close and did everything together, but as Virginia developed she had competed vigorously for his attention and pushed Vanessa into the background.

Both sisters worshipped Thoby, as did many of his friends. Lytton Strachey's admiration for him overflowed:

> He has a wonderful and massive frame and a face hewn out of the living rock. His character is as splendid as his appearance and as wonderfully complete. In fact, he's monolithic. But if it were not for his extraordinary sense of humour, he would hardly be of this world.[4]

Virginia and Vanessa felt protected by his presence. He provided a balance at Gordon Square. His high standards and disapproval of anything too unconventional ensured social boundaries. When he died in 1906 those boundaries became fluid, and nowhere more than in the field of sex. While Thoby lived, sex was never discussed; afterwards it was rarely absent. Many years after his death Thoby emerged from Virginia's mind as the heroic Percival, worshipped by the characters in *The Waves* – all of whom were aspects of Virginia.

Virginia was content that their lives continued unchanged indefinitely. She had material and emotional security and enough freedom to expand herself. Her peace of mind was broken one afternoon in 1905 when Vanessa, 'stretching her arms above her head with a gesture that was at once reluctant and yielding, said, ". . . Of course, I can see that we shall all marry. It's bound to happen."' Virginia's anxiety was immediately aroused and a black cloud gathered on the horizon. She sensed a fresh loss, 'a horrible necessity impending over us; a fate would descend and snatch us apart, just as we had achieved freedom and happiness'.[5]

Virginia's own marriage appeared remote, almost absurd. None of Thoby's friends attracted her physically. Secretly, she considered marriage to be 'a very low-down affair', linked to high society, and 'if one practised it' it would be 'with young men who had been in the Eton Eleven and dressed for dinner'.[6]

Clive Bell first proposed to Vanessa in July 1905, and was politely turned down. She wanted no immediate change. Her work was going well and that April her portrait of Lord Robert Cecil's wife had been exhibited at the New Gallery, which led to further commissions. In the summer she founded the Friday Club, where artists could meet to discuss and exhibit their work. Marriage would interrupt and impede her ambitions. Besides, she still needed to watch over Virginia.

Clive proposed again a year later. This time Vanessa's refusal was firmer but scarcely final, for even while saying 'no' she told him she liked him better than any other man. Her confusing behaviour suggests her own confusion in the summer of 1906. At heart she was beginning to want marriage; she was 27 and emotionally ready, and she found Clive attractive and their interests were alike. She now believed marriage to him could help rather than hinder her painting, but she still hesitated because she feared the effect on Virginia and her sister's ability to fend for herself. Virginia was beginning to lead a more independent life, but there were still occasions when she became 'absolutely out of touch with reality', and Vanessa had to take 'her baby' in hand.[7]

She was beginning to feel the strain. She was much better balanced than Virginia, but she too was genetically predisposed to the Stephen family depression. That September, when all four Stephens, accompanied by Violet Dickinson, set off on holiday to Greece, Vanessa was already clinically depressed. Thoby and Adrian went on ahead, while Vanessa, Virginia and Violet Dickinson travelled by train to Brindisi and thence to Patras by boat. The two groups met up at Olympia.

Vanessa became increasingly unwell and unable to cope with the journey, and spent much of the time resting. When she reached Athens she collapsed, and it took a fortnight's rest and four glasses of champagne a day before she was well enough to be carried on to a boat bound for Constantinople and the Orient Express. When she arrived home she found Thoby, who had returned a week earlier, seriously ill in bed with typhoid fever – at first mistaken for malaria. She was put to bed at once and not allowed to see him. She was still there when Thoby died from the disease on the 20 November.

Thoby's death shocked Vanessa back into life. In the course of depression underlying conflicts often resolve themselves. The mind clears and a firm decision presents itself, ready-made as it were. So it was with Vanessa. Two days after her brother's death she agreed to marry Clive Bell. Two weeks later she was well enough to stay with a friend in the country, happier than she had been for a long time. She and Clive were married in St Pancras Register Office on 7 February 1907.

Virginia dealt with the loss of Thoby and Vanessa's marriage surprisingly well. She was deeply upset by Thoby's death, but her distress was offset by the shock of the announcement of Vanessa's engagement. She alternated between anger and despair. She desperately wanted to be mothered but there was no one to hand. Violet Dickinson had also developed typhoid and was seriously ill at home in bed.

Virginia now began an elaborate correspondence with her, pretending that Thoby was alive and making good progress, sending daily accounts of his doings. 'Thoby is going on splendidly. He is very cross with his nurses because they won't give him mutton chops and beer' (25 November). 'He asks daily after you . . . and how many spots you had and what your tem is' (29 November). The 'game' continued for almost a month, until Violet read of Thoby's death in the *National Review*.

> We had to do it [Virginia explained]. I never knew till this happened how I should turn to you and want you with me when no one else could help. This is quite true, my beloved Violet, and I must write it down for once. I think of you as one of the people . . . who make it worthwhile to live and be happy.[8]

Virginia's fabrication was both the desire to keep Thoby alive, holding back his death with her pen, and an obtuse way of wishing for Violet's full recovery; for at that time of loss Violet seemed her only comforter. In a revealing letter, written halfway through the hoax, Virginia wrote:

> My plan is to treat you as a detached spirit; maybe your body has typhoid; that is immaterial (you will be glad to hear). I address the immortal part and shooting words of fire into the upper aer [sic] which spirits inhabit. They pierce you like lightning, quicken your soul; whereas, if I said How have you slept. and What food are you taking, you would sink into your nerves and arteries and your gross pads of flesh, and perhaps your flame might snuff and die there. Who knows?[9]

Over the next months Virginia was tense and irritable. She had difficulty in sleeping, 'and drugs are worst of all', she told Violet.[10] She raged against those family well-wishers who told her it was time for her to follow her sister's example and marry: 'Is it crude human nature bursting out? I call it disgusting.'

At Vanessa's register office wedding she was 'numb and dumb', and ten days later she still could not realise what had happened. Much of her anger was displaced on to Clive.

> When I think of Father and Thoby and then see that funny little creature twitching his pink skin and jerking out his little spasms of laughter I

wonder what odd freak there is in Nessa's eyesight.[12]

She felt lost when Vanessa decided Virginia and Adrian must leave 46 Gordon Square to the Bells and find a place of their own.

Virginia's ill humour was enhanced by the 'spring melancholia' but as this receded and her mood improved her attitude began to change. By April she had found a house for herself and Adrian in Fitzroy Square and begun to acknowledge Vanessa's happiness in marriage. Two months later she decided Vanessa 'might marry twenty Clives and still be the most delightful creature in the world. And I like him better too.'[13]

Vanessa went out of her way, just as Stella had done, to make Virginia feel welcome and as much loved. They met almost daily, shared their experiences and laughed and delighted in each other's company. Vanessa needed the stimulation and humour of her sister as much as Virginia her affection. Much as she loved Clive, Vanessa missed Virginia. 'Don't starve or do anything foolish', she warned, adding wistfully, 'you aren't at all to be trusted and I see quite plainly that you'll have to take up your abode with me again before very long.'[14]

Vanessa's sexual awakening had a striking effect on her looks and behaviour. She became noticeably bawdy, often shocking more conventional acquaintances, as though she needed to assert her new-found sexuality. Perhaps subconsciously she also wanted to trumpet her superiority to Virginia and emphasise she had come into her own. Virginia was amused and apparently unembarrassed, but neither she nor Vanessa discussed their sexual lives. Virginia did not ask Vanessa about her honeymoon and whether sex was pleasant or painful. Details of sexual intercourse did not really interest her; indeed her physical libido was never very strong and she looked at sex from a largely intellectual standpoint. She could sometimes be outrageously vulgar but lacked the bawdy humour of Vanessa.

Thoby's death brought the sisters closer to his friends. Formality was discarded and everyone became on Christian name terms. Lytton Strachey circulated a collection of indecent poems among the group. Gossip became the major topic of conversation, along with sex. No one was invited to Gordon Square or Fitzroy Square unless they were Bloomsbury material: intellectual, literary, radical, amusing, and preferably scatological.

Strachey became an intimate of both sisters. Vanessa thought the world of him: 'He came after Thoby's death, and was such an inexpressible help . . . we loved him very much.' However, it was with Virginia that he was particularly close. Both were witty and clever, and equally malicious when together, intellectual, widely read and ambitious. They found each other uncommonly sympathetic; as she later told Vita Sackville-West, 'We fitted like gloves.'[15]

Virginia admired Lytton but feared his tongue and went out of her way to impress. She liked the speed and agility of his mind: 'It is an exquisite symphony his nature when all the violins get playing . . . so deep, so fantastic.'[16] Like her he was thin-skinned and often out of step with the rest of the world, and he confided his unhappiness to her, talked freely of his homosexual affairs, and discussed his work. She based the character of St John Hirst in *The Voyage Out* on him. 'I envy everyone,' Hirst declares. 'I can't endure people who do things better than I do.'[17] Nor could Virginia and their rivalry added to the attraction between them. The attraction was almost entirely intellectual and held little or no sexuality but by 1909 Vanessa, wanting to see Virginia married and 'out of her hair', was telling her sister that Lytton would make a good husband. Lytton's long affair with Duncan Grant had just ended and in the course of sharing his grief with Vanessa, he may have hinted at the possibility of marriage to Virginia and received some encouragement. Whatever the reasons, Lytton proposed to Virginia who, to his horror, immediately accepted. There was a flurry of excuses, Virginia gracefully agreed to his withdrawing the proposal, and their relationship continued, undisturbed.

Vanessa's first child, Julian, was born on 4 February 1908. Vanessa developed postnatal depression, not bad enough to attract medical attention but sufficient to lower her self-confidence and leave her tired and worried. She was, in fact, depressed after each of her three pregnancies; a combination of genetic vulnerability and unhappy circumstances.

Clive's reaction to his son's arrival upset Vanessa. He was jealous and rejecting, constantly complaining of the time Vanessa gave to Julian, and how hideous the child was. Had Julian been a girl he might have behaved better. Vanessa believed a male child represented competition and brought out the worst in him. He complained of the noise, the mess, the incessant demands. He refused to hold the child and insisted on sleeping in a separate bedroom.

His behaviour was not unexpected, given his nature and background, but it opened Vanessa's eyes to her husband's immaturity. From then on, very slowly, their marriage deteriorated.

Vanessa's depression only served to increase Clive's fractiousness. Feeling inadequate as a mother, afraid of neglecting and failing the child, she fussed over him far more than was necessary and insisted on doing everything herself, wearing herself out. She became over-possessive of Julian, behaviour which was to endure and never failed to irk Virginia and irritate Clive.

Virginia's response to Julian's birth was lukewarm. The infant's demands for immediate attention reflected her own need. She, not Julian, she maintained, was Vanessa's 'first born'.[18] Once more she felt separated from her sister and her jealousy was barely hidden: 'Its voice is too terrible . . . like an ill-omened cat. Nobody would wish to comfort it or pretend it was a human being.'[19] Her exclusion from her sister's life was painfully apparent, she told Clive: 'I seem often to be only an erratic external force, capable of shock but without any lodging in your lives.'[20]

The flirtation between Clive and Virginia began when they were all on holiday at St Ives that May. Virginia had already begun to edge in that direction for, on 15 April, she wrote to Clive, 'kiss her

[Vanessa] most passionately in all my private places – neck, and arm, and eyeball, and tell her – what new thing is there to tell? How fond I am of her husband?'[21]

The St Ives boarding house echoed to the cries of Julian and the landlady's noisy two-year-old son. Clive and Virginia took refuge in long walks together along the cliffs and across the moor. They talked of books, gossiped about friends, laughed and joked and set out to impress each other. Never before had they been alone together for so long. Clive was an amusing, stimulating companion and Virginia, when on form, was captivating. He was a natural flirt. Virginia was an attractive woman, and when elated she was irresistible. At a party fellow guests fell under her spell and, 'listening to her, forgot love affairs, stayed on and on into the small hours.'[22] She was flattered by Clive's attention; 'my head spins – I feel above the Gods,' she told him.[23]

Clive has been blamed but it is just as likely that Virginia made the first moves and Clive responded. Thrown together, Vanessa tied down with Julian, it was almost inevitable they should become involved. Clive may have wanted to make love to Virginia but his conscience and, perhaps even more, the likely consequences of stirring strong emotions in Virginia stopped him. He had, after all, seen her in Paris just before she went mad in 1904, and observed her occasional wild flights of fantasy at Gordon Square.

However, Clive became deeply involved with Virginia, and eventually lost his way. What began as a lighthearted diversion from the trials of fatherhood turned into a disturbing obsession, which led ultimately to the breakdown of his marriage. He became restless and unsettled, wanting the unobtainable, pursuing the forbidden. He continued the pursuit but with no end in sight, and when Virginia offered to kiss him he backed away. Virginia was more amused than disappointed. Clive's timidity reassured her that she was in control of the relationship. 'We achieved the heights then,' she told him triumphantly.[24]

Sexual exploration and sisterly rivalry played a part at first but, essentially, Virginia wanted to win back her sister. As time progressed Virginia began to see the relationship with Clive as a means of achieving this: to possess Clive's love would be to possess her sister's. Her thinking was childlike. In no way did she wish to separate husband and wife. She wanted simply to be part of their marriage, to love husband and wife as one. Clive would be the carrier of Virginia's passion for her sister: 'Kiss my yellow honey-bee,' she ordered him.[25]

Vanessa became aware of the entanglement before long and was hurt and angry. She felt betrayed by the two people she most trusted, and was confused as to their intentions. She now saw the moral weakness and self-indulgence at the centre of Clive's easygoing nature, and her respect and affection waned. Virginia was the main offender in her eyes, although she was unsure whether her sister was being deliberately wicked or playing a fantasy game. She knew Virginia well enough to believe she was not in love with Clive and that there was no sexual intimacy, but that, if anything, only added to her exasperation. In the end she decided Virginia had created a make-believe world.

Vanessa withdrew and concentrated her affection on her son. She avoided any scene or direct confrontation with Clive or Virginia. She never mentioned the affair to either, for it was not in Vanessa's nature to have rows. Her reaction to a painful event was always to withdraw and hide her feelings, to avoid angry scenes which could risk destroying important relationships. She preferred to suffer in silence rather than risk confrontation. Virginia would always be important to Vanessa and she would never cease to care for her, but from then on she was wary of her sister. In one important respect, Virginia and Clive shared a deep interest which did not concern Vanessa: literature. Clive introduced Virginia to the modern French novelists and she came to respect his opinion. This side of their relationship developed in a constructive way, free of neurotic complications, and before long she was talking to him of her problems with the novel.

She had begun to write 'Melymbrosia', which became *The Voyage Out*, at the end of 1907. It had been germinating for some time and, once started, she wrote with intensity, her imagination flowing. Clive was of great assistance when she ran into difficulties. He was an excellent critic, with no axe of his own to grind, and Virginia trusted him enough to show him each instalment of the first draft as completed.

Clive, like Violet Dickinson, believed in Virginia's genius and he took immense pains over his criticism. Virginia needed to feel her novels had the backing of someone whose judgement she respected. Clive was hardly the father-figure Leonard Woolf was to become, but concerning 'Melymbrosia' Virginia saw him as a man of stature. 'Ah, how you encourage me!' she told him gratefully. 'It makes all the difference.'[26] Her genuine need for Clive's encouragement complicated their affair, prolonged it and led Clive to mistake Virginia's gratitude and partial dependence for deeper feelings.

Virginia was damaged by the involvement. The initial excitement soon gave way to a painful sense of guilt towards Vanessa: 'that turned more of a knife in me than anything else has ever done.'[27] Her cyclothymic swings were exacerbated; the intensified spells of depression in late winter and early spring, and hypomanic outbursts in summer, began to cause concern. She still had calm periods, but these too were liable to be disturbed by some incident with Clive that provoked jealousy and outbursts of temper. There was no one to intervene, to advise caution, to prevent the reinforcement of the mood cycle. Had Vanessa stood her ground, read the riot act and told Virginia to stop, the relationship might have ended at once. Virginia would have recognised reality and the harm she was doing to herself and her sister. She and Clive might have continued their co-operation on the novel but not their neurotic interplay.

Disaster is certain when a manic depressive is allowed to slide inexorably out of control. A manic depressive often knows he is helpless to halt the gathering storm, but will respond to firm intervention in the *early* stages. Vanessa, alas, unlike Leonard Woolf, was unable to act, and her passivity encouraged her sister's destructive behaviour and fuelled manic depression.

In September 1908 Virginia went with the Bells to Tuscany. She was still mildly 'high' from the summer and on at least two occasions she and Clive ended up screaming at one another in the street, and rowing noisily when Virginia objected to his kissing Vanessa. She accompanied them again the following year to Florence but there were such 'stormy squalls' that she cut short the holiday and returned home alone.

At the end of that year, shortly before the spring melancholia, she became over-excited. On Christmas Eve she impulsively decided to go to Cornwall on her own for a few days, and it was soon after her return home that she was persuaded by her brother Adrian to join him and three friends in the Dreadnought Hoax.

A telegram was sent to HMS *Dreadnought*, the flagship of the British home fleet then anchored at Weymouth, advising the Admiral of a visit by the Emperor of Abyssinia and four of his entourage. The group, all disguised by dark greasepaint and wearing flowing robes, were met by a guard of honour at the station and escorted round the ship by the captain, Adrian being the interpreter and using what one sailor called 'a rum lingo'. Virginia remained silent, which is perhaps why they escaped detection. They got back safely and all would have been well had not one of the party informed the press, whereupon a storm broke over their heads.

Knowing Virginia's vulnerable state, Vanessa had tried to dissuade Virginia from taking part but to no avail. By March Virginia was on the verge of a breakdown: headaches, insomnia, reluctance to eat, and explosive irritability. Vanessa summoned Dr Savage and on his advice she and Clive took Virginia to Studland for rest and quiet.

The improvement was short-lived and, as summer neared, signs of hypomania, mixed with depression, began to appear. Vanessa, who was in the final months of her second pregnancy (perhaps a last attempt to keep her marriage going) was by now very anxious. Again acting on Dr Savage's advice, she and Clive took Virginia to a rented house near Canterbury, but she continued to cause alarm; excitement and agitation were followed by exhaustion, 'numbness and headache'. Vanessa returned to London after a fortnight to prepare for the delivery, leaving Clive and Virginia together, hardly an ideal arrangement. She spoke to Savage who, persuaded of the danger, arranged for Virginia to enter Miss Thomas's nursing home at Twickenham for a 'slightly modified' rest cure. Virginia reluctantly agreed, and several times during the six weeks' treatment she threatened to leave. 'I really don't think I can stand much more of this,' she wrote to Vanessa at one stage, 'all this eating and drinking and being shut up in the dark . . . in bed alone here for four weeks.'[28]

But she put on weight and was considered well enough to leave in mid-August. Accompanied by Miss Thomas – who seems to have been captivated by her patient – she went to Cornwall on a three-week walking convalescence. She was still unstable and liable to a 'bad night', or a sudden flight of fantastic ideas, but insight and self-control were slowly returning. She wrote to Clive from Gurnards Head, 'I feel a great mastery over the world. My conclusion upon marriage might interest you. So happy I am it seems a pity not to be happier.'[29] A week later she joined the Bells at Studland. Despite a furious row there with Clive, provoked by him, she continued to improve and returned to London in October. Chastened by the breakdown and now conscious of the risk she was running, she heeded Dr Savage's warning that London life would soon unsettle her, and began searching for a country 'refuge'. She found Little Talland House in Firle, near Lewes, and thus began her association with East Sussex and the Downs.

Chapter Seven

Gender and Sexuality

Quentin Bell was born on 19 August 1910. There were no complications but Vanessa was tired and depressed and glad of the customary month in bed, relieved that Virginia would be in Cornwall for most of the lying-in period. Throughout the pregnancy she had watched her sister slipping towards madness, comforting her one moment and having to defend herself against abuse and 'uncontrolled passion' the next. Clive, although recognising that Virginia was ill, had done little to support his wife and relieve the pressure. His tolerance for stressful problems was low, and Vanessa's only ally in the struggle had been Dr Savage.

A month of rest and relative quiet gave Vanessa time to reflect on her current life. She saw it was unsatisfactory; she had too little time to paint, Clive did not provide the companionship and support she wanted, and, above all, the strain of Virginia was becoming almost unbearable. Much as she loved Virginia she could not continue to mother her at the cost of her own family and career. But she could see no solution and, characteristically, displaced her worries onto the new child, convinced he was failing to eat and losing weight. The doctors did not understand what lay behind her obsession and Clive, of course, was a broken reed, unable to bear Quentin's cries. Vanessa grew ever more miserable and distraught. It was at this low point that Roger Fry entered her life.

She had met him earlier in 1910. At the age of 44 he had also reached a crisis point in his life; his wife had developed schizophrenia, from which she would not recover, and he had recently resigned from his post as buyer to the Metropolitan Museum in New York. Enormously energetic and enthusiastic and never at a loose end for long, Fry had arranged an exhibition of contemporary European art – including artists such as Picasso, Matisse, Gauguin, Cézanne, little known in England at that time – to be held in London at the Grafton Galleries. The first exhibition of Post-Impressionist paintings opened in November to a mixed chorus of abuse and praise and created an immediate sensation.

Both Bells, but particularly Clive, were involved in helping with the exhibition, and during that autumn Roger Fry was a frequent visitor to Gordon Square. One evening, when Clive was away and Vanessa and Roger were alone together, she discovered 'something of his power of sympathy', and on a sudden impulse unburdened herself to him.[1] The relief was enormous, and the effect long-reaching.

A growing intimacy and companionship with Fry, together with the excitement of the exhibition, temporarily lifted Vanessa's gloom:

> that autumn . . . everything seemed springing to new life . . . all was a sizzle of excitement, new relationships, new ideas, different and intense emotions all seemed crowding into one's life. Perhaps I did not realise then how much Roger was at the centre of it all.[2]

Roger Fry fell in love at once. Vanessa moved more cautiously and at first would not admit to herself she loved Roger. That April she and Clive travelled to Turkey with him to look at Byzantine art. At Broussa Vanessa collapsed after a supposed miscarriage. In all probability, the conflicts and strain of the journey brought out lurking depression and, coinciding with premenstrual tension and heavy bleeding, released panic attacks. Breathless and hyperventilating, she was terrified and unable to move, but in no danger. Roger seems to have recognised this. He took charge and quickly calmed her and restored order.

Virginia was at home when she heard the news and, fearing the worst, hurried to Constantinople. There she found her sister prostrate but tranquil, being nursed by Roger and preparing to return home on the Orient Express.

Vanessa's depression lasted over two years. The emotional conflicts which had released the 'black Stephen madness', required time for resolution. During this period she came to love Roger passionately. She leant heavily on him, relying on his judgement and understanding, and put herself into his care. She trusted him implicitly and allowed herself to love him. The emotional turmoil eased and she released herself from Clive. For as long as possible she kept the affair hidden and the marital break-up, never total, was gradual.

Clive reacted predictably to Roger's intrusion with jealous outbursts and demands that Roger stay away from Gordon Square, but his attempts to regain Vanessa's affection were wasted. She wanted her marriage to continue, for conventional and financial reasons, but only on an asexual basis. She wanted Clive to remain a husband in name and to stay within the family circle, but nothing more. She succeeded. The Bells never divorced.

Virginia was quick to detect what was happening, and regarded the relationship with surprise and some disapproval at first. Her first thought was that once again she had lost her sister, for Vanessa had become more reserved, partly because of depression but also for fear of Virginia influencing Roger. But this time Vanessa had no cause for alarm. Roger's attachment as unassailable.

Virginia's interest in Clive waned steadily, although his continued for her, but they remained close friends. Throughout the summer of 1911 she was restless and her behaviour erratic, moving between depression and hypomanic excess. Vanessa no longer attempted to watch over her and Virginia was left with no protector. She bathed naked in the Cam with Rupert Brooke (it was an innocent outing), and fraternised with the 'Neo-Pagans', squabbled with Adrian and contemplated living away from him. She finished the seventh or eighth draft of her novel. She seemed to be going nowhere. She was '29 and unmarried – a failure'.[3]

Virginia's gender was not in doubt. She felt herself to be an attractive woman. She might play with the idea of androgyny but she could not imagine being 'more than half a man', as Katherine Mansfield did,[4] nor did she desire to put on male dress. On the other hand she was sexually attracted to women. She could appreciate male beauty and enjoy a chance touch, but any hint of sexual interest brought down the shutters.

Her first real crush in adolescence had been on the older Madge Vaughan – echoed in Clarissa Dalloway's memories of Sally Seton – and that had been followed by her need for a maternal protector and a sensual relationship.

Vanessa's marriage made Virginia examine her sexuality. No man attracted her physically, apart perhaps from Clive, although she liked male company and preferred the male mind. Several men between 1908 and 1911 were interested in marrying her, but the only one acceptable as a husband had been Lytton Strachey, a confirmed homosexual, suitable because he was 'the perfect female friend'.[5]

Men lacked the gentleness and sensitivity of women, in Virginia's opinion. A man always wanted power, however gentle and understanding he might be on the surface, and a husband would try to dominate his wife. Sexual intercourse lay at the centre of the marital struggle, and must end in a wife being subjugated and humiliated. The prospect terrified Virginia. If she could not be in control, sex was unacceptable. It was not the physical act of penetration, but the psychological effect of being overcome and defenceless that was so horrifying. Perhaps the fear originated in her half-brother Gerald's fumbling explorations in childhood, but the cause surely lay much deeper; perhaps partly genetic, partly the confusing relationships in early childhood.

Virginia wanted to be married. She hated the idea of living alone. She wanted a marriage that was 'a tremendous living thing . . . not dead and easy'.[6] She wanted an equal partnership, a companionable husband, strong and understanding enough to be mother and father to her, who loved her yet did not make sexual demands, who watched over her and yet allowed her freedom. The choice of husband was limited.

Chapter Eight

Leonard Woolf and Courtship

Leonard Woolf was born on 15 November 1880 into a liberal Jewish family, the third of nine children and the second of six boys. His father had come from a background of East End tailors to become a successful barrister. His mother was a de Jong, Dutch Jews who had established themselves in London in the middle of the last century.

Leonard was always dismissive of his mother, claiming without justification, 'she loved me . . . less than any of the eight others',[1] and he believed he was his father's favourite son, possessing his father's mental gifts and marked out to succeed. These lifelong beliefs, together with his provocative and hurtful behaviour to his mother, suggest, at the least, unresolved childhood conflicts, which may have contributed to his melancholic and solitary nature.

His father's sudden death, when Leonard was 11, plunged the family overnight from wealth into relative penury and a change of lifestyle. His mother Marie Woolf, acting decisively, moved away from their prosperous home in South Kensington to a smaller suburban one in Putney, and decided to spend her available capital on educating her sons. She calculated that, provide some won scholarships, the money would just last out until the eldest were in a position to support the family.

Leonard possessed a huge capacity for work and a determination to succeed. At school he swept the board academically. He won a scholarship to St Paul's and, from there an Exhibition to Trinity College at Cambridge University. He was by nature an intellectual, but he was also an all-round sportsman; as a result, instead of the bullying usually meted out to swots, he gained a measure of popularity. Nor did he encounter any personal anti-Semitism, a remarkable escape given the widespread prejudice of the period and a tribute to his charm and the 'carapace' he erected. Yet his popularity at school was not accompanied by any close friendships and he brought no school acquaintances home. He was proud of being a Jew and very conscious of belonging to that race, but from his teens he seems to have felt ashamed of the habits and settings of his home. From early on he looked upon himself as an outsider, and even in the body of his family he felt himself to be different, a critical yet uneasy observer, never fitting in, always criticising his mother's 'dream world of rosy sentimentality', upsetting her and disturbing himself in the process.

Cambridge determined the direction of Leonard's life. There he discovered an exciting new world of the intellect and the company of like-minded friends. For the first time in his life he felt himself to be one of a group, accepted and on the inside. They included the men who went up to Cambridge in 1899 with him: Lytton Strachey, Clive Bell, Virginia's brother Thoby Stephen, Saxon Sydney Turner; as well as Maynard Keynes – who began at King's College three years later – and a number of dons.

Leonard and his friends tirelessly debated and railed against what they saw as hypocritical Victorian standards and beliefs. They were all atheists in search of honesty and truth, 'arrogant, supercilious, cynical, sarcastic'. Leonard, Strachey and Saxon Sydney Turner would walk at night through the cloisters to listen to the nightingales and return, arm-in-arm, chanting Swinburne, prior to meeting in one or other's rooms to debate weighty moral issues.

It was a joyful time and academic work took second place.

Leonard worked but ceased to 'swot', no longer driven to achieve the top-ranking place. He suddenly grew up and rejected many of the values and standards of his family, replacing them with those of his Cambridge friends. He abandoned Judaism in his last year at school – as all the Woolf children did in time, to their mother's disappointment – and during his first undergraduate year proclaimed himself an atheist, utterly opposed to any organised religion.

Quite suddenly, in his second year, Leonard was devastated by a profound sense of emptiness; his life seemed pointless and he began questioning his existence. He could 'find no place for and no explanation of my life or my mind in this fantastic universe' . . . 'Doubt came upon me black as Hell.'[2] Faced with an existential crisis, he became depressed and, for the only time in his life, self-pitying.

Leonard was an usually self-contained man, but throughout his life he needed an example and a cause to centre himself on. Prior to Cambridge he had his idealised father, who 'worked so hard and so continually', and 'whose code of personal conduct [was] terrific'.[3] Leonard had worked flat out at his prep school and St Paul's to succeed and win an Exhibition because it was what his father would have done and, like him, he was 'something of a Puritan'. When he abandoned Judaism he was also discarding an idealised part of his father, and signalling the need for a new ideal, a belief or philosophy from someone he could revere and who might give him a clear sense of direction. His friends stimulated and delighted him, and gave him a newfound sense of intimacy, almost of family, helping to bring Leonard's familiar world to an end. But none was able to help him in his mental struggle or even to understand the problem. He turned to his elder sister Bella, but her advice to 'follow the light and do the right' was unilluminating to someone already groping in the dark.[4]

Two events occurred in 1902 which brought Leonard peace of mind. He was elected to the Apostles, and he came to know the philosopher G. E. Moore.

The Apostles were members of the Cambridge Conversazione Society, better known as 'The Society'. A secret society which had existed since 1820, it met behind locked doors on Saturday evenings, when essays were read and moral questions argued. Discussions were inspired by the 'spirit of the pursuit of truth', and members were expected to speak freely and with absolute candour. To be invited to become an Apostle meant you were not only regarded as highly intelligent and intellectual, but fit company for an élite. At one time or another the Society included some of the best Cambridge minds. Fitzjames Stephen had been an active Apostle but his younger brother Leslie, to his chagrin, was never invited because of his prickly manner. Nor was Thoby Stephen, although Lytton Strachey considered proposing him for membership and later regretted not having done so.

Leonard and Lytton Strachey were elected in 1902. An Apostle remained one until he 'took wings' and resigned, and the Society included men of all ages and repute. Leonard, for instance, continued assiduously to attend Apostle dinners after his marriage, provoking Virginia to refer banteringly to them as 'the feast of the brother Apostles'.

In 1902 the Society included Bertrand Russell and G. E. Moore. Russell remarked, 'It was owing to the existence of the Society that I got to know the people best worth knowing,'[5] a view both Leonard and Lytton would have echoed. It was now they became friends with G. E. Moore. They sat at his feet, accompanied him on his walking holidays in the vacations, and absorbed his philosophy. His *Principia Ethica* became their Bible. His influence on Leonard was immense. Moore removed the 'obscuring accumulation of scales, cobwebs and curtains' from his eyes and revealed, so it seemed, 'the nature of truth and reality, of good and evil character and conduct', replacing what Leonard termed 'the cant of Jehova and Christ' with 'the fresh air and pure light of common sense'.[6]

Alas, the idyllic life did not encourage Leonard to work. He had been expected to obtain first class honours in his final examination, and he too anticipated a good enough pass to obtain a Fellowship but, in the event, his results were indifferent and a Fellowship became out of the question. He decided to spend a fifth year at Cambridge reading for the Civil Service Examination, but his feet were not yet firmly on the ground; his mind was still with the Apostles, and he failed to do the necessary cramming. The outcome was that he came 65th in the pass list, too low for an interesting post in the Home Civil Service. The shock of failure hit him hard and left him bemused. He toyed with the idea of teaching and even resurrected the childhood dream of becoming a barrister like his father, but he was finally brought down to earth with a crash by his elder brother Herbert – the 'head' of the family, who had left school at 16 to work on the Stock Exchange and help out his mother – who told him sharply that he was now expected to contribute to the family finances. He decided to take an appointment in the Colonial Service and, applying for Ceylon, to his surprise and initial dismay, was accepted. In October 1904 he sailed from Tilbury Dock and landed in Colombo on 16 December.

Cadet Woolf was posted to Jaffna in the Northern Province of Ceylon. The contrast between Cambridge and the parochial society of sahibs and memsahibs he now encountered was huge. At first he felt lost without his friends and the convivial Cambridge lifestyle, and clung on to his closest friend Lytton Strachey, writing him long letters about his new life, his despair and the physical and mental hardships of a colonial civil servant. In return he demanded every piece of Cambridge news and gossip. To his family, however, he wrote in an entirely different vein, and Leonard's letters home are chatty and full of interesting and amusing anecdotes of his life.

In his new surroundings, Leonard initially experienced a sense of *déjà vu*, as of returning to life at school. To be seen to be an intellectual was to put oneself outside the pale, and he had to hide his introspective and natural inclinations and assume the outward trappings of a 'jolly good fellow'. He played a good game of tennis, which he enjoyed, was a competent bridge player, and he made himself take part in the evening ritual of whisky and soda and 'British conversation'. Leonard possessed considerable charm when he exerted himself, particularly for women, and as he was young and presentable he was quickly accepted socially. He encountered no anti-Semitism. Arrogant, conceited and quick-tempered as he was, he kept his temper well under control and his often uncomplimentary opinion of his colleagues to himself.

As at school, work became his *raison d'être*; his old drive to succeed, which had been lost in the Apostolic heavens of Cambridge, returned in full force. He coerced the authorities at Jaffna to give him greater responsibility, and within a short time he had proved so efficient and reliable that his boss, the government agent, a man Leonard liked but considered lazy and indecisive, came to look on him as indispensable. When the government agent was promoted to Kandy he insisted on Leonard being transferred with him, which was very much to Leonard's benefit. Leonard continued to do most of his boss's work, working a ten- or eleven-hour day, seven days a week, with such conspicuous success that in the summer of 1907 he was promoted to Office Assistant to the Government Agent.

Leonard's outstanding abilities and energy attracted the attention of the Acting Governor of Ceylon, Sir Hugh Clifford, who enjoyed the climate and entertainment of Kandy and spent a good deal of time there. Clifford took to Leonard and used him on a number of important occasions. He was so impressed with his competence that he had him promoted to Assistant Government Agent to the Hambantota District in the Southern Province. It was exceptionally rapid promotion, after only four years' service, and it made Leonard by far the youngest A.G.A. in the country. The promotion, predictably, generated resentment among some of his colleagues. The Government Agent of the Southern Province, Leonard's immediate superior, for whom Leonard had little respect, considered him a 'jumped-up' favourite, and was openly antagonistic.

In Hambantota, Leonard was solely responsible for the administration of an area of over one hundred thousand people. He was all things to all men: policeman, magistrate, judge, vet, adjudicator, customs officer, taxman, planner and keeper of the peace. The work was immensely hard and often dangerous; comforts were primitive; malaria, along with a range of other tropical diseases and parasites, was endemic. Leonard had to rely entirely on his own resources. He rarely saw another European. There were no railways and few made-up roads. He rode everywhere, and when on circuit his diet frequently depended on what he shot.

He fell in love with the country and became fascinated by the Sinhalese and their way of life. He set about improving their lives; opening schools, developing irrigation schemes, combating poverty and disease. He learnt Sinhalese and Tamil, and it became his passion to understand the people and the structure of their lives and relationships in the villages. He became so involved that he rarely recalled the pleasures of Cambridge, and his letters to Lytton Strachey dwindled to a mere trickle. His empathy with the villagers was remarkable strong, as the reader of Leonard's novel *The Village in the Jungle* will recognise.

Leonard's life in Hambantota was given over to work. Every day, from the time he got up to the moment he went to bed, was concerned with some problem. He exalted his work to a mania, and became obsessed with the need for efficiency, of finding the quickest, most methodical and economical way of tackling a task. He was determined to make his district the most efficient in the island. His pride in completing a census of the district and wiring the result to the authorities in Colombo before anyone else gave him immense satisfaction. He changed the way the goverment salt industry was organised, battled against rinderpest which was ravaging the district, and gained the reputation for being a fair-dealing if hard police magistrate. When he left Hambantota after three years to return home on leave, he had achieved much, and was held in high esteem by the administration in Colombo.

Success was only achieved at a cost to himself and the villagers. His drive for efficiency often became an end in itself. He allowed his impatience and arrogance to triumph over his humanitarian side; efficiency became the be-all and end-all of action. He was prone to trample over traditional native ways when they appeared inefficient and cumbersome and to replace them by Western methods. He played the 'strong man' and often aroused resentment and dislike. More than one person complained to the Governor and asked for his dismissal. Years later, looking back on that time, Leonard admitted he had been 'too ruthless – both to them and myself'.[7]

Leonard was never ambitious in the conventional sense of seeking high position, wealth and honours. He despised such aims. His drive came from wanting to be as perfect as possible in his work, and to be recognised as 'best'. He believed, long before Hambantota, that he was more able than most of the Europeans he encountered, and towards the end of his service he was liable to show it, making little effort to hide his contempt. On at least one occasion he was rebuked by the Governor for writing rude comments on orders received from his G.A., and instructed to show 'more restraint and discretion'.[8]

Three years of near-isolation from European life inevitably increased Leonard's introspective nature and his intolerance for fools. During that time he was a large fish in a small pond, and his word was virtually law among the natives. He loved them as children and came to understand them, much as he did his pets, and he expected the same obedience. He was beginning to assume the mantle of the all-wise dictator, but even before he left Ceylon he had begun to recognise this and question his role.

How could he justify governing another race? What right had an Imperial power to impose its standards on another culture? British rule kept the peace in Ceylon and brought progress to its 'less civilised' peoples, yet was it morally right? Did he want to continue to rule over these people as proconsul? As a highly successful civil servant it was likely that when he returned to Ceylon after his leave he would be promoted to Central Government in Colombo and, in time, progress to Colonial Secretary or even Governor. The thought depressed him. He would have to mix, put on his carapace, suppress his arrogance, and adopt a 'good fellow' approach to life. He would be expected to join in the social life of Colombo; tennis and bridge, billiards at the Club, the interminable gossip and 'filth'. The prospect was unappealing. Yet he was reluctant to abandon the achievements of seven years and start afresh.

Leonard left Colombo on a year's leave on 24 May 1911 with a divided mind and a sense of uncertainty.

He returned to the family home in Putney. Almost nothing had changed in his absence: there was the same surburban atmosphere, thick dark curtains, heavy furniture, the photographs and porcelain knick-knacks, his brothers and sisters joking and disputing, all presided over by his mother radiating 'rosy sentimentality'. A 'mixture of reality and unreality, of familiarity and strangeness'. overcame him. [9] Sitting at the dinner table that first evening he felt claustrophobic and homesick for Ceylon. In his mind's eye he saw the large open room of his Hambantota bungalow, and heard the waves of the Indian Ocean pounding the shore below. The walls of the Putney dining room closed in on him and, for a moment, he thought to catch the next boat back. He felt unsure of himself, who he was or what he was doing there. He forced himself to concentrate his thoughts. He was home, the responsible Jewish boy, the good son who had proved himself and become a sahib, his mother's pride and joy; but the acclaimed Administrator of Hambantota seemed far off.

Cambridge and the Apostles were soon in the forefront of his thoughts, and three days after the homecoming he went up to Cambridge to stay with Lytton Strachey and renew friendships. Initially, Leonard was apprehensive, fearing he had changed and become a dull being, but Lytton welcomed back the friend who had been 'absolute Lord of ten million blacks in the middle of the desert', with open arms.[10] Leonard had not changed at all, Lytton declared, apart from his 'long, drawn, weather-beaten face' and habit of speaking 'very slowly, like one re-risen from the tomb – or rather on the other side of it'.[11] He went to a gathering of the Society and immediately found himself back in the familiar stimulating environment he had left behind in 1904; the same friends, almost the same intellectual disputes. Leonard's gloom vanished overnight. He sought out his old acquaintances, including Moore, and was infinitely reassured to find them 'unchanged and unchanging', holding to the same truths and values.

Leonard decided to forget his doubts about Ceylon and his future and for the first six months of leave give himself up to enjoyment. He spent a week walking on Dartmoor with Lytton and Moore, and three weeks in Scandinavia with his brother Edgar. The remainder of 1911 was a time of 'unmitigated, pure, often acute, pleasure', such as he 'had never had before'. Much of this pleasure came from his growing friendship with Virginia, Clive and Vanessa.

Leonard dined with Vanessa and Clive in Gordon Square on 3 July, three weeks after his arrival home, and afterwards Virginia, Duncan Grant and Walter Lamb joined them for coffee and talk. It was, Leonard later decided, 'the beginning of what came to be called "Bloomsbury"'.

Leonard was captivated by what he found at Gordon Square. When he had last dined there in 1904 with Thoby and his sisters, the atmosphere had been formal and reserved. It was 'wonderfully different' in 1911, freer, more friendly, less inhibited. Leonard felt immediately accepted, at once on intimate terms with the Bells, taken into a society, unimaginable in Ceylon, where people said exactly what they thought on any topic, be it literature or sex, and women participated as passionately and freely as men. Formality was banished, everyone was on first name terms, and kisses were preferred to handshakes.

The contrast between the Stephen sisters in 1906 – so aloof and reserved and, to Leonard, almost unapproachable – and the witty, friendly women Leonard encountered in 1911 amazed him at first. Eight years earlier he had secretly fallen in love with Vanessa, partly because of her looks – her features were 'more perfect, her eyes bigger and better, her complexion more glowing'[12] than Virginia's – but mainly because she looked so like her brother Thoby and possessed something of his 'monolithic' aura. Thoby had been a close friend. His imposing presence and immensely good nature had made him an object of hero worship to many of his friends, including Lytton Strachey. Leonard's admiration contained little or no homosexual attraction but it did include envy of Thoby's family background. Meeting his sisters and father in Thoby's rooms in 1903 had been an unforgettable experience, and when he learnt of Thoby's death in 1906, he had felt a huge sense of loss, for Thoby was 'above everyone in his nobility'.[13]

Leonard's interest in Vanessa in 1903 had been little more than a reflection of his feelings for Thoby and all that he represented. Brother and sister symbolised an ideal world, one where he might live by writing, surrounded by like-minded friends. Virginia had scarcely registered with Leonard at that time; she was simply Vanessa's sister. When he met her again in 1904, just before leaving for Ceylon, she had been silent and gloomy and left little impression.

Lytton had kept Leonard up to date on all the Stephens while in Ceylon. He knew of Vanessa's marriage to Clive Bell, but not until 1909 did Virginia become of interest. Then, Lytton had mischievously written of Virginia's entanglement with Clive and described the holiday she and the Bells had had in Italy, adding,

> That little canary-coloured creature we knew at Trinity . . . how does he manage to attract the two most beautiful and witty women in England.[14]

Three months later Lytton suggested Leonard should marry Virginia before it was too late. Amused but intrigued, Leonard wrote back, 'Do you think Virginia would have me? Wire to me if she accepts. I'll take the next boat home.' To his astonishment he then learnt Lytton had himself proposed marriage to Virginia, been accepted, and immediately 'got out of it . . . it would be death if she accepted me.'[15]

Lytton now redoubled his urgings to Leonard to marry Virginia, as though his proxy. 'Marry her', he urged. 'If you came and proposed, she'd accept. You would be great enough and you'll have the immense advantage of physical desire.'[16] Leonard was too busy in the jungle and by-ways of Hambantota to take the matter any further. Perhaps he would propose when he returned home on leave but, he told Lytton with some prescience, marriage holds such 'ghastly complications'.[17]

Leonard had a strong heterosexual drive, unlike many of his Apostolic friends, with no overt homosexual leanings. Ceylon began his sexual education. Young civil servants were expected to copulate but not to marry or become engaged, and Leonard followed tradition. He had sex with prostitutes and one or two outlandish but enthusiastic women and, for a time, shared his bungalow with a concubine, but he was always troubled by post-orgasmic depression, the plunge from violent pleasure into despair, and he worried over separating love from lust. He had 'an absurd, amusing and romantic affair'[18] with the seventeen-year-old wife of a 'boring Ceylon planter',[19] but when it ended he concluded it was degrading to be in love, 'since 99 per cent of it is always the desire to copulate, otherwise it is only the shadow of itself'.[20]

Leonard was attractive to women, not least because he enjoyed the 'undiluted female mind, as well as . . . the female body'. Women, he believed, were gentler, more sensitive, more civilised than men, and he liked communicating, listening and experiencing 'the female quality of mind'. Once only, in Kandy, was Leonard near falling in love, with the teenage daughter of a tea planter, but again he found the relationship 'pretty degrading', and he had to 'behave like a gentleman' lest he be pushed into marriage.[21]

Increasingly, however, he saw that marriage could rescue him from his loneliness and depression. Others, apart from Lytton, thought the same. Leonard's sister Bella took him to task and told him he required 'someone to turn to' to relieve his gloom and recommended 'a very special sort of girl . . . strong-minded and clever and a sense of humour. If you marry a weak character, you'll squash her. You *must* marry someone who can hold her own with you and yet be good-tempered.'[22]

Perhaps Leonard remembered that advice when he entered Gordon Square. He was certainly well primed, and he was immediately drawn to Virginia. Virginia was, in turn, interested in Leonard and, encouraged by Vanessa, invited him for a weekend at her cottage in Firle. Leonard was committed to other arrangements and had to refuse, but the idea of marriage was already in his mind, for on holiday he told his brother about Virginia and discussed the problems marriage would bring. On returning home, Leonard engineered another invitation from Virginia and on 16 September, together with Marjorie Strachey, Lytton's sister, and Desmond McCarthy (an Apostle and friend of Moore) he went down to Firle for the weekend.

Their friendship prospered. In November Virginia moved with Adrian into a four-storey house in Brunswick Square, and arranged to let out the top floor to Leonard. By now Leonard was in love. He felt a deep affinity with Virginia. They thought alike and had the same ideals. Each wanted to write. Both rejected religion and bourgeois values and wanted a 'civilised' life. They were, Leonard believed, 'mind to mind and soul to soul'.[23]

Leonard decided on marriage. If Virginia accepted, he would resign from the Colonial Service; if she refused he would return to Ceylon. He proposed to her on 11 January 1912. Virginia procrastinated; she was unsure and must have time. What Leonard did not know was that the Spring Melancholia was gathering force, heightening her anxiety and reinforcing her uncertainty. Depression gathered and at the end of January, unable to sleep, headachy and agitated, she was forced to spend a week in bed. She was still unwell and very erratic in mood when, with Vanessa, she gave two housewarming parties at Asham, a remote old farmhouse near Firle on which the sisters had just obtained a five-year lease. Her behaviour worsened. Savage was consulted, and Virginia went back to the Twickenham nursing home for ten days' rest. Visitors and letters were forbidden, and Leonard's first news of Virginia's progress was a hypomanic note, written immediately after her return to Brunswick Square:

> I shall tell you wonderful stories of the lunatics. Bye the bye, they've elected me King. There can be no doubt about it. I summoned a conclave and made a proclamation about Christianity.[24]

It was funny, but just a little bizarre.

No alarm bell seems to have rung for Leonard, although he knew about the 1904 breakdown. He was already too committed to Virginia to draw back, and he considered Virginia's behaviour to be due to 'nerves', which would calm down once she decided about marriage. She simply needed more time. By now Leonard's leave was almost up. He applied for an extension but, because he refused to give a reason, this was withheld. On 25 April, encouraged by a letter from Virginia, he took the plunge and resigned from the Ceylon Civil Service although, he told Virginia, he expected no decision from her until she had finished *The Voyage Out*. He was certain she loved him.

Leonard's resignation – finally accepted on 7 May – helped Virginia make up her mind. He had given up a brilliant career for her sake, proof enough of the strength of his love, despite knowing her to be so difficult to live with and so very intemperate. But even more important was her improving state of mind. As the summer hypomania neared, her spirits rose and her anxieties lessened. On 29 May she told Leonard she would marry him.

Virginia was thirty years old, 'getting on a bit', as the Stephen matrons would have told one another, and she did not want to find herself 'a melancholy old maid'. She was often exasperated living with Adrian, but the prospect of living alone was worse. She was still attractive – an old friend, Sydney Waterlow, had proposed marriage only two months before Leonard – but Leonard was the first man since Lytton to whom she could imagine being married. What was also important was Vanessa's approval.

Vanessa was utterly weary of bearing the responsibility of

(left) Virginia's father, Sir Leslie Stephen. (Hulton Getty)

(below) Virginia with her father, photographed in 1902. (Hulton Getty)

Vanessa Bell. (Hulton Getty)

(left) Vita Sackville-West. (Hulton Getty)

(below) Leonard Woolf reading with John Lehmann, managing director of Hogarth Pr (Corbis/Hulton Getty)

Portraits of Virginia Woolf. (Hulton Getty)

watching over Virginia. She believed marriage to the right man would give her sister stability, and she had strong backing from Dr Savage. Leonard impressed her as 'one of the most remarkable and charming people I know'. She did all she could to encourage Virginia, at the same time telling Leonard he was 'the only person I know whom I can imagine as her husband.'[25]

Virginia's elated mood at the end of May made her confident and decisive and allowed her to say 'yes' to Leonard, but below the surface strong anxieties remained.

No sooner had she decided than she began to see Leonard as having Jekyll and Hyde identities. On the one hand she saw Leonard as sensitive and protective, strong, firm, trustworthy, an ideal companion, devoted to her, having much in common with her lovable, literary father and her adored brother Thoby, one of his 'great friends'. She told Violet Dickinson, 'There is something very like Thoby about him, not only in his face. I feel I shall get fearfully spoilt.'[26]

This idealised brother/father figure could be replaced in Virginia's mind, when anxious, by an unpleasant image of masculine brutality, male lust for power, threatening. She recalled Thoby's description of Leonard, 'A Jew . . . so violent, so savage',[27] and Lytton telling her Leonard was like Swift and would murder his wife. She alternated between 'being half in love' and wanting to be with Leonard, and the 'extreme of coldness and aloofness'.[28]

She soon brought up her anxiety about sex, and told Leonard she felt no physical attraction; when he kissed her she went cold. The strength of Leonard's desire frightened her; 'Is it the sexual side which comes between us?' she asked.[29] Leonard looked on Virginia's frigidity as little more than the customary behaviour of an upper-class English virgin, but he held himself back despite his desire for her having 'grown far more violent as my other feelings have grown stronger'.[30] Virginia's tension eased and soon they were addressing one another by the pet names of 'Mongoose' (Leonard) and 'Mandril'.

Virginia was no more anti-Semitic than most of her class. She and

Vanessa and their friends were all liable to make remarks that today would be offensive but were then taken as amusing rather than malicious. As late as 1930 Virginia was capable of telling Ethel Smyth that Jews 'pullulate, copulate and amass . . . millions of money',[31] yet when Hitler came to power three years later she vehemently condemned Nazi anti-Semitism.

That the Jew, as an outsider, is a ready-made scapegoat needs no emphasis. Virginia for a time came to link Leonard's Jewishness with his sexuality; 'I feel angry, sometimes, at the strength of your desire', she told him. 'Possibly your being a Jew comes in also at this point. You seem so foreign.'[32] Such an attitude could not continue if the engagement was to survive. Virginia made a psychological leap and displaced her anxieties from Leonard onto his family. Henceforth, anti-Semitic remarks were reserved for them: 'How I hated their nasal voices, and their oriental jewellery, and their noses and their wattles.'[33] Her vitriol was directed particularly at Leonard's mother who, Virginia sensed, wanted to dominate and put 'her claws in me . . . the horror of family life and the terrible threat to one's liberty that I used to feel with Father, Aunt Mary or George' came back.[34] Tension between the two women grew in the two months before marriage and culminated in a row, with Virginia refusing to have her future mother-in-law at the wedding. Marie Woolf was dreadfully upset; it was 'an unheard-of slight'.[35]

Leonard colluded with Virginia in what can only be described as a *folie à deux*. He sided with Virginia and, not unreasonably, Marie Woolf believed Virginia had taken Leonard away from his family. For Virginia, Leonard was no longer the threatening Jew. Now, when she described him to her friends he was transformed from the man who shot tigers, 'hung black men' and ruled Empires, into 'a penniless Jew'.

Virginia's summer hypomania gave her energy and zest but led to exhaustion and tension. She and Leonard embarked on a round of visits and introductions to family and friends and, in addition, Virginia worked hard to finish the final draft of *The Voyage Out*. As insomnia and headaches developed, Leonard took charge for the first time, persuaded her to become 'a comatose invalid', and took her to Brighton for a recuperative weekend. He was by now 'extremely uneasy' about Virginia's health and went to see George Savage. Dr Savage was very friendly, but impressed Leonard 'much more as a man of the world than as a doctor'.[36]

Savage was then 70 and at the top of his profession, having recently been knighted for his work, and elected the first president of the new section of psychiatry at the Royal Society of Medicine. He was an enthusiastic mountaineer, and his exploits in the Swiss Alps had resulted in his getting to know Leslie Stephen. His remarkable ascent of the Gablehorn from the Trift Glacier at a time when Leslie was President of the Alpine Club was recorded in the *Alpine Journal*. For many years he was a member of the Sunday Tramps, which Leslie had founded, who would walk twenty or more miles a day.

Savage dealt with Jim Stephen when Virginia's cousin developed manic depression, and by the time Julia Stephen died he was well acquainted with most of the family. He may even have been asked for advice on Virginia in 1896 although no record of such exists. He treated Virginia through the 1904 breakdown and saw her, both socially and professionally, over the next eight years. Vanessa always went to Savage for help when worried by her sister's mental state. She liked and respected him – as a family friend he would take no fees – but when she herself became depressed in 1911 she consulted a younger, more detached specialist, Maurice Craig, perhaps wisely recognising she was too close to Savage for his professional comfort.

Savage was a competent, if not very imaginative, psychiatrist. His experience was wide, his opinions conventional, in line with those of the older, renowned Henry Maudsley. Although he modified some of his views for the twentieth century he still believed that women had weaker minds than men and 'cannot be relieved of the duties of motherhood'. Too much education and mental activity were unhealthy for young females, liable to 'develop into insanity', and they were 'peculiarly vulnerable to mental illness in puberty, menstruation, pregnancy and childbirth'.

Savage had no doubt that 'an insane or nervous disposition' could be inherited, and believed that patients from 'neurotic stock' were liable to go 'out of their minds'. Marriage should be forbidden to those with a history of periodical mental illness. 'There is a grave risk in those adolescents who at puberty and with adolescence have periods of depression and buoyancy', he wrote, and advised all those contemplating marriage to someone with such a history to think long and hard before deciding. As a footnote he added, 'suppression of the facts as to such attacks should really be a ground for declaration of nullity'.[37] He expressed this opinion only one year before his interview with Leonard.

Savage told Leonard that Virginia suffered from 'neurasthenia, and not manic depressive insanity', and that marriage and children would do her 'a world of good'.[38] What had happened to his professional consistency and integrity?

The term neurasthenia was introduced by the American neurologist George Beard in 1869, and for a time it was used for all mental illness except insanity. It was seen as a disease of modern civilisation, respectable and lacking the stigma of madness. For some years neurasthenia was an immensely popular diagnosis but by 1912 medical belief in it as an entity was already fast waning, and today it is forgotten.

Savage knew that Virginia had recurring periods of 'depression and buoyancy' and had been insane, yet he confidently said she suffered from neurasthenia. Had he diagnosed manic depression he would have been obliged to follow his own advice and warn Leonard of the dangers of marriage and the future. As it was he was able to maintain that marriage and children would do Virginia 'a world of good'. Perhaps he eased his conscience by reflecting that neurasthenia was 'the soil from which all mental illnesses spring'; but it must have been hard to reconcile his view that 'marriage should never be recommended as a means of cure . . . or a relief for so-called neurasthenia' with his advice to Leonard.[39]

Did Savage deliberately mislead Leonard? Was he medically negligent? He would be judged so in today's courts, but at the time he may simply have seen himself being economical with the truth. He liked the Stephen family and wanted to see his friend Leslie's daughter fulfilled in marriage and motherhood. He considered she led an undesirable destabilising style of life, and he hoped marriage to a reliable man could be her salvation. His professionalism took second place to his emotions on this occasion and led him to lose his objectivity. It would have been better to have discussed the problem frankly and fully with Leonard. The facts would hardly have stopped Leonard from marrying and he would have responded by trusting Savage thereafter.

Virginia at first was as optimistic about her future health as Savage: 'I shall never be ill again because with Leonard I get no chance,' she confided to Janet Case.[40] She and Leonard were married on Saturday 10 August at St Pancras Register Office, while a thunderstorm raged prophetically overhead. They spent the weekend at Asham and several days at Holford in the Quantock Hills before embarking on a gruelling tour of Provence and Spain, and thence by boat and train to Italy, finishing up in Venice. They returned to London at the beginning of October.

Chapter Nine

Marriage – The Second Major Breakdown, 1913

The honeymoon was both a success and a failure. They talked a great deal, explored the towns, walked in the mornings and read or wrote in the afternoons. Virginia completed *The Voyage Out*. Leonard finished *The Village in the Jungle* – which Virginia thought 'amazingly good'[1] – and began *The Wise Virgins*. They were compatible as companions and Virginia enjoyed being 'chronically nomadic and monogamic'. But sexually their relationship was troubled. Leonard's attempts to make love had brought on 'such a violent state of excitement' and hysteria 'that he had had to stop'.[2]

Without having been an accompanying fly on the wall it is impossible to know what transpired in the Woolfs' bedroom. One can guess, however, a possible sequence of events. Virginia was anxious and feared Leonard as a sexual lover. Jekyll threatened to become Hyde. Leonard restrained himself, probably for several days. He tried to talk Virginia's fears through and reassure her, but her anxiety was too deep for her to respond rationally and she remained tense. Leonard felt growing exasperation and helplessness. Finally, sometime in the first fortnight, Leonard lost patience and attempted intercourse forcefully. The effect, to judge from Leonard's account, was explosive. Leonard may have partially penetrated, and then ejaculated prematurely and lost his erection in the face of Virginia's hysteria and panic.

Virginia wrote from Spain to her friend Ka Cox on 4 September to say she had lost her virginity, adding:

> Why do you think people make such a fuss about marriage and copulation? Why do some of our friends change upon losing chastity? Possibly my great age makes it less of a catastrophe, but certainly I find the climax immensely exaggerated. Except for a sustained good humour (Leonard shan't see this) due to the fact that every twinge of anger is at once visited upon my husband, I might still be Miss Stephen.[3]

Leonard's sexual experience had come from Singalese prostitutes and enthusiastic 'amateurs'. Then he had been concerned mainly with reaching a climax, not with pleasing the woman, and afterwards he had been assailed by a sense of 'degradation'. Leonard assumed that virgins were naturally cold, but lost their frigidity once aroused in married life. He had no one to discuss sexual problems with. Strachey and Moore were out of the question and Clive Bell, who could have given him good advice, was bitterly jealous; his scurrilous remarks about Leonard had made both Leonard and Virginia angry. Bella might have helped but she was abroad with her husband.

In December, Leonard and Virginia went together to ask Vanessa's advice. Unexpectedly, she was not only unhelpful but made her sister feel humiliated and angry.

> I perhaps annoyed her [Vanessa reported to Clive] but may have consoled him [Leonard] by saying that I thought she never had understood or sympathised with sexual passion in men. They were very anxious to know when I had my first orgasm.[4]

There is a ring of triumph behind Vanessa's words. After the trouble and hurt Virginia had caused, it must have been gratifying to inform Clive that Virginia was sexually inadequate. Virginia might be the more gifted and clever, but Vanessa was the better woman.

Virginia's sexual rejection of Leonard, in such contrast to their close companionship, affected him profoundly. A partner's resistance stimulates some people, but prolonged and bitter rejection inhibits and eventually takes away desire and a man's potency. By the end of the honeymoon Leonard had probably ceased to be sexually aroused by Virginia, and may even have been impotent in her presence. Certainly all attempts at sexual intercourse were 'abandoned quite soon'.[5] Lust had been removed from love. Thereafter Leonard seems to have displaced all his sexual drive into work. He never had an affair; and even his relationship with Trekkie Parsons, after Virginia's death, was without sex.

Leonard was ashamed and resentful. He had failed as a man and if that were widely known, he would be ridiculed. Frustration made him restless, which perhaps explains why the honeymoon couple rarely stopped for more than a night or two in any town. When they finally reached Venice, before returning home, Virginia was ill, headachy, exhausted and reluctant to eat. Forced to rest for a week she was content to let Leonard take charge and feed her on 'buttered toast, cakes and ices'. Leonard was changing from a lustful husband into a maternal protector.

Leonard poured his emotions into *The Wise Virgins*, which he wrote at great speed, as though under pressure.

Harry, Jewish, dissatisfied with his life, is the central character living with his family in suburbia. He meets the gentile sisters Camilla (Virginia) and Katharine (Vanessa), and is drawn to Camilla: fascinating but frightening to young men, possessing purity, coldness, of hills and snow – something that might at any moment break out destructive of you – of her'. Harry can imagine kissing Katharine, but Camilla seems beyond reach: 'fine ladies and Dresden china don't kiss'. The sisters 'had no blood in them' and were 'cold, pale souls'. Harry then switches his attack and pours scorn on his mother, Mrs Davis, who is unambiguously Marie Woolf: 'a handsome large woman – big curved nose, the curling full lips, great brown eyes, a . . . sing-song nasal voice – talked trivialities'.[6]

Friends and relatives thought badly of Leonard for publishing the novel in 1914, but no amount of criticism would deflect him. Virginia did not read the book until 1915, just before she became manic.

Virginia, despite recurrent headaches, coped with moving house from Brunswick Square to rooms in Clifford's Inn, near Fleet Street, but by January cyclothymic depression was so exacerbating her symptoms that Leonard began keeping a daily record. He told Vanessa of his worries and sought her view on the dangers of Virginia becoming pregnant. The two sisters had in fact recently talked over the question of pregnancy, and perhaps Vanessa had even proffered advice on intercourse. Vanessa was surprised to discover that Leonard had strong objections, for she knew that both Savage and the nursing home matron Jean Thomas thought Virginia would benefit from motherhood. 'I wonder why Leonard has gradually come to think childbearing so dangerous?', she asked Virginia at the end of January.[7]

Leonard had by now convinced himself that Virginia would not 'be able to stand the strain and stress of childbearing'.[8] He again consulted Savage, who 'brushed my doubts aside', and Leonard sought other medical advice: Maurice Craig, who was currently treating Vanessa for depression; Maurice Wright whom Leonard had consulted over his familial tremor; and Theo Hyslop, a writer of eccentric articles on women. Maurice Wright agreed with Savage, but Hyslop sat on the fence and suggested delaying a decision. Craig, however, who was by far the best qualified and most impressive of the three, agreed strongly with Leonard. Leonard also saw Jean Thomas, a suggestible woman, and easily persuaded her to change her mind. Leonard, when his mind was made up, was a formidable force and he eventually won Vanessa round to his way of thinking. He had no doubts; the doctors 'confirmed my fears and were strongly against her having children'.

Virginia now knew that Leonard was determined to stop her

having children, although what they discussed between themselves is unrecorded. Leonard reported each new piece of 'expert' advice but Virginia was too depressed and demoralised to protest. She fell back on fantasy, as when Thoby died, and in April she told Violet Dickinson:

> We aren't going to have a baby, but we want to have one, and six months in the country or so is said to be necessary first.[9]

Her resentment as buried beneath depression, but she was very angry with Leonard, was he was to discover, and furious with the doctors. Fourteen years later she told a friend, 'I'm always angry with myself for not having forced Leonard to take the risk in spite of the doctors.'[10]

Virginia's desire for children was not deeply rooted. She expressed a wish for them only when she was depressed. Waking in the early hours, tossing and turning, she tormented herself: 'I wish I were dead . . . Vanessa. Children. Failure.'[11] She envied Vanessa with her children round her: 'a little more self-control on my part and we might have had a boy of twelve and a girl of ten.'[12] She took a different line when in high spirits: then she scarcely wanted children; life was too short. She had to write.

She enjoyed Vanessa's children when they were older, especially her niece Angelica, but not over prolonged periods. When her sister asked her to look after her two boys during her last confinement (admittedly it was in the vulnerable month of January), Virginia took to her bed and the boys had to go elsewhere. The presence of children of her own would have hindered Virginia's creative life and been a health hazard.

Leonard was right to doubt Virginia's ability to cope with childbearing. The risk of breaking down in the first two weeks after childbirth is greater – almost 25 per cent more – for a woman who has had an episode of manic depression, or a strong family history of the disease. Profound hormonal changes occur in a woman after delivery: the fall in circulating oestrogen levels affects the neuro-transmitter patterns in the brain and results in varying degrees of depression. Many mothers experience 'post-natal blues', but these are short-lived. A woman with manic depressive genes is liable to become far more disturbed. Vanessa was depressed after each of her three children, and the chances of Virginia becoming mad after childbirth were high.

However, a manic depressive breakdown after childbirth is not entirely due to genetic influence, and emotional factors play an important part. Studies of puerperal illness often overlook their importance, because it is difficult to measure subtle emotional stress. Such 'life events' as death and divorce, or a husband's alcoholism, are easily recorded, but how accurately can a researcher measure reluctance to become a father, the aggressive fantasies of a pregnant mother-to-be, or ambivalent feelings towards a husband?

The cyclothymic Sylvia Plath, for instance, was depressed after each of her two children. Her marriage appeared outwardly stable but below the surface she was angry, envious of her husband Ted Hughes's success as a poet and gloomy about her own work. A probing search will show that most manic depressives who develop post-natal illness harbour resentment towards the partner. Those who remain well, or suffer no more than short-lived minor depression, are generally at peace with themselves and their partner at the time of delivery.

Many manic depressives are cheerful during pregnancy; cyclothymic swings stop or lessen, probably because of changing hormone levels. After birth the cyclothymic rhythm resumes, and if delivery coincides with the time of an expected swing, the post-natal reaction is potentiated.

Every post-natal manic depressive illness involves the interaction of cyclothymic, hormonal and emotional factors, and it is always difficult to predict the outcome of a pregnancy. It is impossible to *know* how Virginia would have reacted to childbirth. She could have been well during the pregnancy, and with a supportive Leonard in attendance at delivery might have had no serious after-effects, particularly had the baby been born in summer. But Leonard's ban on motherhood may have had causes other than concern about Virginia. Perhaps he wanted to avoid the spoiling effect children might have had on his own as well as Virginia's life and work. He enjoyed training his pets, but what he termed 'the much less attractive and savage human baby' was a different matter.[13] Accommodation in the early years of marriage was cramped, and finances were not good enough to cover a full-time nanny, so essential for Virginia. Leonard would have needed a more substantial income, and that would have entailed doing less congenial work.

Virginia's mental state continued to deteriorate. Writing with 'a kind of tortured intensity', she finished revising *The Voyage Out*, and Leonard delivered the manuscript to Gerald Duckworth's publishing firm at the beginning of March.[14] It was accepted, and at once Virginia's anxieties came to centre round the novel, its possible reception of scorn and derision. She lay awake at night worrying over the book. She ate little, headaches were severe and she became more and more indecisive. She clung to Leonard, reluctant to let him out of her sight.

Leonard believed *The Voyage Out* to be the root cause of Virginia's distress. Vanessa thought the same. She told Roger Fry that Virginia's 'worrying over what people will think of her novel . . . seems really to be the entire cause of her breakdown'.[15] But the novel, although some cause of anxiety, was not the chief reason for Virginia's turmoil, but rather a focal point for the gathering storm.

In a sense, every manic depressive breakdown reflects battle with a close companion, suppressed anger, fear of rejection, resentment struggling against love. As the cyclothyme's mental defences crumble, perplexity grows and behaviour becomes increasingly inconsistent. In 1904 Virginia had struggled with Vanessa, driven her away, clung to her, pleaded for affection, abused her. In 1913 the pathological process was slower, but the pattern was the same. All Virginia's major breakdowns had their beginnings in the cyclothymic depression of late winter/spring, and with each one went powerful emotional conflicts.

Leonard, in 1913, ruled his marriage as he had the natives in Ceylon. He tolerated no disagreement; on important issues he was sure he knew best for Virginia. Virginia was at first angry. Leonard's highhanded action in stamping her unfit for motherhood, his bullying manner, enraged her. Yet she had to keep her feelings under control, for Leonard was her vital protection, and the more depressed she was the greater her dependence. She clung to Leonard, unable to work, convinced she was a burden, was ruining his life, that he should leave her. She ate almost nothing, slept for no more than an hour or two at a time, and was so 'terribly depressed' that Leonard feared suicide. He made her see Savage and on 25 July she reluctantly agreed to go back to the Twickenham nursing home.

Anger against Leonard surfaced after a few days in the nursing home; she did not trust him, did not love him, doubted his love, wanted separation. Leonard was extremely upset and tried to discover the cause:

> If I *have* done anything wrong to you and which has displeased you, you would tell me, wouldn't you? I do adore you so, Mandy, that I would do anything to change any beastliness in myself, if I knew how it had shown itself.[16]

He stayed away from the nursing home for several days, probably on medical advice, and his absence, in conjunction with rest and isolation, halted the paranoid outbursts. Contritely, she assured him,

> nothing you have done, since I knew you, has been in any way beastly – how could it? You've been absolutely perfect to me. It's all my fault . . . I do believe in you absolutely, and never for a second do I think you've told me a lie. Goodbye, darling Mongoose – I do want you and I believe in spite of my vile imaginings the other day that I love you and that you love me.[17]

Virginia left the nursing home on 11 August, seeming to be a good deal better, and she and Leonard went to Asham for a fortnight. But no real improvement was possible in so short a time, and she quickly returned to agitation and depressive thinking. Leonard was completely out of his depth, helpless to counter Virginia's delusional ideas, only with difficulty able to persuade her to eat and rest.

Dr Savage had made the fatal mistake of bargaining with a seriously depressed patient, an extraordinary error for someone of his experience, and another sign that his judgement was distorted by his friendship. To persuade Virginia to have treatment he had promised she could go away for a holiday with Leonard in August, although he must have known she would not be well enough.

Leonard was understandably reluctant to take Virginia away, but Savage said his promise must be kept; to break it would bring on a crisis and risk suicide. He was wrong, clinically inept and weak. He should have insisted on Virginia going back to the home for further treatment, and if she had refused – unlikely had he been firm – he should have threatened to send her to a mental hospital; as a suicide risk, he had the power to do so. Ill as she was, part of her was probably still in touch with reality and would have been relieved by firm direction.

Leonard took Virginia to the village inn where they had stayed on their honeymoon, an unwise choice, perhaps. Virginia rapidly became worse. She believed people were watching and organising plots against her. Everywhere was threatening and alarming. Every shadow and creak had meaning. Sleep was impossible without a drug, and Leonard doled out a sleeping pill, Veronal, each night, keeping the supply locked in his case. Mealtimes were battles which Virginia increasingly won; Leonard, she protested, was forcing her to eat unnecessarily. Leonard, in desperation, appealed to Vanessa, who wrote telling Virginia to 'be sensible and don't make things difficult for Leonard . . . he is far more sensible than you are, and trust him to know how to get things right'.[18] It did not help.

Leonard cut short the holiday and returned to London. Once there, to Leonard's surprise and relief, Virginia agreed to see Dr Henry Head. Head was more a neurophysiologist than a clinical psychiatrist. His chief work before the war had been concerned with sensation, but later he became interested in shell shock and co-operated with W. H. R. Rivers, the psychotherapist. The Woolfs had heard of him through Roger Fry, whose schizophrenic wife he had seen, and Virginia's resistance may have been overcome by learning that Head was also a poet.

Head at once recognised the seriousness of the situation and advised Virginia's immediate admission to a nursing home. She would 'get perfectly well again if she followed advice', rested in bed and ate well for a few weeks. It was no different from the rest cure that Savage would have prescribed, but there was no realistic alternative treatment. Virginia appeared to acquiesce, and when Leonard brought her back to Gordon Square he was relieved to observe how calm she was. He left her in the bedroom with a friend, and with Vanessa went to see Savage to explain why they had bypassed him and gone to Dr Head. Left alone for a moment, Virginia opened Leonard's unlocked case, found the Veronal and swallowed a large dose. She became deeply unconscious, and thirty-six hours elapsed before she awoke.

It would be unfair to criticise Head, who was not consulted again, for he could have done little more. A sudden calm in someone deeply depressed is a danger sign, a signal that suicide is a strong possibility; once the decision to die has been decisively taken, agitation disappears. Virginia had decided to kill herself, and she planned her action deliberately. Leonard normally made sure his case was locked and it was a curious oversight for so careful a man; but given the strain he was under, not extraordinary.

A suicide attempt often lifts depression, sometimes for good if the time is ripe, but usually any improvement is transient. When Virginia recovered she seemed tranquil for a few days, but then agitation and depression began to reappear Her attitude to Leonard, however, changed, and anger and paranoia gave way to a childlike need for him. She wanted Leonard to be continually with her, and would only eat if he fed her, encouraging her with each mouthful.

George Duckworth lent the Woolfs his country house for the emergency. Nurses were in attendance day and night. At times Virginia objected violently to them and demanded Leonard alone look after her. At other times she was silent and withdrawn, lying motionless on her bed, expressionless, passively resistant, taking up to two hours to eat a small meal. Leonard was exhausted but he never lost patience or rebuked her, and always encouraged her with soothing words and touches. He recognised that 'if left to herself she . . . would have gradually starved to death'. Over the years Leonard came to believe Virginia had 'a taboo against eating'. It was, he wrote, 'extraordinarily difficult ever to get her to eat enough to keep her strong and well'.[19] Leonard perhaps overemphasised the problem, partly because he believed her mental stability depended on maintaining a 'good' weight, but also because Virginia became noticeably more anorexic when there was tension between them.

Virginia slowly improved. In mid-November she moved from Dalingridge Place to Asham with two nurses in attendance, and in February she was well enough to give up the last one. Depressive thoughts, verging on the delusional, came and went and she continued to cling to Leonard and ask his forgiveness, repeatedly telling him, 'how much I am grateful and repentant. You have made me so happy.'[20]

Leonard, understandably, had almost reached the end of his tether. For months he had had to remain in the sickroom, listening, pleading, encouraging, supervising eating and toilet, urging her to be calm and take her medicines (bromides, chloral, Veronal), watching for danger signals. By March he was suffering from painful tension headaches and had lost a considerable amount of weight. Reluctantly, he was persuaded to leave Virginia in the care of Vanessa and two friends, and go away to recuperate with Lytton Strachey. Virginia immediately felt lost and anxious:

> If you could have seen my sorrow after you went you would have no doubts about my affection [she wrote]. Old Mandril does want her Master so badly and last night his empty bed was so dismal, and she went and kissed the pillow.[21]

Leonard responded reassuringly,

> Don't think, dear one, that I'm ill. I'm not . . . But I'm lonely without you. You can't realise how utterly you would end my life for me if you had taken that sleeping mixture successfully or if you ever dismissed me.'[22]

By June Virginia was well enough for Leonard to leave her alone at Asham for a day or two, having promised to be in bed by 10.25 each night, drink a whole glass of milk in the morning, have breakfast in bed and 'to be wise and to be happy'.[23] She and Leonard went for a holiday to Northumbria in August, just after the declaration of war – which had no obvious effect on Virginia – and on her return her recovery *seemed* complete. It was not.

Leonard had given up their rooms in Cliffords Inn in early 1914. Virginia was now keen to resume life in London, but Leonard was convinced that all excitement had to be avoided and he refused to consider living in central London. At first Virginia stood her ground, but she admitted she was liable to become intoxicated 'by the delights of chatter',[24] and eventually accepted Leonard's choice of Richmond, close enough to London for work, but too far out for hectic social life. They took lodgings there and began house-hunting, and at the beginning of 1915 began negotiations for the lease on Hogarth House, a large Georgian country house built in 1720, and now divided in two.

On 23 February, breakfasting in bed and talking to Leonard, Virginia suddenly became violently excited and distressed. She believed her mother was in the room and began talking wildly to her. It was the beginning of mania. Leonard was caught unawares although, in fact, there had been small but cumulative warning signs of mental trouble from the beginning of January. Headaches had returned and Virginia was sleeping badly. More ominously, she had bouts of irritability, disinhibition, and fleeting paranoia.

Her diary, which she had resumed that January and which ended on 15 February, records, 'I begin to loathe my kind' (3 January); 'I do not like the Jewish voice' of Flora Woolf (4 January); and on 9 January, after passing a line of imbeciles, 'They should certainly be killed.' A noisy quarrel with Leonard broke out at the end of January, which lasted all morning.

What were the emotions that pushed Virginia into madness? Why did she develop mania rather than depression? And why was it ushered in by an hallucinatory encounter with her mother?

Leonard believed the imminent publication (in March) of *The Voyage Out* caused the outburst but there is nothing to suggest she was unduly anxious about the book. She mentions the novel only once in the diary, at the end of January, when she wrote, 'Everyone, so I predict, will assure me [it] is the most brilliant thing they've ever read, and privately condemn, as indeed it deserves to be condemned,' not an attitude anticipatory of mania.[25]

More interesting is why the spectre of Virginia's mother materialised. Hallucinatory figures do not usually appear without cause, in the absence of intoxicants. However mad someone may be, the spectre has to be summoned or provoked into appearing by word or deed which, by association, releases powerful emotions.

There is no record of what the Woolfs were discussing that morning at breakfast; perhaps the move to Hogarth House, talking about her family. Sex was often in Virginia's thoughts at that time. She was fascinated by Lytton Strachey's sister's infatuation with an older married man, 'the great affair of her life'.[26] She was taking an undue interest in a tumultuous affair Clive had been having with Molly MacCarthy: 'as I could have foretold, after violent scenes . . . they have parted'.[27] Three days after the hallucinatory scene, by now calmer but still clearly hypomanic, she told Lytton Strachey:

> Let us all subscribe to buy a parrot for Clive. It must be a bold primitive bird, trained of course to talk nothing but filth, and to indulge in obscene gestures . . . The fowl could be called Molly or Polly.[28]

It may be significant that Virginia read *The Wise Virgins* for the first time on 31 January. She records she 'was made very happy by it', although there is little in the book, other than Leonard's rudeness to his mother, that might have pleased her. She made no reference to Leonard's portrayal of her (Camilla's) sexual inadequacy, although it must surely have disturbed her.

The spectre of her mother created violent distress in Virginia. Julia stood for Victorian standards, female domesticity, a home run by the woman and ruled by the man, a concept long rejected by her daughter. Did Julia's ghost tell her she was a failure as a woman? Did Julia's words merge with Leonard's, that she was frigid and unfit for motherhood? Virginia was angry, yet over the following three days she idealised her marriage: 'our happiness is wonderful'.[29] It was followed by furious rage against Leonard.

A week after her mother's appearance Virginia erupted into full-blown mania and nurses had to be summoned. She went into a nursing home while Leonard moved into Hogarth House, and joined him there, in the care of four nurses, on 1 April. She was difficult to restrain and talked incessantly, hardly making sense, her voice trailing off into incoherent mumbling. She barely slept, scarcely ate or drank, and resisted violently all attempts to feed and clean her until, growing exhausted, she gradually subsided into stupor. She lay 'like a stone statue', her lips occasionally moving soundlessly, withdrawn into a world of her own.[30] Three or four days later she slowly began to return to life. She now responded to questions and co-operated with the nurses, but she remained wary of Leonard and bristled whenever he came near.

Over the following two months, Virginia's mood was a mixture of depression and euphoria. Often she was reasonable, but she was also unpredictable, liable to sudden outbursts of violence. Her hostility to Leonard continued and for a time she was so vicious towards him that he dared not enter her room. She said 'the most malicious and cutting things', which distressed him to breaking point.[31]

Very gradually Virginia's anger faded and the symptoms of the illness, although not its memory, ceased. In September she was able to stay at Asham with Leonard and one nurse, and in the New Year she began leading a normal if sheltered life at Hogarth House.

Chapter Ten

Inner and Outer Worlds

After three years of mental illness, Virginia struggled to make sense of the experience. It had been an horrific time yet she had known moments of 'exquisite happiness',[1] and glimpsed truths about herself and ideas for her writing. It taught her 'a good deal about what is called oneself',[2] and it gave rise to the 'poems, stories, profound and to me inspired phrases' which she would develop in the future.[3] She had come to recognise the creative power in her mental depths and that, as a novelist, she needed both inner and outer worlds. As an essayist and reviewer she was placed firmly in reality. As a novelist she had to let herself down, as she put it, into the depths, and return to reality with whatever she found.

Genius needs the subconscious, but whatever comes up is valueless without intellectual discipline. An artist with schizophrenia, never fully in touch with reality or in control of his mind, cannot create in any meaningful sense. Leonard was wrong in his belief that Virginia was never sane. Had she not been sane for most of her marriage she could never have written what she did.

At first she 'was so tremblingly afraid of my own insanity',[4] that she drew back from exploring her mind, but the desire for 'goblin fruits' was often strong and she longed for their refreshing taste.[5]

In 1917 she began to write *Night and Day*. It was what Leonard called a factual novel, without disturbing material; she deliberately kept off 'that dangerous ground'. Writing the novel gave her self-confidence and even before she finished, new ideas came bursting into her mind, 'all in a flash, as if flying, after being kept stone-breaking for months'. There followed 'The Mark on the Wall', 'Kew Gardens', 'The Unwritten Novel', short stories that showed her how she might embody all her 'deposit of experience in a shape that fitted it'. By January 1920 she had arrived 'at some idea of a new form for a novel'.[6]

She was now secure enough to welcome subconscious sources of inspiration. Many of her works were made up as she lay in bed with depression; ideas effortlessly presented themselves, to be stored for later use. Music, especially the late quartets of Beethoven, could also have this effect, as could walking alone, through the old parts of London, or across the Sussex Downs.

Virginia's need to write was, among other things, to make sense of mental chaos and gain control of madness. Through her novels she made her inner world less frightening. Writing was often agony but it provided 'the strongest pleasure' she knew.[7]

Leonard believed his wife's sensitivity to criticism was liable to make her ill; every time she finished a novel, depression followed. It is true she was sometimes depressed during the proof-reading stage and while waiting for publication, but this was as much due to what was going on in her life as to the novel. Leonard invariably overlooked such stresses; perhaps because he was often involved.

When Virginia started a novel, she was excited but relaxed and usually stable. In the final stages, when she repeatedly revised, she often did become exhausted and depressed. Yet she was never in danger of serious depression from the writing itself. No author becomes mad writing a book, although he may write the book because he is on the brink of madness and subsequently goes mad. Virginia was apprehensive when she completed a novel, but once Leonard praised the work Virginia was able to relax.

After 1916 Virginia saw Leonard in a new light, had 'a child's trust in Leonard'.[8] He was the strong linchpin, able to control her gyrations, the adored father and maternal protector in one. She gave way to him on anything touching her health, but he was also a trusted friend to whom she could tell everything. No longer had she to hold back her feelings; when she was angry she said so. She was sure of their love. 'Darling love, I kiss thee', she wrote when he went away for a night to lecture, and promised to eat 'exactly as if you were here', despite weighing 40 pounds above her normal weight, and being 'hardly able to toil uphill'.[9] She and Leonard cuddled and kissed but there was no attempt at sexual intercourse. Virginia had chosen her 'narrow, virginal bed',[10] and Leonard, after being so battered emotionally by Virginia, was unlikely to have wanted to share it.

Leonard loved Virginia, but looked on her as a child, 'never completely sane',[11] needing to be closely watched and protected. He ensured she maintained her weight, and at the first sign of headache or insomnia made her rest and stop imaginative writing. A sudden flight of fancy in conversation was a warning sign of hypomania, a need for rest and quiet, although often it was no more than Virginia enjoying herself in company. He strove to keep Virginia within the bounds of reality. At his instigation she joined the Richmond Branch of the Women's Co-operative Guild, and for four years she organised guest speakers and presided over monthly meetings at Hogarth House.

It was largely to provide Virginia with a practical occupation as far removed from the imagination as possible that in March 1917 Leonard bought a small hand-printing press and installed it at home – the beginning of the Hogarth Press. The Woolfs taught themselves to print and, by July, were proficient enough to publish the first Hogarth booklet containing a short story by each.

It proved to be a brilliant move. The Press gave Virginia valuable occupational therapy for many years. She came to look on printing and bookbinding and despatching orders as 'the sanest way of life. If I were always writing I should be like an inbreeding rabbit – my progeny becoming weakly albino'.[12] The Press also had the great advantage, once big enough to publish her books, of removing the need of submitting her work to other publishers. In time it became a lucrative source of income, although as the volume of work increased, so did the demands on the Woolfs' time. As early as 1920 they brought in a part-time manager, the first of several, and a later source of considerable contention.

Leonard's life was intensely busy. He thrived on hard work. At the outbreak of war he was commissioned by the Fabian Society to research the causes of war and its prevention and, working 'like a dedicated mole', his report as published in 1916. Almost overnight he became an authority on the subject and related issues. That work was followed by another detailed study on *Empire and Commerce in Africa*, which came out in 1920 and led to him becoming the Labour Party's expert on Imperial Affairs and, in 1924, Secretary of the party's Advisory Committee on Imperial questions. Virginia respected his work, although she took little real interest in the politics, and she regretted that Leonard's 'poetic side' was ' a little smothered in Blue-book, and organisations'.[13]

Leonard's early ambition to write novels had had to be abandoned at the outbreak of the war, and later on he came to recognise he was better suited to writing about politics and world affairs. None of that brought in much money and most of Leonard's income in the early years of marriage, which was supplemented by Virginia's trust income of about £300 a year plus what she earned, came from journalism and reviewing.

Vanessa and Clive had partially separated during Virginia's breakdown. In 1916 Clive was living on his own at Gordon Square, and Vanessa had moved, with her sons, to Suffolk to be near the painter Duncan Grant. She was still very tied to Roger Fry but their sexual relationship had ended, with some bitterness on his part. As Vanessa had recovered from the long drawn-out depression she had become increasingly drawn to Duncan, and when he responded – partly, one suspects, because an affair with Adrian Stephen was finishing and being replaced by one with David Garnett – she fell in love. Duncan and Garnett were fruit picking on a Suffolk farm in the hope of avoiding conscription into the army.

Virginia missed her sister deeply; the stimulation provided by their rivalry, their understanding and affection for each other, the laughter and sense of the absurd – what Leonard called silliness – and the scandalous gossip which set Virginia's fantasies flying. She made Vanessa promise to write at least twice a week, and before long she was badgering her to leave Suffolk and move to Sussex near her.

She and Leonard visited Vanessa in the summer, and at once Virginia felt more alive and her imagination moved into a higher gear. Ideas for *Night and Day* began to form, with Vanessa the model for Katharine Hilbery. 'It's fatal staying with you, you start so many new ideas', Virginia told her.[14] 'You stimulate the literary sense in me as you say I do your painting.'[15]

Leonard never inspired a novel, although he provided Virginia with the outline of several characters – Peter Walsh in *Mrs Dalloway*, Louis in *The Waves* – but, much more important, he gave her the consistent background against which she could develop her writing. Without Leonard there would have been no Virginia Woolf as we know her.

Virginia searched the Sussex countryside and found a farmhouse to rent within easy bicycling distance of Asham, just a mile from Firle; very solid and simple with 'flat walls in that lovely mixture of brick and flint',[16] the perfect house for Vanessa's needs. It was Charleston. Vanessa needed little persuasion, and when Duncan Grant and David Garnett obtained exemption from military service she moved there with them in October.

Leonard had mixed feelings about Vanessa living on their doorstep. He thought her too scatty, frivolous, and liable to make her sister dangerously excited. He recognised Virginia's need for Vanessa and their mutual devotion, but he was afraid she might undermine Virginia's stability. He also disapproved of the *ménage à trois*, not so much on moral grounds but because he foresaw the difficulties Vanessa would be facing, and feared these would rub off on Virginia.

Leonard's disapproval was soon noticed by Vanessa. She wrote to Lytton Strachey:

> I think the Woolves have a morbid terror of us all – I can't think why. They seem to think we should contaminate the atmosphere and bring wicked gaieties into Virginia's life. If they could only see the quiet lives we lead! Surely the downs are wide enough for us all and they needn't fear a constant flow in and out of Asham a long as Woolf is in it.[17]

Lytton was inclined to agree: there was 'some pollution theory in the background' of Leonard's mind.[18]

The tension between Leonard and Vanessa never came into the open or disturbed Virginia. Subconsciously it may have pleased her, since it meant Vanessa could not touch her relationship with Leonard. Vanessa might mutter about Leonard's lack of humour and his seriousness, and Leonard would criticise Vanessa's friends or the frequency with which the Bell children visited and disturbed the peace – but not enough to upset Virginia. She remained well, and cyclothymia was no more than a gentle swell in 1916 and 1917.

However, depression at the beginning of 1918 was unusually severe and sent her to bed for more than a week. Leonard was vexed to discover she had lost weight, and despite the problems of wartime rationing, organised extra milk and took her to Asham to rest. She was out of action for almost a month. Leonard attributed most of it to Virginia finishing *Night and Day*, but the significant stress probably originated from Vanessa, who was desperately trying to become pregnant; she wanted a son by Duncan, and that March she conceived.

Clive was officially the father, and that pretence was kept up for nearly twenty years, even to the child. Virginia probably learnt the truth in the last three or four months of the pregnancy. She was always disturbed by Vanessa's pregnancies. On this occasion, once her depression had passed, Virginia wrote prolifically all through 1918. She finished *Night and Day* in November at a gallop, and new ideas and stories followed, almost as if Virginia had to give birth to her literary children before Vanessa.

Angelica was born on Christmas morning at Charleston. Vanessa had anticipated a boy – she thought Duncan would take more interest in a son – and was put out when a girl arrived. She had insisted on being delivered at home (the colours of her bedroom were so much more sympathetic than those of the nursing home), but conditions verged on the chaotic. New servants were unreliable; one had to be dismissed for stealing, and a nurse left the day she arrived, horrified by what she encountered.

Vanessa had not been well during the pregnancy. She had quarrelled with Roger, who was still bitter at being ousted, and in September she threatened to miscarry. Halfway through the pregnancy Duncan told her that sexually their relationship was at an end, and he was not in love with her. She was left unsupported, anxious and liable to bouts of breathlessness and panic.

Virginia had promised to have Julian and Quentin for the first fortnight of the confinement, but signs of depression began immediately. She complained of toothache, a tooth was immediately extracted, headache followed, and she was in bed for much of January. The boys had to go to their father in Gordon Square.

Vanessa's depression came to focus on the infant. She was convinced the baby's crying was due to serious indigestion, and demanded the child be given castor oil and grey powders (a mixture of mercury and chalk). The doctor refused, a row built up, and in the end a more understanding female doctor was found who calmed mother and child. It was several months before Vanessa regained her composure, and Leonard would not allow Virginia to visit until early March.

Virginia's depression was followed by mild hypomania – the pattern that occurred after Julian's birth – and in her fantasy she took over Angelica. She suggested the name and went on to say, 'she is going to think me something more than an Aunt – not quite a father perhaps, but with a hand (to put it delicately) in her birth'.[19]

Hypomania persisted for much of that summer The lease on Asham had come to an end and Virginia, searching for a replacement, heard of cottages to rent near St Ives that D. H. Lawrence had once lived in; without seeing them she immediately made an offer. As a weekend holiday home the distance from London made the scheme wholly impractical and the plan was soon dropped.

A few weeks later Virginia went to Charleston and quarrelled with Vanessa over 'Kew Gardens'. Vanessa, who had illustrated the book, complained that the production was shoddy and she would not illustrate any more of Virginia's books; in her opinion 'an ordinary printer' was preferable to the Hogarth Press.[20] Virginia was 'stung and chilled' by the attack, and in a fury, hypomanic and resentful, rushed into Lewes and recklessly bought the Round House, a converted windmill beside the castle wall. It was not at all what the Woolfs wanted – it lacked a 'country garden' – but she bought it on the spot, barely stopping to look at the house, with no thought of consulting Leonard beforehand.

Leonard was outwardly polite and reasonable, but as he made his reservations felt Virginia's ebullience ebbed, and she began to regret her impulsiveness. On the way to show Leonard the Round House, they saw an estate agent's notice announcing the forthcoming sale of Monks House, Rodmell, a small village nearby. It seemed like a message from heaven: 'An old-fashioned house standing in three-quarters of an acre of land to be sold with possession'. 'That would have suited us exactly,' Leonard said regretfully, and Virginia at once determined to make amends.[21] She went next day to Rodmell, where she found a run-down house in much need of repair: small rooms, narrow stairs, an outside WC, no bath or hot water, but attractive views and surroundings and a pretty garden. Leonard could become 'a fanatical lover of that garden', Virginia immediately thought, and Leonard agreed. They bought the house for £700 and moved there in September, by good luck disposing of the Round House without loss.

Leonard's tactful handling of the episode was immensely reassuring to Virginia. He had not been angry or rejecting; on the contrary he had discussed his feelings in the most reasonable manner and never once upbraided her. Her sense of security was reinforced by their joint purchase of Monks House.

Leonard's life had become dominated by politics and international events. His work on the causes of war and colonial problems had made him a name, and he was firmly in the Labour Party camp. He believed passionately in the need for collective security and worldwide disarmament, and he saw capitalism and the Conservative Party as the opponent. He was convinced that if nations continued in their old nationalistic ways another world war was inevitable and civilisation would be extinguished. He held his belief in the League of Nations as fanatically as Virginia's great-grandfather Jem Stephen had believed in the abolition of slavery.

In May 1920 he agreed to stand 'rather half-heartedly for Parliament', as Labour Party candidate for the combined English Universities. He had initially hesitated because becoming a Member of Parliament seemed 'the acme of futility and boredom . . . his only function being to record his vote at the next division',[22] but his reservations also reflected doubts about the possible effect on Virginia. Her health influenced all his decisions; at various times he refused invitations to India and Africa, which he would have accepted but for fear of destabilising her.

Although neither Virginia nor Leonard said so, she was unenthusiastic about his undertaking a parliamentary career. It was obvious to that astute observer Beatrice Webb, who took Virginia to task at a luncheon party she gave in February and told her firmly, 'it was wrong to prevent Leonard from going into Parliament.'[23]

However, when Leonard was a candidate Virginia supported him, although she did little to hide her dislike when she accompanied him to Manchester to meet his constituents. She ridiculed the statue of Queen Victoria in the square 'looking like a large tea cosy', and laughed at Wellington, 'sleek as a mastiff with paw extended'; everyone she met was 'lower middle class, no sprinkling of upper class'; the dons and their wives had 'no surface brilliancy, not a scrap of romance'. Why had she come? she was asked; 'Oh, for the fun of spending £10 in Manchester and seeing the zoo.' Had she been 'a scatterbrain' she asked herself when she returned home? Yes, but then none of the Mancunians had read her books.[24]

Virginia was beginning slowly to mature and become aware of some ill-defined need for a more sensual love, akin to her love for Vanessa, to supplement but not replace Leonard's love. 'If one could be friendly with women, what a pleasure – the relationship so secret and private compared with relations with men,' she wrote in her diary.[25] It was not so much sex she was seeking as an intimate relationship which 'managed to make life seem a little amusing and interesting and adventurous.'[26] Katherine Mansfield, with her vivid past, attracted her, but Katherine was too elusive and ill for Virginia to grasp.

Ottoline Morrell seemed a possibility. She was the sister of the Duke of Portland, and had 'the head of a Medusa'.[27] She was six feet tall and angular, with equine-like teeth, but she had great charm and her striking appearance was exaggerated by flamboyant clothes and vast hats, and rather badly dyed red hair. This eccentric woman, renowned for her parties and generosity, had 'something Elizabethan' about her and was fascinating to many people. She had a number of lovers, including Bertand Russell, and liked to surround herself with creative individuals.

She and Virginia, who was nine years younger, had first met in 1909. Then, Virginia had sung her praises to Vanessa, to be warned that Ottoline was known for her lesbian tendencies. It was untrue but it added to her attractions.

After her breakdown, Virginia resumed the friendship and was much taken with her.

> I was so much overcome by her beauty, that I really felt as if I'd suddenly got into the sea and heard the mermaids fluting on their rocks . . . she has red-gold hair in masses, cheeks as soft as cushions with a lovely deep

> crimson on the crest of them, and a body shaped more after my notion of a mermaid's than I've ever seen . . . swelling but smooth [she told Vanessa].[28]

Ottoline, who had a protective side, was intrigued by Virginia and encouraged the friendship, but she was too woolly a thinker for Virginia's taste, nor did she want to step into the role of maternal protector. By 1925 Virginia was 'rather overcome by her ravaged beauty and desperation, and humility',[29] and by then she was already becoming involved with Vita Sackville-West.

Chapter Eleven

Creativity

The years 1920–25 were years of change for Virginia. It was an intensely creative period. Virginia's experiments with short stories led on to *Jacob's Room*; 'to have the same rhythmic flow as the short stories, one thing opening out of another: a kind of tunnelling process'. She wrote *Jacob's Room* between April 1920 and November 1921, despite interruptions through illness, and began 'Mrs Dalloway in Bond Street' the following April, a short story which grew into *Mrs Dalloway*.

Despite or perhaps partly because of this creative activity and progress, during 1921 and 1922 Virginia was continually beset with tension symptoms and depression and had to spend much time in bed. She rested for most of the summer of 1921:

> with wearisome headache, jumping pulse, aching back, frets, fidgets, lying awake, sleeping draughts, sedatives, digitalis, going for a little walk and plunging back into bed again – all the horror of the dark cupboard of illness once more displayed for my diversions.

But like Elizabeth Barrett Browning, she recognised that illness had its compensations:

> to be tired and authorised to lie in bed is pleasant . . . I can take stock of

> things in a leisurely way. Then the dark underworld has its fascinations as well as its terrors.[1]

By that autumn she was feeling well, but three months later, in January, cyclothymia caused her 'to tumble into bed with the influenza' and, for the next eight months, one symptom continually followed another.[2] Her temperature rose and fell, her heart raced, pains racked her body. Organic disease was sought and she saw a variety of specialists. One found a focus of septic infection which he was sure was the source of the trouble and pulled out three healthy teeth. Microbes were swabbed and grown from her throat and made into a vaccine, which was then injected into her. Tuberculosis was suspected and 'they vaccinated a guinea pig with my spittle. It died',[3] but not from TB. Heart and lung diseases were incriminated. Her general practitioner, who may have privately suspected a psychological cause, protected her from more draconian measures. Gradually in 1923 the tension lifted and apart from a short-lived but alarming mad episode in October, Virginia remained well until the affair with Vita Sackville-West developed in 1925.

None of the specialists suggested a psychological cause for Virginia's ill health. Maurice Craig acknowledged that the mind could affect 'any or all of the organs of the body', but he was not consulted at this particular time.[4] He might have saved the Woolfs their fees, but he is unlikely to have uncovered the psychological cause. He never discussed Virginia's feelings with her, but concentrated his attention on weight and sleeping habits. He looked on fatigue as a major cause of mental illness, for it permitted 'toxins to invade the system, and a vicious circle of cause and effect was formed'. The yearly attack of influenza, Craig explained to Virginia, 'poisoned her nervous system'. Sleep was 'the only certain means of restoring wastage' and he advocated the liberal use of hypnotics. He advised her always to have a sleeping draught at the bedside 'to take at the least wakefulness'.[5] She obeyed, but later on was often reluctant to do so because of the drug's after-effects, which included 'a head like wood' and made 'our breakfast fiery'.[6]

But perhaps that was better than the exhaustion which followed a sleepless night. She told her friend, the composer Ethel Smyth, 'I did not take chloral at 4.30 this morning – but lay wide-eyed; and rather doubt if chloral isn't the less drugging of the two.'[7]

Craig was not alone in avoiding discussion of the emotions, for that had long been the habit of psychiatrists. Although the isolation that was part of a rest cure usually resulted in a patient developing a strong dependence, the doctor was expected to remain god-like and detached, avoiding emotional subjects and restricting himself to rules for a healthy future life.

By the 1920s psychodynamic ideas were beginning to penetrate British psychiatry, but Craig had little time for them. He 'left psychoanalysis to its particular exponents, and would content himself with suggesting that many of the patients they claimed to have cured would probably have shown as good or better results under some other treatment.'[8]

Virginia never became dependent on any doctor, certainly not Craig. She accepted him because Leonard respected and regarded him as 'the leading Harley Street specialist in nervous and mental diseases'.[9] Having succeeded Savage to the prestigious post of psychiatrist to Guy's Hospital, he had built up the largest consulting practice of his time. He looked the part: a distinguished man, 'tastefully neat' in his dress, authoritative and sure of himself, a thoroughly conventional doctor.[10]

Virginia could never have opened herself up to Craig. He represented everything she hated about bullying male authority. She fused him with Savage, and the two became Sir William Bradshaw in Mrs Dalloway:

> worshipping proportion, Sir William not only prospered himself but made England prosper, secluded her lunatics, forbade childbirth, penalised despair, made it impossible for the unfit to propagate their views until they, too, shared his sense of proportion.[11]

There is no record of Virginia seeing Craig, or any psychiatrist after 1920. She relied on the family doctor to look after her. Male practitioners mostly made little impression, and after returning to

London she had a woman doctor, Dr Elly Rendel, whom she liked and trusted and may have occasionally confided in, for Elly had the enormous advantage of being Lytton Strachey's eldest sister's daughter, and was therefore almost part of the Bloomsbury circle.

Virginia's symptoms in the 1920s came more from tension than depression. She felt frustrated and under-stimulated, bored by suburban life. 'Here I sit at Richmond, and like a lantern stood in the middle of a field my light goes up in darkness.'[12] She felt life was passing her by: 'out here no one comes in to waste my time pleasurably'.[13] She looked enviously at Vanessa, 'astride her fine Arab, life I mean', and told her:

> Yes, I was rather depressed when you saw me – what it comes to is this: you say, 'I do think you lead a dull respectable absurd life – lots of money, no children, everything so settled: and conventional. Look at me now – only sixpence a year – lovers – Paris – life – love – art – excitement – God! I must be off.' This leaves me in tears.[14]

Virginia was always gloomy when she returned to Richmond from Rodmell; 'one lives in the brain there – I slip easily from writing to reading with spaces between of walking'.[15] Friends came to stay and she was near Vanessa. Richmond had nothing to commend it. She could not face 'a life spent, mute and mitigated, in the suburbs, just as I had it in mind to go full speed ahead'.[16]

She determined to move to London, and was angered by Leonard's opposition. She was convinced that his reasons were selfish. He maintained, through thick and thin, that her health would quickly deteriorate living in London, and bring on another bout of madness. As it was, whenever she went to London for a party, he was like an anxious father, immediately on the telephone if she was late home, 'expressing displeasure. "Very foolish . . . your heart bad"', and she returned feeling guilty and resentful.[17]

Eventually, faced with Leonard's trump card for the umpteenth time, Virginia exploded. She would no longer let him use her health as an excuse for doing what *he* wanted. Because he liked living in the suburbs and disliked the social life which she found so necessary, he wanted to bring her down to his level:

> to catch trains, always to waste time, to sit here and wait for Leonard to come in . . . when alternatively, I might go and hear a tune, or have a look at a picture, or find something at the British Museum, or go adventuring among human beings . . . now I'm tied, imprisoned, inhibited For ever to be suburban.[18]

Virginia's anger overflowed. It was a far cry from 1913 when she had silently given in to Leonard's decision against motherhood and her suppressed anger had fermented into madness. She demanded he examine himself and their differences. He was too much of a puritan, of a disciplinarian.

> There is [she told him] a very different element in me; my social side, your intellectual side. This social side is very genuine to me . . . It is a piece of jewellery I inherit from my mother – a joy in laughter, something that is stimulated, not wholly or vainly selfishly, by contact with my friends. And then ideas leap in me. Moreover, for my work now, I want freer intercourse, wider intercourse . . . In Richmond this is impossible. Either we have arduous parties at long intervals, or I make frenzied dashes up to London, and leave guiltily as the clock strikes eleven.[19]

Leonard dug his heels in, but slowly came to recognise that Virginia could not be dissuaded, that it could be dangerous to continue opposing her. The turning point came in October when Leonard was late returning to Monks House. Virginia, who had been tense for most of the day, became agitated, and suddenly associated Leonard's absence with the violence of the wind and rain, and the deaths of 41 miners in a recent coal pit disaster, and the sudden death of a distant relative.

It was a wet blustery night, and for no good reason she set out across the fields to meet the bus Leonard might be on. It was empty. 'The old devil has once more got his spine through the waves', she thought. Then, she

> became physically rigid. Reality, so I thought, was unveiled. And there was something noble in feeling like this; tragic, not at all petty. Then cold white lights went over the fields, and went out; and I stood under the great trees at Iford waiting for the lights of the bus. And that went by; and I felt lonelier. There was a man with a barrow walking into Lewes, who looked

> at me. But I could toy with, at least control all this, until suddenly, after the last likely train had come in I felt it was intolerable to sit about, and must do the final thing, which was to go to London. Off I rode, without much time, against such a wind; and again I had satisfaction in being matched with powerful things, like wind and dark. I battled, had to walk; got on; drove ahead; dropped the torch; picked it up, and so on again without any light. Saw men and women walking together; thought you're safe and happy, I'm an outcast; took my ticket, had 3 minutes to spare, and then, turning the corner of the station stairs, saw Leonard, coming alone, bending rather, like a person walking very quick, in his mackintosh. He was rather cold and angry (as perhaps, was natural). And then, not to show my feelings, I went outside and did something to my bicycle . . . All the way back . . . I was feeling My God, that's over. I'm out of that. It's over. Really, it was a physical feeling, of lightness and relief and safety, and yet there was too something terrible behind it – the fact of this pain, I suppose; which continued for several days.[20]

Virginia's frustration and anger – always a dangerous emotion for a cyclothyme – had pushed her into short-lived madness. Cyclothymic swings were unusual and never large in October and there was no dangerous potentiation of emotional forces. Madness lasted no more than a few hours, although after-effects lingered for several days. Leonard, who must have been shaken to encounter a wet wild-looking Virginia, was finally forced to accept the need to move to London.

As she searched for a suitable London house Virginia felt 'ten years younger'.[21] She looked into the future, convinced that 1924 was 'almost certainly bound to be their most eventful year.' On 9 January the Woolfs obtained a ten-year lease of 52 Tavistock Square and Virginia's excitement rose; so much lay ahead, 'music, talk, friendship, city views, books, publishing, something central and inexplicable, as it hasn't been since 1913.'[22] Spring melancholia was light. Even Leonard's initial pessimism and gloom, and his retiring to bed for four days with 'flu, failed to disturb her. When he solemnly told her his worst fears were coming to pass and visitors and social life were beginning to take up most of the day and interfere with work, she laughed loudly and told him he was imagining it all.

In fact, once Leonard was accustomed to the new home he found it far more convenient for his work than Richmond, and the Hogarth Press fitted easily into the basement of Tavistock Square. Virginia's health showed no sign of deteriorating. If anything, her stability was strengthened by her 'victory' over Leonard. She was writing *Mrs Dalloway* at this time and Clarissa Dalloway says of Peter Walsh (Clarisa's old lover, not unlike Leonard) there must be

> a little licence, a little independence between people living together day in and day out in the same home; which Richard [Clarissa's husband] gave her and she him . . . But with Peter everything had to be shared; everything gone into. And it was intolerable.[23]

Chapter Twelve

Vita Sackville-West

Virginia first met Vita Sackville-West in December 1922 at a dinner party given by Clive, but the two did not begin to know one another until 1924. Virginia fell passionately in love and, in December 1925, they became lovers.

It was an extraordinary but necessary development in Virginia's life. She did not contrive to fall in love with Vita. Love came naturally, for Virginia was now psychologically ready for a sexual relationship and was sufficiently emancipated and secure with Leonard to allow her emotions freer rein.

Virginia could never have been promiscuous; for her, a sexual relationship had to co-exist with love. A lover, of necessity, had to be a woman, for Leonard was far too important for Virginia to risk upsetting through an affair with another man, even had she been attracted to one. She was still capable of flirting occasionally with Clive, but no more. She knew that Leonard would not tolerate a male rival. On the other hand Virginia sensed, not without qualms at first, that Leonard could accept her involvement with another woman, and not see it as threatening their marriage or affecting his position.

Vita, that 'lovely, gifted aristocratic Sackville-West', attracted

Virginia from their first meeting.[1] Vita's manner – 'no false shyness or modesty' – and her aristocratic background, 'all those ancestors and centuries, and silver and gold', captured her imagination.[2] 'Snob as I am, I trace her passions 500 years back and they become romantic to me.'[3]

Vita invited Virginia to Knole, the great house where she had been born and which she loved. They lunched with Vita's father, Lord Sackville, the third Baron, and among others, Geoffrey Scott, Vita's only heterosexual lover, whom she was in the process of ditching. Afterwards, as Virginia travelled home in the train, absorbed in Vita's ancestors and the wonders of Knole, the thought struck her that Knole was 'capable of housing all the desperate poor of Judd Street' (a slum area of Bloomsbury);[4] an observation worthy of Leonard, and a reminder that he was never far away.

She was intrigued by Vita's reputation as a lesbian, so 'violently Sapphic', and the still fresh stories of her notorious affair in 1920 with Violet Trefusis. 'I will tell you a secret', she told her dying friend, Jacques Raverat; 'I want to incite my lady to elope with me next.'[5]

Vita was married to Harold Nicolson, himself a homosexual. Physical sex between them had ended, but their marriage was firmly anchored and neither was disturbed by the other's sexual encounters. Vita was much the stronger character, but she looked to her husband to rein her in and prevent impulsive actions which she would later regret. There were obvious similarities between the Nicolsons' and Woolfs' marriages, which perhaps Virginia was underlining when she told Vita 'in all London, you and I alone like being married'.[6]

Virginia saw Vita from many angles: 'a ravishing beauty and commanding presence';[7] a 'race horse' with 'no sharp brain';[8] 'virginal, savage, patrician'.[9] Above all she saw her as a maternal protector: 'open the top button of your jersey', she told Vita, 'and you will see, nestling inside, a lively squirrel, with the most inquisitive habits, but a dear creature all the same.'[10] The affair took two years to mature, and by the beginning of 1925 Virginia knew she was in love. She thought of Vita much of the time, desiring to go with her 'at once into the silent dusk', but she was uneasy over Leonard's possible reactions. As much to involve Leonard as to please Vita, she suggested Vita write a book for the Hogarth Press, and in September 1924 the manuscript of *Seducers in Ecuador*, dedicated to Virginia, was delivered in person. The book sold well, like most of Vita's works, appealing to a wider readership than Virginia's novels, but both women knew without question that Virginia was the better writer.

Leonard regarded Vita as a 'sentimental, romantic, naive and competent writer', 'an animal at the height of its powers, a beautiful flower in full bloom'.[11] He seems to have liked her well enough from the beginning and never came to see her in any way as a rival. She had, he thought, a 'manly good sense and simplicity about her'.[12]

Leonard had a theory that women developed 'little bursts of passion for one another' which might last 'for a day or two up to, sometimes, twelve months' before becoming close friends or drifting apart,[13] and he seems to have seen Virginia's interest in Vita at first in that light, along the lines of her friendships with Ottoline Morell and Katherine Mansfield.

Throughout 1924 and 1925 Vita flirted with Virginia and raised her expectations. 'Will you ever play truant to Bloomsbury and culture, I wonder, and come travelling with me? . . . I would rather go to Spain with you than with anyone,' Vita wrote early in the friendship, adding provocatively, 'You like people through the brain better than through the heart – forgive me if I am wrong.'[14] Virginia at once took up the challenge: 'It [your letter] gave me a great deal of pain – which is, I've no doubt, the first stage of intimacy – no friends, no heart, only an indifferent head. Never mind: I enjoyed your abuse very much.'[15] She visited Vita's home, Long Barn, and Vita came to stay the night at Monks House. By the end of 1924 Vita was constantly in her thoughts. In a last-ditch attempt to hold back her infatuation, she told herself Vita was 'like an over-ripe grape in features, moustached, pouting, will be a little heavy', but it was too late. 'I like her; could tack her on to my equipage for all time . . . if life allowed, this might be a friendship of a sort.'[16]

1924 was a mentally stable year and Virginia wrote *Mrs Dalloway* 'without a break from illness'[17] but 1925 was very different, and Virginia was frequently ill. Cyclothymic depression continued from mid-January until early March and was deep enough to keep her in bed and limit her activities. She recovered in time to go on holiday with Leonard to Cassis in the South of France. It was a great success, she noted, a sure sign that her marriage was secure.

> L and I were too too happy, as they say [she wrote in her diary on 8 April]. Nobody shall say of me that I have not known perfect happiness, but few could put their finger on the moment, or say what made it. Even I myself, stirring occasionally in the pool of content, could only say, but this is all I want; could not think of anything better, and had only my half superstitious feeling as the Gods who must, when they have created happiness, grudge it.

She crossed her fingers to add, 'Not if you get it in unexpected ways though.'[18]

The lift of mood was prolonged, and even the death of her friend Jacques Raverat, with whom she had corresponded with unusual intimacy during his slow death from multiple sclerosis, failed to dampen her spirits:

> I no longer feel inclined to doff the cap to death [she wrote]. I like to go out of the room talking, with an unfinished casual sentence on my lips. This is the effect it [his death] had on me – no leave taking, no submission – but someone stepping out into the darkness – more and more do I repeat my own version of Montaigne: 'It's life that matters.'[19]

She saw little of Vita during the first half of 1925. Both women were busy writing, and Vita was finally disposing of Geoffrey Scott. *The Common Reader* and *Mrs Dalloway* had been published and acclaimed. Virginia was pleased by Morgan Foster's praise, and puzzled by Vita's comment on the novel, unsure how to take ' will-of-the-wisp, a dazzling and lovely acquaintance'.[20] Ideas for *To the Lighthouse* had been forming for some time and she was impatient to begin, but there were too many diversions. During that summer she seemed in perpetual motion; she did not 'get any idle hours . . . heaven knows we have had enough visitors.'[22]

The Woolfs went to Monks House in August. It was an exeptionally hot summer. On 19 August the traditional birthday party for Virginia's nephew Quentin, on this occasion combined with Maynard Keynes's marriage to Lydia Lopokova, was held at Charleston, where Virginia was the life and soul of the party. The heat and noise and exhaustion proved too much and she suddenly fainted. Afterwards, lying in bed with headache and aching limbs and frightening bursts of racing pulse, she blamed herself: 'Why couldn't I see or feel that all this time I was getting a little used up and riding on a flat tyre?'[23] Depression followed the hypomania and, because of her exhaustion, was prolonged; she was in and out of bed for much of the next six months, and was not fully well until the following March. Depression was not severe and the headache and insomnia were often little more than a nuisance, and did not suggest danger, but Leonard was worried and insisted on rest and quiet. Virginia, however, was unable to relax. She desperately wanted to see Vita; 'I try to invent you for myself,' she wrote from her sick bed.[24]

Vita was gratifyingly concerned over Virginia's illness, wanted to visit at once, but Leonard would allow no visitors until *he* thought she was better. He attributed the relapse, as he saw it, to the strain of *Mrs Dalloway*, and he gave no hint of suspecting Vita. When Vita was finally allowed, Virginia's satisfaction was enormous, and she incautiously revealed the depth of her feelings, 'blurted out "truths" which the cautious respectability of health conceals'.[25]

Virginia was improving when, on 13 October, she heard that Harold Nicolson was going to Teheran as Counsellor at the Embassy and Vita would be joining him. She was 'filled with envy and despair',[26] and at once fell back into bed, panicky, 'a good deal of rat-gnawing at the back of my head'.[27] Leonard and the doctor forbade all activity, including writing letters, but she was allowed to receive them, and was hugely relieved to learn that Vita would not be leaving until January. But for the next two months she was a semi-invalid, her activities severely curtailed by Leonard.

Leonard finally came to acknowledge the force of Virginia's feelings for Vita. To his credit he at once did everything in his power to help his wife. He wrote to Vita – it was not unusual for Leonard to write for Virginia when she was ill – emphasising how much her visits meant and how much she would be missed.

Vita came at once in response to Leonard's letter. The two women had tea together, and when Virginia mentioned that her doctor had advised her to go away, Vita immediately invited her to convalesce at Long Barn, adding, 'I shall be alone after Harold has gone' (he left for Persia on 4 November).[28] Virginia was put into a state of dithering excitement, unable to make up her mind. She wanted to accept but feared she might disappoint Vita, and the thought of leaving Leonard frightened her. She waited nervously for Vita to confirm the invitation although, as Leonard pointed out, Vita had made it clear she wanted her to come; Virginia had only to choose a date.

When no letter arrived, and Vita failed to make an expected visit – impossible because of thick fog and illness – Virginia sank back into bed 'like a tired child', wanting to 'weep away this life of care . . . If I do not see her now, I shall not – ever; for the moment of intimacy will be gone next summer.'[29] She felt neglected, unwanted, unloved. Leonard told her she was behaving like a silly child, and that she should make arrangements to go to Long Barn. 'By God – how satisfactory after, I think, twelve years, to have any human being to whom one can speak so directly as I to L!' she wrote in her diary.[30]

The next day Vita's letter explaining her absence arrived and at once, spurred on by Leonard, Virginia wrote, 'Would you like me to come to you for a day or two, if you are alone, before the 20th?'[31] Vita was delighted, and on 17 December Virginia travelled down to Long Barn and spent three days alone with Vita. Leonard joined them on the 19th and Vita drove them back to London next day.

Virginia was in love. She revelled in the 'glow and the flattery and the festival'.[32] Above all, she basked in Vita's love. 'These Sapphists *love* women; friendship is untinged by amorousity,' she noted approvingly.[33] But passionate as she felt, she remained in control of herself. Part of her stood back and observed:

> What is the effect of all this on me? Very mixed. There is [Vita's] maturity and full-breastedness; her being so much in full sail on the high tides, where I am coasting down backwaters; her capacity, I mean, to represent her country, to visit Chatsworth, to control silver, servants, Chow dogs; her motherhood (but she is a little cold and offhand with her boys), her being, in short (what I have never been), a real woman. Then there is some voluptuousness about her; the grapes are ripe, and not reflective. No. In brain and insight she is not as highly organised as I am. But then she is aware of this, and so lavishes on me the maternal protection which, for some reason, is what I have always most wished from everyone. What L gives me, and Nessa gives me, and Vita, in her more clumsy, external way, tries to give me.[34]

Leonard, who had sent Vita instructions to ensure Virginia went to bed early, was pleased by the all-round improvement. 'Flu came in January, but it was a mild dip and Virginia was well enough to dine with Clive and Vita and Leonard shortly before Vita left for Persia. Her departure left Virginia lost in 'a dim November fog; the lights dulled and damped'. Vita might not be clever but she was 'abundant and fruitful; truthful too. She taps so many sources of life; repose and variety . . . I feel a lack of stimulus, of marked days, now Vita is gone.'[35] She conjured up the 'candlelight radiance', Vita 'walking on legs like beech trees, pink glowing, grape-clustered, pearl hung' that was 'the secret of her glamour'.[36] But every now and again she reassured herself she loved Leonard deeply, that Leonard remained the linchpin of her life; 'one has room for a good many relationships'.[37]

Leonard made no difficulties. Had he done so the affair would probably have finished, leaving Virginia resentful and unstable, and Vita would have retreated, afraid of Leonard's wrath. Whatever his deepest feelings Leonard tolerated the affair; he would return uncomplainingly to London after a weekend at Rodmell, leaving Virginia to stay on and spend a night or two alone with Vita, and he would raise no objections to her visiting Vita at Long Barn. If he suspected the sexual nature of the friendship, he wisely never discussed the matter, despite gossip at Bloomsbury gatherings. Clive had the bad taste – not unusual in Bloomsbury – to ask Vita at a New Year's Eve party if she had slept with Virginia; to which she returned a virtuous 'No!'[38]

Vanessa learnt of the affair early on, for not only did Virginia have a need to share the secret but she wanted to boast of her conquest:

> Vita is now arriving to spend two nights alone with me – L is going back. I say no more, as you are bored by Vita, bored by love, bored by me . . . Still, the June nights are long and warm, the roses flowering, and the garden full of lust and bees.[39]

Leonard would have been inhuman not to have felt an occasional spark of jealousy. He accepted Vita, and if she irritated him, he kept it hidden, hiding resentment behind boredom. Vita was half-afraid of him, such a 'funny, grim, solitary creature',[40] she told Harold, and she sometimes hesitated to telephone Virginia in case Leonard answered. But she made huge efforts to be friendly. She gave the Woolfs a spaniel bitch puppy to which Leonard became devoted. Her books sold well and made money for the Woolfs, and she remained loyal to the Hogarth Press despite Leonard's penny-pinching ways, and higher offers from other publishers.

Virginia was quick to notice Leonard's resentment, real or otherwise. Although she told herself that, 'whatever I think, I can rap out, suddenly to L',[41] she tried to hide the depth of her feelings, unlike Vita who held back few secrets from Harold. Occasionally, if she thought Leonard had been boorish with Vita, she criticised him for spoiling the visit by 'glooming'. After one such occasion he reacted by telling her their 'relations had not been so good lately', and she was left feeling 'an elderly, fussy, ugly, incompetent woman, vain, chattering and futile'.[42]

Their quarrels never lasted long, but Virginia determined to be 'more considerate of Leonard's feelings, and so keep more steadily at our ordinary level of intimacy and ease: a level, I think, no other couple so long married reaches and keeps so constantly.'[43] She took the precaution of arranging for Vita's more revealing letters to be sent under cover of uncompromising ones which could safely be shown to Leonard.

After Vita's departure for Persia, Virginia's depression lingered on for another six weeks. Then, in March, as though a dam had been opened, depression gave way to hypomania; energy returned two-fold and she resumed writing *To the Lighthouse*, 'never have I written so easily, imagined so profusely'.[44] By mid-April she had finished the first part and begun the second; 'Why am I so flown with words and, apparently, free to do what I like?' she asked herself.[45]

Vita returned home on 16 May. Virginia was apprehensive: 'The shock of meeting after absence; how shy one is'.[46] But once they met, shyness gave way to joy, not due to 'egotism but your seduction', she told Vita. So excited and wakeful was she that another 'dribbling little temperature' and 'nerve exhaustion headache' forced her to return to bed. It was short-lived but she continued to do too much and exhaust herself. Leonard was censorious and tried to restrain her, but she felt at one with the 'Spirit of Delight',[47] free, capable of anything. She turned her attention to home comforts. She had already spent some of her profits from writing on modernising Monks House, putting in two lavatories and a bath and a hot water system. She wanted to be comfortable, and Vita to be impressed, and now with this in mind she bought new armchairs and rugs. A row blew up with Leonard who wanted to spend available money on the garden, but Virginia stuck to her guns and won the day.

Vita returned to Persia on 28 January 1927, having spent the morning with Virginia, infatuated. 'What intelligence – what perception. Sensitiveness in the best sense, imagination, poetry, culture . . .'[48] 'I really adore her. Not "in love" but just love – devotion.'[49] Harold in Teheran was unusually jealous, although he termed it 'self defence', and urged Vita to be careful; although 'from your point of view, I know that the friendship can only be enriching'. He was 'a little anxious about it from her [Virginia's] point of view as I can't help feeling that her stability and poise is based on a rather precarious foundation.'[50] Vita assured him she would tell him of any 'muddle with Virginia'.[51] Despite Virginia missing Vita the spring melancholia was minimal; she felt sure of Vita and at ease with Leonard, and she was engaged in finishing *To the Lighthouse*. Leonard enthused when shown the manuscript; 'much my best book, and it is a "masterpiece" . . . a psychological poem.'[52] She worked on the proofs, but always at the back of her thoughts was Vita. In February she 'came out', with 'the most important event in my life since marriage – so Clive described it';[53] her long hair was cut off and, she told Vita, shingled and bingled. It was a signal to all three of her protectors that she was leaving childhood behind. One night in March, she thought up 'a whole fantasy . . . an escapade after these serious, poetic, experimental books whose form is always so closely considered'. It would be fun, written 'at the top of my speed . . . Sapphism is to be suggested. Satire is to be the main note – satire and wildness.'[54] By October the ideas had crystallised into *Orlando*.

Vita returned in May with Harold, who had completed his tour of duty in Persia. The excitement proved too much and within a short time Virginia had 'a very sharp headache' and an erratic jumping pulse. Leonard forced her to rest; 'a good thing in some way', she admitted, 'for I got control of society at an early stage, and circumvented my headache, without a complete smash'.[55]

It was gratifying to have Vita home but Virginia found Harold's presence at Long Barn irritating, despite his friendliness. More than a hint of resentment lies behind Virginia's diary entries: 'a spontaneous childlike man',[56] 'flimsy' compared to Leonard (who in turn thought him 'too commonplace').[57] Virginia was also sensing a sexual restlessness on Vita's part, which made her feel 'elderly and valetudinarian'.[58]

In October Virginia began *Orlando,* a never-ageing Vita who changes from male to female, beginning with the year 1500. As she wrote, 'it rushed off like a rocket',[59] and she finished it by March. The book started as 'a joke',[60] but became what Nigel Nicolson has called 'the longest and most charming love letter in literature'.[61] Virginia told Vita, it is about 'the lusts of your flesh and the lure of your mind . . . Shall you mind?'[62] Vita was entranced: 'what fun for you; what fun for me. You see, any vengeance that you ever want to take will be ready in your hand.'[63] *Orlando* was published that October, dedicated to Vita.

Leonard was not upset, and Virginia was surprised how seriously he took the book, his opinion being that it was 'in some ways better than *The Lighthouse*'.[64] Perhaps it was his way of avoiding any embarrassing discussion. The person most upset was Vita's mother, who called Virginia a 'wicked madwoman' and tried ineffectually to prevent the book being reviewed.[65]

That July Virginia spent a weekend at Long Barn, where Vita confessed to having spent a night with Mary Hutchinson, Clive's ex-mistress. Virginia tried her best to see it as a passing peccadillo, but warned Vita to take care lest she find Virginia's 'soft crevices lined with hooks'.[66] When a more serious affair with Mary Campbell, wife of the poet Roy Campbell, threatened, Virginia became alarmed. She told Vita:

> Never do I leave you without thinking it's for the last time since I am always certain you'll be off and on with the next . . . since all our intercourse is tinged with this melancholy on my part. Perhaps we gain in intensity what we lack in the sober comfortable virtues of a prolonged and safe and respectable and chaste and cold-blooded friendship.[67]

Vita's affair caused trouble. Roy Campbell found out and threatened murder and suicide, and an alarmed Vita confessed everything to Virginia, tempering the blow by swearing that Virginia remained 'absolutely vital'. Virginia was only partly mollified, and for some years, until she began to come to terms with what was clearly the inevitable, depression was frequent and often prolonged.

At the end of September Vita and Virginia spent a week together in France. The holiday had been planned and discussed for months. Virginia very much wanted to go, but was worried by '7 days alone with Vita', in case they 'found each other out'.[68] She was also very anxious at separating from Leonard for so long. She dithered, and in the end Vita and Leonard both had to push her. Her 'separation anxiety' was huge She wrote home every day and once, when Leonard's letters failed to arrive, she sent a telegram asking what was wrong. Her letters were full of endearments. She longed to be reunited with her 'daddie'.[69] 'I don't think I could stand more than week away from you, as there are so many things to say to you, which I can't say to Vita.'[70] But she enjoyed the holiday, and so did Vita. Vita fussed over Virginia 'like a perfect old hen'. They had separate bedrooms, and when a thunderstorm broke one night Vita went immediately to Virginia's room to comfort her. Vita found the combination of 'that brilliant brain and that fragile body very lovable – so independent in all mental ways, so dependent in all practical ways'.[71]

Vita had by now lost sexual interest in Virginia. Initially she had been physically attracted, but it was Virginia's mind and character that really held Vita. She saw Virginia as 'a mental thing, a spiritual thing if you like, an intellectual thing, and she inspires a feeling of tenderness . . . She makes me feel protective. Also she loves me, which flatters and pleases me.'[72] Vita was incapable of maintaining a passionate relationship for long. She needed the 'buzz' of intense involvement, and as the excitement fell away the relationship changed to one of friendship only. Most of Vita's lovers were dependent women looking for a mother-figure. She was 'St Anne, her Demeter, lover, mother',[73] to Mary Campbell. Margaret Voight, another lover, wrote in language Virginia would have recognised: 'I wish I were three years old and that I could crawl into your arms and just stay there while you take on the *régie* of my life.'[74]

Virginia, as she learnt of each new affair, poured 'rage hot as lava' on Vita and lectured her to change her ways.[75] She scorned the 'schoolgirl nonentities' Vita involved herself with, but eventually she was forced to recognise that Vita was not going to change. She tried rationalising their relationship:

> the gnawing down of strata in friendship; how one passes unconsciously to different terms, takes things easier; don't mind at all hardly about dress or anything; scarcely feel it an exciting atmosphere, which too, has its drawbacks from the 'fizzing' point of view: yet is saner, perhaps deeper.[76]

Harold Nicolson had been posted to the embassy in Berlin in 1927 and Vita stayed with him that winter. The Woolfs planned to visit them in the New Year, but Leonard was already regretting it. He knew of Vita's affairs, and was worried by Virginia's erratic moods and tension. When he could not persuade Virginia to postpone the trip he insisted she warn the Nicolsons that she *must* have a quiet time.

His instructions were ignored, or Virginia never passed on his message and in Berlin Leonard became increasingly angry with the Nicolsons. They in turn were irritated by Leonard's bad temper, and his boorish refusal to attend a lunch party Harold had arranged in their honour. Virginia was embarrassed and upset by Leonard: 'I shiver at the thought of our behaviour,' she told Vita. 'You and Harold were such angels.'[77] She was also upset at never having Vita to herself. Only once did the two women dine alone together, and the occasion proved highly disturbing to Virginia; she questioned Vita repeatedly about her sexual involvements, and demanded proof that Vita still loved her. Vita was evasive and Virginia was not reassured.

Two days later, on the overnight ferry home from the Hook of Holland, Virginia swallowed a large quantity of Somnifen (containing the barbiturate Veronal) given her by Vanessa against seasickness. She sank into semi-coma and Leonard could barely rouse her:

> it was with the greatest difficulty I got her into the train, as she could hardly walk and was in a kind of drugged state . . . The giddiness lasted off and on for about twenty-four hours.[78]

Virginia maintained she took no more than the prescribed dosage, but the evidence points to an overdose; either through carelessness or perhaps as a *gesture* to Vita, a warning and an appeal. Leonard blamed the incident, and Virginia's subsequent depression, on the Berlin 'racketing', but ignored the effect his own behaviour may have had. Vita scoffed at Leonard's explanation; to hear him talk, she told Virginia, 'you might have spent every night for a week till five in the morning indulging in orgies'. The real cause of the trouble, said Vita with tongue in cheek, was partly the 'flu but mainly Virginia's 'suppressed randiness'.[79]

Virginia was laid up for six weeks, but depression was not severe and the time resting was not wasted, for it released a stream of creative thoughts; she composed *The Waves* 'hour after hour', and *A Room of One's Own* wrote itself as she lay in bed; 'I was like a water bottle turned upside down.'[80]

Virginia tried distancing herself from Vita. She would

> enter a nunnery these next months; let myself down into my mind . . . I am going to face certain things. It is going to be a time of adventure and attack, rather lonely and painful I think. But solitude will be good for a new book. Of course, I shall make friends. I shall be external outwardly. I shall buy some good clothes and go out into new houses.

She inspected her life and her marriage. Her miseries were really very small ones, 'and fundamentally', she told herself,

> I am the happiest woman in all WC1. The happiest wife, the happiest writer; the most liked inhabitant, so I say, in Tavistock Square. When I count up my blessings, they must surely amount to more than my sorrows.[81]

Virginia eventually accepted Vita's philandering, but she could not reconcile herself to the thought of sharing Vita's love with another woman. Of all Vita's lovers, it was Hilda Matheson, the Director of Talks at the BBC, she loathed most. Vita tried to play down the attachment, but Virginia remained 'worried and angry and hurt and caustic about this affair'.[82]

> These Hildas are a chronic case; and as this one won't disappear and is unattached, she may be permanent. And like the damned intellectual snob

> that I am, I hate to be linked, even by an arm, with Hilda . . . A queer trait in Vita – her passion for the earnest middle-class intellectual, however drab and dreary.[83]

Vita herself was withdrawing. In May 1930 she bought Sissinghurst Castle and set about restoring it and, with Harold, creating the renowned gardens. It became her permanent home after two years. Only once did Virginia stay there, when she slept in the absent Harold's room, but she and Leonard occasionally went there for the day. Jealousy and doubts obtruded from time to time, and brought on headaches and 'galloping horses'.

In July 1931 Virginia pronounced 'Potto' – a primitive monkey, Vita's nickname for her – to be dead. 'You have not been for a month', she told Vita, 'and I date his decline from your last visit. As he died his last words were, "Tell Mrs Nick that I love her . . . she has forgotten me. But I forgive her."'[84] Potto revived at the last moment. The friendship continued, and although they met at decreasing intervals they remained important to one another. Vita's words after Virginia's suicide, 'I might have saved her if only I had been there',[85] were not entirely an ignorant boast, although a mad Virginia, whom Vita had never known, would have been very different from the familiar Potto.

Between July 1929 and the summer of 1931 Virginia was writing *The Waves*. It was more difficult than anything she had attempted before; 'the play-poem idea; the idea of some continuous stream, not solely of human thought, but of the ship, the night etc. all flowing together.'[86] As she finished the book she knew, triumphantly, she had 'netted that fin in the waste of waters', which she had seen 'passing far out' on completing *To the Lighthouse*.[87] The fin, rising from her subconscious depths, symbolised 'something in the universe that one's left with'.[88] Writing the book was at times agonising but there were moments of ecstasy when she was carried outside herself. As she wrote the last ten pages she felt she was being taken over by huge universal forces; stumbling 'after my own voice, or almost after some kind of speaker (as when I was mad). I was almost afraid, remembering the voices that used to fly ahead.'[89]

She wrote to a rhythm, not to a plot – she worried lest readers should find it incomprehensible. The rhythm of the waves on the seashore reflected, perhaps, the rhythm of the deep subcortical areas of her brain.

> I like to flash and dash from side to side, goaded on by what I call reality [by which Virginia meant the subconscious]. If I never felt these extraordinary pervasive strains – of unrest, or rest, or happiness, or discomfort – I should float down into acquiescence. Here is something to fight: and when I wake early I say to myself, fight, fight. If I could catch the feeling, I would: the feeling of the singing of the real world [the subconscious] as one is driven by loneliness and silence from the habitable world.[90]

In creating *The Waves* Virginia dredged her mental depths: 'one goes down into the well and nothing protects one from the assault of truth'.[91] The first draft needed so much concentration; so many ideas kept welling up to be hammered into shape. Depression interrupted the work from time to time, but the breaks were valuable in solving the insoluble. When faced with a mental block she thought, '6 weeks in bed now would make a masterpiece'.[92]

Leonard regarded *The Waves* as a masterpiece, Virginia's greatest book. Vanessa was 'overcome by the beauty . . . it's quite as real as having a baby or anything else, being moved as you have succeeded in moving me'.[93] Her friend Ethel Smyth found it 'profoundly disquieting, sadder than any book I ever read'.[94] Only Vita thought it 'boring in the extreme'.[95] Virginia hid her disappointment in jocularity, and told Vita's son that his mother believed 'only a small dog that had been fed on gin could have written it'.[96] Six weeks after the publication of *The Waves*, in October 1934, headaches and exhaustion forced Virginia to lead 'a hermit's life, without pleasure or excitement', until the end of the year.[97]

Ethel Smyth was a well-known if minor composer when she swept into Virginia's life in 1930 and became an important friend, providing love and adoration. Her warmth and interest in Virginia, feminism, honesty, intelligence and eccentricity, perhaps even her age, encouraged Virginia to bare her soul to Ethel. Ethel also had that essential 'maternal quality, which of all others I need and adore . . . for that reason I chatter faster and freer to you than to other people'.[98]

Ethel was besotted by Virginia. Almost at once she made Virginia 'a declaration of violent but platonic love', she had 'never loved anyone so much'.[99] She was nearly 72 when they met, and deaf enough to need an ear trumpet. She had lesbian leanings but sex was never an issue in her relationship with Virginia. Convinced that her musical reputation had suffered through being a woman, she was an extraordinary being: massively built, with a huge head and a 'humane, battered face', egotistic, warmhearted and quarrelsome.

She helped to keep up Virginia's morale as Vita retreated. For Ethel, Virginia came before everyone and anything else. When ill and confined to bed, Ethel rushed to her bedside. Virginia loved her for it: 'I can't tell you, Ethel, how I adored you for that dash here – for two hours only – how it kindled and enraptured me to have you by me.'[100] She craved such affection, and formed a 'limpet childish attachment' to Ethel.

There were occasional setbacks. Once, Ethel sent Virginia a picture of a sick monkey, with a note telling her all her ills 'spring from liver', calomel would cure her. 'After swallowing this terrific insult to the celebrated sensibility of my nervous system; Virginia forgave her.[101]

Chapter Thirteen

Threat of War

Leonard, through his committee work and writings, sought to widen the Labour party's international and imperial horizons, and gain support for the League of Nations. He worked prodigiously hard; much of his aggression, and perhaps his sexual energy, were displaced into work. He rarely lost his temper, and his celibacy probably added to his 'grimness'.

Until the 1930s the Parliamentary Labour party voted consistently for disarmament and measures to strengthen the League. The Party held power briefly in 1923 under Ramsay MacDonald, and again in 1929 when they came back as a minority government. Leonard's hopes of radical change ended with the world financial crisis and the depletion of Britain's gold reserves in 1931. The Cabinet split over proposed cuts in public expenditure, especially unemployment benefits, and Ramsay MacDonald resigned. A National Coalition government, made up largely of Conservatives, was formed next day with MacDonald at its head. Leonard was incensed by MacDonald's 'betrayal' of the Party; there was never 'a more treacherous man'. His despair was complete when the Labour Party was routed at the General Election that followed. They would remain weak and divided for years to come.

Leonard barely had time to adjust to these catastrophic changes when Japanese troops occupied Manchuria and went on to invade China. It was the first important challenge to the League of Nations and called for effective action, but the League's response was pathetically inadequate, a disappointment to those who had put their faith in collective security, and a taste of what lay ahead. Neither Russia nor America, the two powers best placed to intervene, were members of the League and Britain had no intention of taking military action. The League simply criticised the use of force and avoided branding Japan an aggressor.

Uncharacteristically, Leonard brought up the subject of the Sino-Japanese conflict at a dinner party given by Clive, and was shouted down by everyone there, including Virginia, who thought 'war is the dullest of all things'.[1] Thus began for Leonard the years of horror as he watched the League disintegrate and war approach.

The Hogarth Press was expanding, almost too rapidly for the Woolfs' liking. It was no longer just a therapy for Virginia, an interesting diversion for Leonard, but a successful and prestigious publishing firm; the 1925 list contained thirty-four books. Over the years the Press published works by many distinguished writers and best sellers, and from 1924 the Press was responsible for the International Psycho-Analytical Library, which included Freud and prominent analysts.

As early as 1920 Leonard was complaining of the amount of work, that the Press 'was beginning to outgrow its parents'.[2] Leonard was entirely responsible for all the management and business side. Virginia set type, bound books, and parcelled them up, but her strength lay in judging the manuscripts which came in. She had no business sense, although plenty of ideas that she expressed when in high spirits, and which Leonard patiently listened to and ignored.

Virginia benefited from the Press. It prevented her 'brooding and gives me something solid to fall back on'.[3] It relieved her of the anxiety of submitting her novels to another publisher, although by 1926 she felt confident enough to 'doubt if Heinemann or Cape would much intimidate me'. But eventually she began to tire of reading manuscripts, and the Woolfs considered selling the Press, or using it solely for her and Leonard's publications. In 1920 they appointed a part-time manager, Ralph Partridge, a bright young man who had just left Oxford. He admired the Woolfs, was ambitious to become a partner in a publishing firm of growing repute, and was intent on doing 'hurricane' business.

Leonard admitted he was never an easy person to work with.[4] He was incapable of giving up the day-to-day running of the Press – he regarded it as his child – and delegating responsibility.

> After a honeymoon period of a few weeks when he would instruct them – the managers – in their manifold obligations with fatherly patience and humour, [he] would become increasingly impatient, intolerant of little mistakes, and testy – indeed often hysterically angry – when things were not going quite to his liking; and when he was testy he could be extremely rude. The result was that each attempt to lift the burden on to a young man's shoulders ended in more time wasted, mainly in altercation, and nerves frayed all round.[5]

Tensions were heightened by the working conditions – untidy, pokey rooms – and by Leonard's parsimony. He ran the Press on a shoestring, and paid his authors little and his managers an almost insultingly low wage. Virginia, who possessed her father's meanness and went along with Leonard's penny-pinching ways, felt impelled on at least one occasion to apologise to Vita for what the Press offered.

Although she always sided with Leonard in disputes, she was often upset by them. On one occasion she walked into the end of 'a terrific quarrel' between Leonard and the manager Angus Davidson over whether or not he had arrived a few minutes late for work, which ended in his simultaneous dismissal and resignation, and everyone being upset. Virginia did not like bullying, which she looked on as a male characteristic, responsible for most of the world's troubles. She could criticise Leonard to his face as 'a tub-thumper, intolerant, arrogant',[6] when she was well, but when depressed she sank under it. She was troubled by the contrasting faces he presented in public and private. He was intolerant and bullied his subordinates, yet he wrote impassioned articles against aggression, and urged men and nations to resolve their differences through rational discussion and compromise.

Leonard's decision to take over the publishing of the International Psycho-Analytical Library was partly prompted by his interest in Freud's work. Leonard regarded Freud as a genius, although not infallible. He was sceptical of some of Freud's hypotheses, but he was prepared to look at colleagues, and sometimes himself, through Freudian eyes:

> I am sure that if one could look deep into the minds of those who are on the Left in politics (including myself), Liberals, revolutionaries, socialists, communists, pacifists, and humanitarians, one would find that their political beliefs and desires were connected with some very strange goings-on down among their Ids in their unconscious.[7]

However, Leonard did not consider analysis for himself (he would have been an impossible analysand, unable to give up intellectual control), although a number of friends took it up. James Strachey, Lytton's younger brother, and his wife Alix, had been analysed by Freud:

> Each day I spend an hour on the Prof's sofa – it's sometimes extremely exciting and sometimes extremely unpleasant. The Prof himself is most affable and, as an artistic performer, dazzling.[8]

Adrian Stephen gave up Law in 1920 and with his wife embarked on analytical training. However, not all Bloomsbury smiled on Freudian theory and methods. Roger Fry, backed by Clive Bell, was incensed by the idea of the artist as neurotic, and art being no more than his unconscious conflicts.

Leonard never considered psychoanalytic treatment for Virginia.

Analysts were practising in London well before her breakdown, but treatment was still experimental and the results unpredictable and, it was said, liable to impair creative work. None of the specialists Leonard consulted for Virginia was *au fait* with psychoanalysis and both Savage and Craig were frankly hostile. Maurice Craig believed she lacked the mental stability to withstand the strain of having distressing ideas dredged up. Alix Strachey, a practising analyst and someone who knew Virginia well, agreed with that view and thought analysis would do more harm than good. Few psychiatrists today would contest that.

If Leonard had suggested psychoanalysis, he would probably have met strong opposition. The possibility of losing the urge to write would have horrified Virginia (it is, of course, an erroneous belief; an artist may be highly neurotic but the quality of one's work does not depend on the neurosis, although that may colour the work). She would have objected to an analyst attempting to break into her privacy. 'There is a virgin forest, tangled, pathless, in each [of us]' she wrote in *On Being Ill*. 'Here we go alone and like it better so. Always to be accompanied, always to be understood, would be intolerable.'[9]

Leonard was impressed by Freud's discoveries regarding the unconscious and he more than half believed that if you punctured a pacifist, out would pour aggression. But he disagreed with Freud over how civilised man learnt to control his aggression and sexual instincts. Freud believed the destructive instincts were repressed into the unconscious in the early years through fear of punishment, and that in the process a sense of sin developed – 'the unhappiness of mankind'. Leonard maintained that such repression was undesirable, for sooner or later it would give way and bring civilisation crashing to the ground with war and anarchy. Only when 'love (in the widest sense) and reason are substituted for the sanctions of fear and sin' will men learn truly to control their instincts and use them for creative and not destructive purposes.[10] 'To be a slave to [a sense of sin] is barbarism; to control it is civilisation. '[11]

Leonard learnt this, he claimed, through training his pets. Training based on fear rather than love resulted in less obedient and affectionate dogs. The same principle must apply to children. When all children can be brought up by enlightened parents and teachers whom they love, there will be no more war. Leonard maintained that he had never known a sense of sin. He had been brought up in a loving atmosphere, and developed into a rational civilised being whose impulses were always under his control. Not everyone would agree with this self-assessment. Leonard may have controlled his sexual instinct, but his aggression was liable to appear in all kinds of 'uncivilised' ways.

In December 1931 the Woolfs learnt that Lytton Strachey was seriously ill with ulcerative colitis; in fact he was dying of cancer of the stomach. In recent years they had seen less of Lytton but he had remained an important friend. Virginia still loved him deeply 'after my Jew. He's in all my past – my youth.'[12] On Christmas Eve they heard he was dying, and they sat talking of 'death and its stupidity'.[13] Virginia asked how Leonard would feel if she died. She felt sure she would die first, yet she wanted to live another twenty years and 'write another four novels'. She wondered about immortality, and questioned Leonard's insistence that death was the end, with nothing beyond. She asked Maynard Keynes's opinion. He was vague: 'I suppose I think something may be continued', but 'death [should] be arranged for couples simultaneously.'[14]

Lytton died on 19 January. Leonard wept briefly and comforted Virginia. They were joined by Vanessa, and the two sisters 'sat sobbing together . . . a sense of something spent, gone.' Lytton had been 'the first of the people one has known since one has grown up to die'. Virginia had adored, feared and admired him. They had talked of everything; 'love and beauty, and prose and poetry'. She knew his complicated love life. He was not a 'protector' in the maternal sense, but he was part of Old Bloomsbury, the 'family' whose love she took for granted.[15]

Dora Carrington had fallen in love with Lytton as a young woman and devoted herself to him, looking after him, an inseparable daughter. Before Lytton died friends predicted she would commit suicide, and on 13 March she shot herself. The Woolfs had visited Carrington the day before her death. Virginia had held her while she wept and confessed she had nothing to live for, causing Virginia to think of her own dependence on Leonard. For a moment she too saw life as 'hopeless, useless, when I woke in the night and thought of Lytton's death.'[16]

Leonard took her to task. Carrington's suicide was 'histrionic' and trivial compared to Lytton's death. They talked again of suicide, 'and the ghosts . . . change so oddly in my mind; like people who live and are changed by what one hears of them'. A week later Virginia was 'glad to be alive and sorry for the dead; can't think why Carrington killed herself.'[18]

Early in 1931 John Lehmann was appointed manager of the Press, and over the following year Leonard was increasingly critical of him. A major row developed and Virginia was bruised by the bickering. It was a relief when Lehmann left, but she was left disturbed by Leonard's 'desire to dominate',[19] to ride roughshod over people, and depressed by 'the inane pointlessness of all this existence; the old treadmill feeling of going on and on, for no reason . . . terror at night of things generally wrong in the universe.' She made herself think of Leonard's 'goodness, and firmness; and the immense responsibility that rests on him', but she

> saw all the violence and unreason crossing in the air: ourselves small; a tumult outside: something terrifying: unreason. Shall I make a book out of this? It would be a way of bringing order and speed again into my world.[20]

Male aggression and unreason angered and frightened her.

> I've been nearer one of those climaxes of despair that I used to have than any time these six years – Lord knows why. Oh, how I suffer! and, what's

> worse, for nothing, no reason that's respectable . . . the incessant rubbing and rasping . . . the whole Press upset, and in process of death or birth, heaven knows which.[21]

That summer of 1932 she saw too many people and wore herself out during the cyclothymic high months. In August another close friend, Goldie Dickinson, died: 'it is thus we die, when they die', she thought.[22] A few days later she fainted in the garden and felt that she too was dying.

One night in November she awoke with her heart pounding, fearing death. She did not want to die, and went to Leonard's bed for reassurance. The turmoil ceased as she lay in his arms; tranquillity returned. Later, she thought:

> I don't think we've ever been so happy . . . And so intimate and so completely entire . . . If it could only last like this for another fifty years – life like this is wholly satisfactory, to me anyhow.[23]

Chapter Fourteen

The Years and *Three Guineas*

Leonard's prolonged frustrations at work brought on psychosomatic symptoms. In January 1933 he began to itch, and was convinced that insects were crawling under his skin. He spent hours picking what he thought were black insects on his neck. Virginia was concerned: 'I can imagine nothing more terrible than to have insects under one's skin – I should see them parading in squads.'[1] She assumed the insects were lice, although in truth she was unable to see any. Their doctor failed to help and eventually sent Leonard to a Harley Street dermatologist, who diagnosed a simple dermatitis and dismissed the idea of bugs out of hand. Within a few days the itch and the imagined insects disappeared.

These symptoms are quite common in old age but in Leonard's case, a mere fifty-year-old, it was a sign of tension. Symbolically, no doubt, they could have been seen as evil forces invading his civilised world.

Hitler became Chancellor of the German Reich at the end of January 1933 and established a one-party system. Leonard was quick to warn of the danger: 'it is one of the most savage and senseless dictatorships that has been tolerated by a civilised

European population for at least two centuries', he wrote in the *Political Quarterly*.[2] He watched with rising alarm as Hitler had himself proclaimed 'Führer of the German Reich', withdrew Germany from the League of Nations, and introduced conscription.

As early as November Winston Churchill was warning of the dangers of Nazi aggression and German rearmament, and the next year the National Government, now under Baldwin, proposed a small increase in the military estimates. They were immediately accused of warmongering by the Labour Party, who bitterly attacked the measure and called for total disarmament.

Although Leonard agreed with the Labour Party policy at that time, he was already beginning to have doubts. He was also concerned by the divisions in the Party, the woolly thinking of some of its members. The extreme left rejected the League as a tool of capitalist countries; the right wing supported the League but objected to sanctions on the grounds they increased the risk of war; die-hard pacifists opposed anything other than passive resistance.

The turning point for Leonard came at the beginning of 1935 when Mussolini's aggressive intentions against Abyssinia became apparent. He saw Mussolini as less of a danger than Hitler, but a bully who would take what he wanted unless faced down. If he violated the Covenant of the League, Italy must face full economic sanctions and if sanctions brought war, so be it. Force had to be met with force, for the sake of peace. The alternative was worldwide barbarism. Leonard's decision did not come easily or quickly for, once accepted, he had to abandon his long-held convictions.

It was perhaps in order to make up his mind that he and Virginia travelled through Germany in 1935. That spring the Woolfs had planned to go to Rome, and their route would normally have taken them through France. Instead, Leonard arranged to travel on the car ferry to Holland and motor across Germany, going through the Brenner Pass. Their friends were alarmed at the risk. Virginia joked that Leonard's nose was 'so long and hooked, we rather suspect we shall be flayed alive'.[3] Quentin Bell thought Leonard 'took an unjustifiable risk with Virginia's nerves',[4] but physical danger never bothered her. As they crossed the German frontier Leonard felt, 'with some disquiet', that he had 'passed in a few yards from civilisation into savagery'. 'Jews [were] not wanted . . . there was something sinister and menacing . . . a crude and savage silliness beneath the surface'.[5]

The journey seems to have resolved Leonard's doubts. He now believed that Britain and France must re-arm and prepare to defend themselves and others against Nazi aggression. He applauded the trade unionist Ernest Bevin for telling the Labour Party Conference – in the course of which he 'battered' the aged pacifist leader George Lansbury to political death – 'if you are going to fight against Hitler, or any other aggressor, you must have arms with which to fight'.[6]

The failure of the League to stop Mussolini in Abyssinia reinforced his new belief; for clearly the League could not deter aggression and prevent war. When Hitler's troops marched into the demilitarised Rhineland that March, Leonard thought not of the League but of alliances and rearmament. He urged the Parliamentary Labour Party to change its line. The increasingly dangerous situation required a new policy: 'mere negative opposition to a policy of rearmament would be sterile and ineffective'.[7] He provoked strong antagonism from many of the members.

Virginia was distressed by Leonard's turn-about, his call to re-arm, preparations for war. She was an out-and-out pacifist. Wars were destructive games invented by men. She simply could not understand 'the fever in the blood' of most males.[8] Women should adopt an 'attitude of complete indifference' to male war-cries.[9] 'Has war ever won any cause?', she challenged Leonard.[10]

Virginia loathed the Nazis as much as Leonard; they stood for brutality, violence, the domestication of women.

> Brutal bullies go about in hoods and masks, like little boys dressed up, acting this idiotic, meaningless, brutal, bloody pandemonium . . . And for the first time I read articles with rage, to find him [Hitler] called a real leader. Worse far than Napoleon.'[11]

She signed anti-fascist petitions and joined committees, while remaining firmly a pacifist, convinced that force should not be used against force. The pen was mightier than the sword, and with that weapon she would fight 'to the death for votes, wages, peace and so on'.[12]

Many of Virginia's friends were pacifists. Aldous Huxley opposed sanctions against Italy because he feared they would result in war. Clive Bell wrote a letter to the *New Statesman* declaring, 'War's so awful it can't be right anyhow', which impressed Virginia; a sign she said, of Clive's 'genuine humanity'.[13]

Another reason for Leonard's decision to travel across Germany may have been to make Virginia recognise Nazi anti-Semitism. I was not something Virginia really felt or understood. She had the conventional disdain of her class for Jews in general but she could not be accused of being truly anti-Semitic. Only gradually did she come to appreciate the basis for Leonard's hatred of Nazi anti Semitism. She met refugee German Jews like Bruno Walter:

> 'You must not think of the Jews,' he kept on saying, 'You must think of the whole state of the world. It is terrible – terrible. That this meanness, tha this pettiness, should be possible!'[14]

Virginia looked forward to seeing Germany. She told a friend there was little danger, 'and it will be the greatest fun',[15] but after three days, angered by the banners stretched across the streets of every town, 'The Jew Is Our enemy', she was thankful to leave behind 'the hysterical crowd' and cross the border into Austria. Both thei nerves were rather frayed, and she was upset by Leonard's tension and gloom.[16] When they got to Rome he was still keyed up and irritable, and Virginia reacted by being 'so difficult to feed tha meals became rather an uneasy problem'.[17]

It was always so when Virginia was angry with Leonard. She wa upset over his reaction to their experiences, his near-certainty that war with Germany had to be faced. She too hated what they had seen, and she now understood Leonard's fear of the Nazis and hi fate under German domination, but she wanted a peacefu outcome, not war. Usually a healthy row would settle thei differences, but on this occasion the problem was too complex.

Leonard grew worried by Virginia's anorexic behaviour and gave her all his attention. His introspectiveness and irritability were replaced by concern and persuasion, and Virginia gradually relaxed. Her anger faded, although the problem remained. Once home, she recorded that 'holidays are very upsetting',[18] the constant motoring was 'intolerable' and she was left with 'a grim wooden feeling'.[19]

She continued to be bothered by talk of war. 'When even I can't sleep at night for thinking of politics, things must be in a fine mess. All our friends talk politics, politics, politics', she told Ottoline Morell. 'All politics be damned.'[20] She got 'into a stew' thinking of war and patriotism, and, seeing the signs chalked up on London walls – 'Don't Fight For Foreigners'; 'Britain Should Mind Her Own Business' – Leonard told her sharply they were 'Fascist propaganda. Mosley again active'.[21]

During 1935 Virginia was revising *The Years*. She had begun the novel in 1932, as an 'Essay-Novel':

> to take in everything; sex, education, life, etc; and come, with the most powerful and agile leaps, like a chamois across precipices, from 1880 to here and now.[22]

Her plan had been to alternate fiction with essay, but she found the method too unwieldy and left out the essays – which were later expanded into *Three Guineas*.

While Virginia was writing *The Years*, ideas for *Three Guineas*, her anti-war book as she called it, kept breaking into her mind and putting her into 'wild excitement'.[23] It was

> like being harnessed to a shark; and I dash off scene after scene. I think I must do it directly *The Years* is done. Suppose I finish *The Years* in January, then dash off 'The War' (or whatever I call it) in six weeks.[24]

Depression built up early in the New Year, Virginia had promised to have *The Years* ready for the printer by 1 February, and despite sleepless nights she forced herself to begin the final revision. Pressure mounted, and was not lessened by Leonard telling her she had not made enough money to pay her share of the household expenses. She concentrated everything on the book, cut out social activities and saw no one apart from Vanessa, but agitation kept breaking through. The novel seemed 'feeble twaddle', and one morning she could no longer face 'such a show up of my own decrepitude', and rushed to Leonard 'with burning cheeks'. He told her, '"This always happens." But I felt, no, it has never been so bad as this.'[25]

On 7 March German troops marched unopposed into the Rhineland. Leonard saw war one step nearer. Virginia watched him being 'rushed and pumped and milked by every ninny on the European situation',[26] and thought:

> how near the guns have got to our private life again. I can quite distinctly see them and hear a roar, even though I go on, like a doomed mouse, nibbling at my daily page. What else is there to do – except answer the incessant telephones, and listen to what L says. [27]

Depression went on building up. Headache forced her to lie prostrate and work for very limited times; at night she woke worrying, sweating, seeing failure, 'the end of civilisation just about to come'.[28] There were moments when she feared for her sanity, when she found herself 'walking along the Strand talking aloud' (although this was not altogether unusual).[29] Remarkably, Virginia managed to complete *The Years*, and sent the last pages to the printers on 8 April. Suddenly she was overcome with agitation. The sight of the proofs sickened her. She stuffed them into a cupboard, unable to face them. Racked by headache, unable to sleep, worrying to no end, she broke down.

Leonard, fearing a serious breakdown, immediately took her to Rodmell and she spent four weeks resting, much of the time in bed. Once she improved Leonard took her to the West Country for a change of scene. She came back to London on 10 June.

The improvement was momentary. Virginia started work on the proofs, but after three days was forced to return to Rodmell. She had 'mornings of torture – pain in my head – a feeling of complete despair and failure'. She attempted to work half an hour at a time. 'Few people can be so tortured by writing as I am. Only Flaubert, I think.'[30] She had lost seven pounds in weight. Leonard, suspecting a return of madness, made Virginia give up all work and rest at Rodmell for the remainder of the summer. She was allowed few friends but she wrote letters, read, admired Leonard's garden flowers, went for gentle walks with Leonard, and lay in bed visiting 'such remote strange places',[31] her head full of 'so many books I want to write'.[32]

Leonard went up to London once a week, otherwise he was with Virginia continuously, attending to her wants, constantly reassuring. By autumn Virginia seemed well enough to resume reading proofs, but at once she was seized with 'stony but convinced despair'.[33] Picking up the proofs she went to Leonard and told him to burn them unread. He was calm and comforting and said that he must first read them. She waited impatiently until 'he put down the last sheet . . . He was in tears . . . it is "a most remarkable book" – he *likes* it better than *The Waves*, and has not a spark of doubt that it must be published.' The effect, like an electric shock (electric shock treatment given towards the natural end of a depression can have a dramatic effect), shook Virginia free of depression. It was a 'miracle . . . the moment of relief was divine'. She hardly knew 'if I'm on my heels or head – so amazing is the reversal . . . I have never had such an experience.'[34]

Leonard was not being entirely honest – he thought the book too long, not as good as her other novels – but he was convinced that unless he gave 'a completely favourable verdict she would be in despair and have a very serious breakdown'.[35] He attributed 'the terrifying time with *The Years* to the crisis of exhaustion and black despair when she had finished a book'; and this time she was 'much nearer a complete breakdown than she had ever been since 1913.'[36] Leonard was wrong on both counts. New Year mood swings were always potentially dangerous when reinforced by strong conflicting emotions, but although Virginia's depression was severe she gave little sign of madness. Perhaps a letter written to Vanessa in July, disinhibited and loaded with references to sex, hinted at hypomania, but her sister would not have thought that too unusual.[37] Suicide never threatened. There were no delusions or hallucinatory voices, no abnormal irritability, no paranoia, and certainly no hostility towards Leonard. She did not cling, as in 1913, and their relationship was unchanged. She missed Leonard when away; 'It's damned dull without you, dearest M . . . Oh how we adore you! How angelic you are to us.'[38] To Ethel Smyth she confessed she was an 'appalling nuisance . . . to L',[39] but she was being realistic, not delusional.

Suppressed anger was a significant factor in the breakdowns of 1904 and 1913–15, but played little importance in 1936. The real strains came from Leonard abandoning his pacifist ideals and advocating war, something she could not accept and yet could not reject outright. The widening divide with Leonard, the seeming irreconcilability of their two positions, made her increasingly anxious. Throughout 1935 Virginia had been building up her 'anti-war' ideas for *Three Guineas*, and this had allowed her to avoid directly confronting Leonard with the problem. As depression gripped and anxiety flooded into the open, her defences collapsed.

It is a truism in psychiatry that the real cause of a mental illness is not always the obvious one. Leonard and Virginia, and their friends, blamed the book for the breakdown, but the novel was a side issue. The main source of her worry concerned Leonard and the threat of war, but most of her anxiety became displaced onto *The Years*.

Frequently the real problem behind mental illness is never exposed and remains a constant source of trouble, but Virginia – and it is an example of the remarkable constructive linkage she had with her subconscious – found a unique solution. In some undirected way most of the emotional charge bound to her conflict with Leonard became transferred to *The Years* – facilitated perhaps by *Three Guineas* having initially been part of the book. When Leonard gave his unreserved approval the effect on Virginia was electrifying; psychologically, it was as though he accepted her anti-war ideals. There was no longer a divide in Virginia's mind. It was 'a miracle'. She felt 'vigorous and cheerful since the wonderful revelation of L's last night. How I woke from death – or non-being – to life! What an incredible night – what a weight rolled off!'[40]

The weight had not rolled off Leonard. Despite looking after Virginia he had contrived to keep in touch with the political and international events. At heart he found them 'very distressing. The Labour Party drives me mad', he confessed.[41] Collective security was 'dead and rotten', and war seemed inevitable.

> The best one can hope . . . is that the guns will not go off or the bombs begin to fall for a year or two, and that something meanwhile 'may turn up'.[42]

In February 1937 he became ill, the chief symptom being pain in the back. A trace of sugar was found in his urine, and various possibilities were discussed; diabetes, prostate trouble, a kidney infection. Virginia was 'devilishly anxious' until a Harley Street specialist found Leonard perfectly healthy, when she experienced a surge of 'extraordinary physical relief'.[43]

The illness was again psychosomatic and disappeared after reassurance, but was replaced by an intensely itching eczema. A holiday in France with Virginia cured him, but over the years eczema returned whenever Leonard was stressed.

Virginia was also worried by Leonard's trembling hands. It was a familial tremor, inherited from his father, and the shaking waxed and waned according to his tension. In 1937 his hands shook so much that he had great difficulty cutting up food, and he was unable to lift a cup without spilling most of it. When she heard from Bernard Shaw, who also suffered from a nervous tremor, of Dr Alexander's treatment, Virginia persuaded Leonard to go to him.

The Alexander Method is based on learning to relax body and mind. Leonard responded well at first and Virginia was excited that Dr Alexander 'was certain of a cure'.[44] She hoped Leonard's prickly moods might also be 'smoothed'.[45] But changing a man like Leonard is almost impossible, and the improvement was temporary.

As 1937 ended Leonard was again crippled by back pains. Kidney disease was suggested and he was put on a strict diet. There was talk of an operation on the prostate, and Virginia was on tenterhooks while doctors argued amongst themselves and 'threatened nursing homes, and all the horrors'.[46] She would rather

her own death than Leonard's. Her relief in mid-January when all tests proved normal was immense.

The enforced rest improved Leonard, but his doctor's continuing suspicion of 'the prostate gland' – that 'perennial horror' – and Leonard's obsession about dying, created a hypochondriacal atmosphere.[47] When a rash developed on his back in November he immediately decided it must come from the prostate, and all the old tests were repeated. As the international situation worsened, his eczema returned, and he was often 'lacerated with his rash'.[48] His gloom was intense. When Beatrice Webb met Leonard at the outbreak of war he 'looked terribly ill' and his tremor was very noticeable.[49] Virginia enjoyed fussing over Leonard, being the 'good wife', acting the 'mother to a hurt and miserable little boy'.[50] It was a relief to worry about his indigestion and low weight instead of herself, and she made him obey doctor's orders, much as Leonard did when she was ill.

Virginia remained well after 1936, disturbed only by brief cyclothymic depressions in the New Year, until 1941. In October she had a sudden impulse to spend a weekend in Paris, but Leonard was too busy and said he would miss her if she went alone:

> then I was overcome with happiness. Then we walked round the square lovemaking – after 25 years can't bear to be separate . . . it is an enormous pleasure, being wanted: a wife. And our marriage so complete.[51]

In July 1937 Virginia's nephew Julian Bell was killed while driving an ambulance in the Spanish Civil War. Vanessa was overcome with grief. She had been particularly close to her eldest son, so much so that Virginia had remarked her nephew seemed more his mother's lover than a son.

Vanessa lay for weeks in bed, unable to face the loss. Virginia immediately went to her aid and for the rest of the summer gave herself up to caring for her sister, visiting her at Charleston almost every day. Only Virginia was able to comfort Vanessa and understand and break through her grief, and Vanessa came to depend on her:

> I remember all those days after I heard about Julian lying in an unreal state

> and hearing her voice going on and on keeping life going as it seemed when otherwise it would have stopped, and late every day she came to see me here [at Charleston], the only point in the day one could want to come.[52]

The letters Virginia sent Vanessa at this time are like the love letters of old:

> If you notice a dancing light on the water, that's me. The light kisses your nose, then your eyes, and you can't rub it off; my darling honey, how I adore you.[53]

The strain of caring for Vanessa did not upset Virginia's balance – by taking attention off herself it may even have been beneficial – but made her irritable with Leonard and 'rather quarrelsome'. Perhaps Leonard, too, was a little put out by all the attention Virginia gave her sister, and she worried; 'Have I the right to leave Leonard alone and sit with Nessa?'[54]

Vanessa slowly returned to life. She was immensely grateful to Virginia for giving so much of herself and making no demands, so unlike her behaviour in the past. On the anniversary of Julian's birthday, Virginia wrote, 'You know I'd do anything I could to help you, and it's so awful not to be able to; except to adore you as I do.'[55] Vanessa replied, 'I can't show it and I feel so stupid and such a wet blanket often but I couldn't get on at all if it weren't for you.'[56]

As soon as Virginia finished *The Years* she began on *Three Guineas*. It absorbed her, 'pressed and spurted out of me . . . like a "physical volcano"'.[57] All her feelings against male aggression and war went into the work, which was enlivened by satire and comical pictures of bemedalled men in peacock-like military uniforms. Men are natural warmongers, she declared; there is for them 'some glory, some necessity, some satisfaction in fighting which we [women] have never felt or enjoyed'.[58] Only when women obtained power and responsibility – provided they were not corrupted into becoming like men – could society hope to change and war be avoided.

Julian's death added fire to her pen. Her nephew had had a 'passion for the art [of war]; and a longing – instinctive and irrational – to fight.'[59] Nothing would stop him. He was heartless in going, knowing how it must torture Vanessa, the waste of his death. 'What made him do it? I suppose it's a fever in the blood.'[60]

The writing brought tranquillity. Virginia felt 'cool and quiet after the expulsion' of so much emotion.[61] She finished the book and showed the manuscript to Leonard, untroubled by their different outlook. Leonard was detached; 'gravely approves *3G*' and judged it 'an extremely clear analysis'.[62] Inwardly he was distinctly lukewarm and he probably agreed with Maynard Keynes, who thought *Three Guineas* 'a silly argument and not very well written'.[63] Virginia had hoped for more praise but she was not dismayed:

> I wanted how violently – how persistently, pressingly compulsorily I can't say – to write this book; and have a quiet composed feeling; as if I had said my say: take it or leave it.'[64]

Critics and friends' reactions to *Three Guineas* were mixed. Q. D. Leavis in the *Scrutiny* condemned it, to Virginia's amusement:

> this book is not merely silly and ill-informed, though it is that too, it contains some dangerous assumptions, some preposterous claims and some nasty attitudes . . . It seems to me the art of living as conceived by a social parasite.[65]

She met Ethel Smyth's accusation of lack of patriotism by,

> Of course I'm 'patriotic': that is, English, the language, farms, dogs, people: only we must enlarge the imaginative, and take stock of the emotion.[66]

Vita disagreed with half of it. Vanessa was ambivalent. She looked on war as 'madness. It's destruction and not creation',[67] and yet Julian's urge to fight had to be respected. If Virginia disagreed, she had the sense to keep quiet, and their newly restored intimacy continued.

The death of Leonard's mother, at 87, in July 1939 affected him deeply. His depression was predictable, given his lifelong ambivalence. He had failed to invite her to his wedding, hurting her deeply, caricatured her as a silly woman in *The Wise Virgins* and, unlike his siblings, failed to acknowledge the sacrifices she had made for her young family. Yet he was always concerned for her well-being, her finances and physical needs, and visited and entertained her regularly.

Marie Woolf blamed Virginia for Leonard's boorish behaviour, believing that Virginia had taken her son away from his family. Virginia had indeed been hostile in the beginning, and encouraged Leonard's childish behaviour, yet in time she came to respect the old lady's qualities, and at the end they were on 'friendly, laughing terms'.[68]

Leonard's gloom persisted. He was 'peculiarly primordially sensitive' to his mother's death,[69] and it had occurred at a particularly difficult time, when the world was reverting to barbarism. The months that followed were 'the most terrible months of my life'.[70]

Chapter Fifteen

War, Depression and Suicide

The war began on 3 September and during the next eighteen months Viginia's state of mind changed three times. Between September 1939 and April 1940, although outwardly relaxed, there was tension below the surface and her customary depression was prolonged from February into early April. The succeeding summer high was extended by excitement of the Battle of Britain into the October/November lift. Then came the final stage of increasing circumstantial depression, which, adding to the January/February cyclothymia, led to her death.

The Woolfs had moved house shortly before war was declared, but their flat in Mecklenburgh Square was unprepared and they were living at Rodmell, commuting to London every fortnight for a few days. Virginia was relaxed; 'If we win – then what?' 'The unreality of force' muffled everthing.[1] She carried coals for newly-arrived evacuees, made black-out curtains, and looked after clerks from the Hogarth Press temporarily staying at Monks House. 'It's hard work talking to clerks. That's been the only work I've done since last week. But you see my little tap dries up', she told Ethel Smyth.[2]

Virginia's tap soon opened. 'Those first days of complete nullity' gave way to 'a pressure of ideas and work'.[3] She took up journalism and wrote monthly articles for the *New Statesman* because 'I shall have to work to make money.'[4] Her concern was not unrealistic, and very different from the depressive delusion of poverty that was to develop in 1941. At the same time she was giving a final polish to the Roger Fry biography, continuing with her memoirs which she had begun in April, moving ahead with *Between the Acts*.

She read a variey of books, and in December began on Freud. She had digested *Moses and Monotheism* in July and now started *Civilisation and its Discontents* and *The Future of an Illusion*, 'to enlarge the circumference, to give my brain a wider scope'.[5] There were perhaps other reasons; continuing concern over war and aggression; remembrance (brought up by memoirs) of her father's rages and the anger they evoked in her; and, by extension, Leonard's aggressive behaviour and her own anger.

She read compulsively at first, 'gulping up Freud'. What he wrote she found interesting but also 'upsetting: reducing one to whirlpool: and I daresay truly. If we're all instinct, the unconscious, what's all this about civilisation, the whole man, freedom, etc?' She liked Freud's 'savagery against God. The falseness of loving one's neighbours. The conscience as censor. Hate.'[6]

Initially, Virginia settled into the new style of life. She could write without interruption, and she told Vita in December, 'I don't think I shall ever live in London again.'[7] Social life was adequate. Friends came to stay, and their days in London were 'hectic'.

That winter was one of the coldest on record; 'Never was there such a medieval winter.' They were sometimes snowbound. Pipes froze. The electricity broke down and they cooked on the fire, 'remained unwashed, slept in stockings and mufflers'.[8] Virginia was irritable and gloomy by mid-January; writing less and worrying about a promised lecture – 'for 5 days I could do nothing but improvise a WEA lecture'[9] – and fearing the Roger Fry book was 'not a book, only a piece of cabinet making, and only of interest to R's friends.'[10] Visits to London

> in nips [became] cramped and creased. Odd how often I think with what is love I suppose of the City: of the walk to the Tower: that is my England; I mean, if a bomb destroyed one of those little alleys with the brass bound curtains and the river smell and the old woman reading I should feel – well, what the patriots feel.[11]

The late winter dip gave rise to 'a queer sense of suspense, being led up to the spring of 1940',[12] and at the end of February 'Virginia retired to bed with headache, insomnia and a fluctuating temperature. 'The Dr now calls it recurring influenza with a touch of bronchitis', she informed Ethel Smth.[13] 'Head a white vapour: legs bent candles. All hope abandoned'.[14] The depression was not severe; she continued to read, and after midday she could write letters but her temperature continued to oscillate, each 'relapse' sending her back to sleep in Leonard's room, until early April.

She had finished Roger Fry and given the manuscript to Leonard before she took to her bed. His reaction, 'a very severe lecture', was unexpected; 'It's merely analysis, not history. Austere repression. In fact dull to the outsider. All those dead quotations'. Virginia felt she was 'being pecked by a very hard strong beak'.[15] The biography is in fact dull and lifeless, but Virginia was still depressed and, knowing the importance she put on his approval, it was a surprising attack.

Virginia was momentarily convinced the book was a failure but suddenly she felt sure that Leonard was 'on the wrong tack and persisting for some deep reason – dissympathy with R? Lack of interest in personality? Lord knows'.[16] The unexpected shock had a therapeutic effect and swept depression away. She saw Leonard in a fresh light; not the authoritarian paternal figure whose approval was so vital, but a hurt and miserable little boy wanting to be comforted. She could now see him, as she could her father, from two angles: 'As a child condemning; as a woman of 58 understanding – I should say tolerating'.[17]

All that summer of 1940 Virginia was in good heart, sometimes teetering on the edge of hypomania, excited by the unfolding aerial drama overhead. The German blitz had begun 10 May and by mid-June French resistance was over. Leonard had an 'incessant feeling of unreality and impending disaster', of living in a 'curious atmosphere of quiet fatalism, of waiting for the inevitable'.[18] Virginia's diary gives a sense of his despair; invasion and defeat almost inevitable, with suicide or death in resisting. When the battle in France opened he told Virginia he had enough 'petrol in the garage for suicide should Hitler win'.[19] Two days later he proposed joining the Home Guard to fight expected enemy parachutists.

Virginia was concerned with the 'vast formless shapes' of events yet her emotions were not deeply engaged.[20] For short spells the war could obsess her, 'then the feeling faculty gives out'.[21] She rejected Leonard's plan of suicide:

> I don't want the garage to see the end of me. I've a wish for 10 years more, and to write my book which as usual darts into my brain.

She pondered on:

> why am I optimistic? or rather not either way? because it's all bombast, this war. One old lady pinning on her cap has more reality. So if one dies, it'll be a commonsense, dull end.[22]

Many friends were as pessimistic as Leonard and talked openly of suicide. Kingsley Martin, the editor of the *New Statesman*, with whom Leonard worked closely and for whom he sometimes deputised, diffused 'his soft charcoal gloom . . . French . . . beaten; invasion here; 5th Column active; a German pro-consul; English Government in Canada; we in concentration camps, or taking sleeping draughts.'[23]

Virginia ridiculed Leonard's proposal to join the Home Guard. The sight of Leonard in uniform and carrying a gun was 'to me slightly ridiculous'.[24] Clive might 'sit up at night watching for Germans in a helmet', but not Leonard.[25] An idea came: 'the army is the body: I am the brain. Thinking's my fighting.'[26] She wanted England to survive, but she remained a pacifist and hated 'the feelings war breeds: patriotism; communal etc. all sentimental and emotional parodies of our real feelings'. She was indignant when

Leonard gave away all their aluminium saucepans 'to make aeroplanes'.[27]

Rodmell was on the flight path to London of the German air force, and Virginia watched dogfights overhead and saw planes shot down. Monks House was rocked by near misses, and in mid-August the roar of planes came so close that she and Leonard lay flat waiting for the blast, convinced 'we shall be broken together'.[28] Next day they had 'the closest shave so far with five bombers, hedge-hopping on their way to London, almost crashing into the dining room.'[29]

The fear was stimulating and she felt, for the first time, 'Now we are in the war. England is being attacked . . . The feeling of pressure, danger, horror.'[30] When twelve Spitfires 'went over, out to sea, to fight, last evening, I had I think an individual, not communal BBC dictated feeling. I almost instinctively wished them luck.'[31] Her fantasies were fired and she wrote to Sibyl Colefax: 'If you hear that Virginia had disarmed 6 German pilots you won't be in the least surprised, will you?'[32] Her sense of history was stirred when Churchill broadcast a warning of imminent invasion, comparing the danger 'with the days when the Spanish Armada was approaching the Channel and Drake was finishing his game of bowls', much as she and Leonard were doing on their bowling green.[33]

The Woolfs regularly played bowls and threw their anxieties into the game. Leonard had never liked losing but Virginia's irritation when defeated only developed that summer. Gloomy and fidgety after one loss she told herself it was because 'I connect it with Hitler'.[34] After losing a game she vowed to play no more, but next day was always eager to resume the contest.

Virginia had often exhausted herself in the past during the summer highs, and had been forced to rest in August and September. In 1940 she remained lively, and only in a letter to Vita at the end of August is there any hint of mental disturbance: 'Dearest', she wrote, 'let me have a line – let us meet next week. But one can scarcely bear it. Only we must. You have given me such happiness.'[35] The letter has a depressed, farewell quality, but it was written after Vita had telephoned to cancel a visit because of a raid and Virginia feared she might be killed any moment. Next day she was apparently cheerful and gave an amusing account of the Dreadnought Hoax to the Memoir Club, but the diary entries have a depressive colouring: 'So lovely an evening that the flat and the Downs looked as if seen for the last time.'[36] 'All writers are unhappy. The picture of the world in books is too dark. The wordless are the happy: women in cottage gardens.'[37] On and off at first, then increasingly as winter approached, one glimpses the gathering depression.

In September the German tactics changed and daylight battles over Rodmell gave way to the nightly drone of bombers *en route* to attack London. On 10 September a time bomb fell on Mecklenburgh Square that exploded three days later and severely damaged the flat, and the Hogarth Press in the basement. The destruction was completed the following month by a landmine falling at the back of the house.

The Woolfs travelled up to inspect the damage. Surveying the mess, Virginia, as much excited as downcast, was exhilarated

> at losing possessions – save at times I want my books and chairs and carpets and bed – how I worked to buy them . . . But to be free of Mecklenburgh would now be a relief; it's odd – the relief of losing possessions. I should like to start life, in peace, almost bare – free to go anywhere.[38]

What most 'raked' her heart was 'the grimy old woman at the lodging house at the back, all dirty after the raid, and preparing to sit out another'; and to see 'the passion of my life, that is the City of London – to see London all blasted . . . the alleys and little courts, between Chancery Lane and the City. I walked to the Tower . . . by way of caressing my love of all that.'[39]

The sight of such destruction set her mind whirling, and the next day she 'suddenly conceived the idea of a new book';[40] 'oh such an amusing book on English literature, the first chapter to be called Anon, the next, The Reader'.[41] Never had she 'been so fertile'. She was 'very happy' as the saying is; and excited by PH' (*Between the Acts*), forging ahead with the novel.[42] On 15 November she had '20 books sizzling in my head at the moment'.[43]

The over-activity ceased and the excitement of war gave way to monotony and boredom. All her life she had needed stimulation to keep up her spirits; it was as essential as food and water. When it had been lacking in the past, Virginia had instinctively manufactured it through her friends, setting off emotional dramas by malicious gossip and 'games playing'. Those who knew her well learnt to be cautious and, as Strachey observed, 'one didn't believe quite everything that came through Virginia'.[44]

Now, however, there were few friends to hand and no gossip, for after September the Woolfs were largely cut off from London and most of their group. Petrol was scarce and it was difficult to travel far by car. Trains were unreliable and uncomfortable. Their resident cook left in September and for the first time the Woolfs were without a live-in domestic. Virginia had a local woman to clean and do some cooking and she initially welcomed the sense of freedom: 'I like being alone in our little boat. I like provisioning and seeing all's ship-shape and not having dependants.'[45] She built up a romantic vision: 'Fish forgotten. I must invent a dinner. But it's all so heavenly free and easy – L and I alone.'[46] But, unlike Leonard, Virginia could not thrive for long on solitude and domesticity; she needed the 'peck and thrill' of social life. To confine Virginia to Rodmell was like putting a skylark into a small cage and ending its song.

Virginia's mental health was always at risk, not only from tensions generated by suppressed emotions such as anger but by the absence of tension; lack of it resulted in boredom and led to depression. Her nervous system required an unusually high level of excitation to function efficiently and healthily, and the difference between optimum and minimum levels for health was narrow.

Virginia struggled to come to terms with Rodmell life:

> Now we're marooned, I ought to cram in a little more reading. Yet why? A happy, a very free and disengaged – a life that rings from one simple melody to another. Yes: why not enjoy this after all those years of the other? Yet I compare with Miss Perkins' [a Hogarth Press clerk] day; public house life and greengrocers.

She wistfully recalled the stimulation of London days. 'Three afternoons someone coming. One night, dinner party. Saturday a walk. Thursday shopping. Tuesday going to tea with Nessa. One City walk. Telephone ringing. L to meetings'. Still, she thought, 'If one lives in a village, one had better snatch its offerings.'[47]

At the beginning of November, after some dithering, she agreed to stand for the Women's Institute Committee and was elected Treasurer. She looked on it as an 'infernal dull bore',[48] but she stuck to it and went on arranging lectures and entertainments right up to the end of her life, seeing the work as therapeutic, keeping her feet on the ground in the way that typesetting and bookbinding at the Press had done.

Contact with old friends was more and more difficult. She kept in touch with Vita and Ethel, but met them only occasionally. It was a problem seeing Vanessa for petrol was so scarce that visits had to be rationed. The shortages of food and labour and the tedium of shopping started to bite:

> So much work to do . . . And so much shopping to do . . . the milk is so cut that we have to consider even the cat's saucer . . . no sugar . . . no pastry unless I buy it ready made. The shops don't fill till midday. Things are bought fast. In the afternoon they are often gone.[49]

Monks House was damp and cold and untidy, and in disarray after December when their possessions from Mecklenburgh Square arrived in several vans. The Woolfs had intended to store most of the four tons of furniture and damp books, and the large printing press, in a nearby farmhouse but, in the event, much of it had to be squeezed into Monks House. Books were piled everywhere. There was scarcely room to stand let alone a space for dirt trays for Leonard's pet kitten. Virginia was harassed 'black and blue with moving',[51] bored and distracted:

> Oh the huddle and hideousness of untidiness – oh that Hitler had obliterated all our books, tables, carpets and pictures – oh that we were empty and bare and unpossessed . . . [52] I see what a working woman's life is. No time to think. A breeze ruffles the surface. No silence.[53]

Leonard was still Virginia's inviolable centre, intellectually the perfect companion, but he was not able to provide the kind of stimulation she required. He was a devoted husband, putting Virginia's health above all else, and usually kept a close, even fussy, watch over her. In 1935 his attention had slipped because of the international crisis and he had failed to notice the early warning signs of serious depression until almost too late; but once alerted he had acted decisively and effectively.

In the winter of 1940 Leonard's attention again started to wander. He was gloomy about the outcome of the war and the future, and felt there was no longer any sense of purpose to his life, no vital work waiting, no urgent summons. Nonetheless he continued to fill his days with work, writing and lecturing, running the Press, involving himself in Rodmell life; he joined the fire service and was clerk to the parish council.

He continued to keep an eye on Virginia, but she seemed to have taken on a new untroubled lease of life with the war. Leonard thought she was 'happier and more serene than was usual with her'.[54] Never sociable, he welcomed their isolation, almost deliberately shutting his eyes to her social appetite, looking on it as beneficial to Virginia's health. Not only did he ignore signs of her growing claustrophobia with village life but positively began to discourage Virginia's attempts to break out. An invitation from Ethel Smyth to spend a few days with her at Woking threw Leonard into such a state that Virginia was taken aback, 'for some occult reason, [Leonard] cries No No No'.[55] She was irritated but hesitated to challenge Leonard. 'I think it's a bad thing that we're so inseparable', she told Ethel, 'but how in this world of separation, does one break it?'[56]

Leonard's reluctance to let Virginia out of his sight amounted almost to separation anxiety, and reflected his depressed state, the presence of the unhappy child glimpsed by Virginia in the past. Insecure, he now needed Virginia in the same childlike way she had clung to him in the early years of their marriage. Subconsciously Virginia recognised this, but she was troubled. She still required a strong reliable husband.

When friends invited her to lunch, along with Clive, she jumped at the opportunity; 'they might be stimulating, and I'm susceptible and they might give me champagne, mentally as well'. Leonard at once objected; it would be timewasting to go; they were uninteresting people. Virginia did not go. She was trapped. 'No audience. No private stimulus'.[57]

The first sign that her depression was developing to a dangerous level came at the end of November when, after hearing Leonard lecture, Virginia made a strangely paranoid entry in her diary:

> I was thinking about Vampires. Leeches. Anyone with 500 a year and education is at once sucked by the leeches. Put me and L into Rodmell pool and we are sucked – sucked – sucked . . . Last night L's lecture attracted suckers . . . Leech Octavia asks to come.[58]

Again, on 13 December Kingsley Martin stayed the night and 'devours sugar and butter . . . Why are we hooked to that large, rather pretentious, livid bellied shark? And must I spend my last years feeding his double row of teeth? . . . at meals he scrapes and sops'.[59] It was understandable to resent sparse rations being gobbled up, but on this occasion Virginia's paranoia reflected a deeper mental disturbance.

Bouts of trembling started to affect her right hand, and she wondered if she was 'becoming palsied'.[60] Reading her parents' letters and father's memoirs for her own memoir was relaxing:

> how simple, how clear, how untroubled . . . He loved her . . . was so candid and reasonable and transparent . . . such a fastidious delicate mind . . . How serene and gay even their life reads to me: no mud, no whirlpools. And so human – with the children and the little hum and song of the nursery.[61]

Virginia looking back on her past through the child's eyes felt comforted; when she looked ahead she saw only darkness.

She was losing weight; eating less but paradoxically thinking about food, savouring each mouthful, making up imaginary meals like a modern-day anorexic, signalling regression. She ended the year quoting Matthew Arnold to herself:

The foot less prompt
to meet the morning dew,
The heart less bounding
at emotion new,
And hope, once crushed,
less quick to spring again.

Civilisation seemed to be ending. She and Leonard went to London in mid-January. Virginia loved the City, 'the passion of my heart' and was intensely upset by the damage. She 'wandered in the desolate ruins of my old squares: gashed, dismantled; the old red bricks all white powder . . . all that completeness ravished and demolished'. On the spur of the moment she went into Buszards 'to eat gluttonously. Turkey and pancakes. How rich, how solid.'[62] 'I have so seldom gloried in food, all alone.'[63] It was out of keeping.

In February she watched two women 'consuming rich cakes . . . They ate and ate . . . Something scented, shoddy, parasitic about them . . . Where does the money come from to feed these fat white slugs?'[64] Food became an obsession. 'I grudge giving away a spice bun.' A week later she was observing

> the shell-encrusted old women, rouged, decked, cadaverous at the teashop . . . I mark Henry James's sentence: Observe perpetually. Observe the outcome of age. Observe greed. Observe my own despondency.[65]

Poverty and death began to preoccupy her. Her diary for 9 January records:

> A blank. All frost. Still frost. Burning white. Burning blue. The elms red. I did not mean to describe, once more, the Downs in snow; but it came. And I can't help even now turning to look at Asheham Down, red, purple; dove blue grey, with the cross so melodramatically against it. What is the phrase I always remember – or forget? 'Look your last on all things lovely.'[66]

> Yesterday Mrs Deadman was buried upside down. A mishap. 'Such a heavy woman,' as Louie [their cleaner] put it, feasting spontaneously upon the grave. Today she buries the Aunt whose husband saw the vision at Seaford. Their house was bombed by the bomb we heard early one morning last week. And L is lecturing and arranging the room. Are these the things that are interesting? That recall; that say Stop, you are so fair? Well, all life is so fair, at my age. I mean, without much more of it, I suppose, to follow. And t'other side of the hill, there'll be no rosy blue red snow.

Shaking off the spectre of death, she added, 'I am economising. I am to spend nothing.'[67]

The New Year cyclothymic depression began to bite towards the end of January and joined forces with the reactive depression that had been building up all winter. Virginia, in a 'trough of despair', told Leonard, 'I think we live without a future . . . With our noses pressed to a closed door.'[68] It was a call for help, warning of trouble brewing, but Leonard believed her gloom to be merely Virginia's usual reaction to revising and finishing her novel *Between the Acts*. The mood lightened after twelve days, but the underlying mental disturbance, which Virginia kept hidden from Leonard, continued inexorably.

Leonard was kept in the dark, and deceived by the absence of the headache which usually heralded her depression although, had he but realised, its very absence was a pointer to the severity of the depression. A painful headache nearly always ushered in Virginia's depressions and persisted until she recovered. But when depression deepened to a more dangerous level, thus threatening insanity, headache gave way to a numb sensation, as though the brain were frozen. Finally hallucinations, the 'visionary' phase of madness, began.[69] In the run-up to the breakdowns of 1904 and 1913 headache had been present only in the very early stages and was absent in the weeks immediately preceding insanity. By contrast it was a prominent symptom during most of the 1936 illness.

Virginia was in control of herself on 11 February when she and

Leonard travelled to Cambridge to inspect the Press's new home in Letchworth and visit old friends. Leonard was satisfied by her apparent enjoyment, but she told Ethel Smyth,

> Ever since we came back from Cambridge – 30 hours in train journeys; £6 on hotel bills; all for Leonard to spend 2 hours in Letchworth – I've been in a fret.[70]

Virginia's reluctance to eat now became more pronounced and Leonard at last became concerned. He tried to cajole and persuade but she 'was very hard to deal with. She lost weight terribly.'[71] Leonard knew the serious consequences of Virginia's losing weight, and he eventually sought advice from Dr Octavia Wilberforce, whom both Woolfs liked.

Octavia lived in Brighton where she practised as a doctor, and lived with the actress and novelist Elizabeth Robins. She was a sensible, attractive, outdoor type, rather dogmatic and prudish, and she detested Freud for 'allowing hugely for sex'. Virginia and she had met in 1937 and discovered they were related through the marriage of Virginia's great-grandfather to William Wilberforce's sister, but not until the end of 1940, when Elizabeth Robins left for America, did they become more closely acquainted.

Octavia had tea at Monks House and fell under Virginia's spell. She was worried by her 'extreme thinness' and 'hands worse than icicles', and arranged to send regular supplies of cream and milk (she owned a herd of Jersey cows) 'in exchange for apples and a copy of Virginia's next book'.[72] Virginia was moved by the 'generosity . . . trouble and the really miraculous gift', but, she confessed, the novel was a 'completely worthless book. I've lost all power over words – can't do a thing with them'.[73] Octavia, as she admitted, was 'very unobservant', and failed to notice the underlying depression, attributing Virginia's words to 'exaggeration'. She diagnosed 'a thoroughly frail creature'.[74]

By the New Year Octavia had become a light in the gathering gloom, a possible maternal figure capable of stirring Virginia's fantasies: 'I've a new love, a doctor, a Wilberforce, a cousin . . . does that make you twitch?!' she told Vita on 19 January.[75] She sought to see more of Octavia and suggested doing a living portrait. 'I think you're very paintable, as the painters say. Now I wonder why? Something that composes well – perhaps reticence and power combined.'[76]

She began to gather details of Octavia's life but, more often than not, Virginia did the talking, mostly about her own family life. By mid-March she was revealing how desperate she felt, 'depressed to the lowest depths'. Octavia still did not recognise the danger signals. She adopted a 'pull yourself together and stop brooding' approach, which did more harm than good. Finally, she upset Virginia very much by admonishing her for spending far too much time thinking about her family; it was 'all nonsense, blood thicker than water – balderdash . . . better to harrow a field or play a game.'[77] Virginia turned away.

Despite trembling hands and 'mornings of torture', Virginia completed *Between the Acts* on 26 February and gave it to Leonard to read. She felt better as the day wore on and by evening managed to read or write a little, but it was increasingly difficult to concentrate. She tried working on simple manual tasks like scrubbing floors and beating carpets, but by March even these activities were becoming too much for her.

On 14 March she lunched at Westminster with Leonard and John Lehmann. When Lehmann congratulated her on the completion of her new novel she became intensely agitated and told him it was no good at all, and obviously couldn't be published.[78] Leonard intervened to say how good he thought the book, whereupon Virginia rounded on him, saying he was wrong. For Virginia to throw out Leonard's praise, normally so vital to her peace of mind, was an ominous sign, on a par with her refusal to eat with him. Leonard was no longer the good parental figure.

By now Virginia was 'as thin as a razor' and had paranoid delusions; her thoughts were racing outside her control, and hallucinatory voices were probably already tormenting and pushing her towards suicide. Even when she came back from a walk 'soaking wet, looking ill and shaken', saying 'she had slipped and fallen into one of the dykes', Leonard 'did not definitely suspect anything'.[79] Not until 26 March could he believe Virginia was 'on the verge of danger'. Then he tried vainly to persuade her to go to bed for a 'rest cure for at least a week'.[80]

The next day, desperately anxious, he insisted on driving Virginia to see Octavia at Brighton. She was angry and hostile to the doctor, reiterating how unnecessary it was to have come. 'All you have to do is to reassure Leonard,' she kept repeating, but eventually she agreed to an examination on condition Octavia promised not to prescribe a rest cure.[81]

Octavia was not a psychiatrist and was out of her depth. Her friendly greeting, 'If you'll collaborate, I know I can help you,' only served to increase Virginia's resistance, for collaboration was *impossible.* No real contact between the women occurred. Octavia was too polite to ask about suicide. Had she done so she might have understood the danger. Many suicide patients freely confess their intention to a doctor who asks, often with some relief, and will even promise to postpone suicide until after their next meeting. Such seemingly bizarre behaviour stems from what persists of the wish to live, and guilt for causing pain to relatives. A promise in such circumstances is usually kept and the doctor may find he has gained his patient's trust and co-operation. He must then act decisively.

Virginia had been contemplating suicide for at least ten days before she drowned herself and had probably already made one abortive attempt. It was too late for Leonard alone to save her. The only way disaster could have been prevented at that stage was for Dr Wilberforce, backed by Leonard, to have insisted on continuous surveillance by trained nurses, if necessary under certification. Neither would have accepted so drastic a move. Virginia and Leonard returned home.

At some point during what must have been a dreadful night of agitation, Virginia came to a firm decision to kill herself. Such a decision always resolves conflict and brings peace of mind. She calmly wrote farewell letters to Leonard and Vanessa, which she left on her writing block. In both letters her deep love for Leonard shines through the depression. To Vanessa, she wrote:

> I feel that I have gone too far this time to come back again. I am certain now that I am going mad again. It is just as it was the first time, I am always hearing voices, and I know I shan't get over it now.
>
> All I want to say is that Leonard has been so astonishingly good, every day, always; I can't imagine that anyone could have done more for me than he has. We have been perfectly happy until the last few weeks, when this horror began. Will you assure him of this? I feel he has so much to do that he will go on, better without me, and you will help him.[82]

To Leonard she wrote:

> I want to tell you that you have given me complete happiness. No one could have done more than you have done. Please believe that. But I know that I shall never get over this; and I am wasting your life. Nothing anyone says can persuade me. You can work, and you will be much better without me. You see I can't write this even, which shows I am right. All I wish to say is that until this disease came on me we were perfectly happy. It was all due to you. No one could have been so good from the very first day till now. Everyone knows that.[83]

Virginia was not entirely sane at this time; much of her thinking was delusional and her feelings were no longer comprehensible. But she could still appear outwardly 'normal'. Leonard found her to be calm and collected on the morning of 28 March before she went out, and anyone meeting Virginia on her way to the river bank would have seen nothing out of the ordinary. Reaching the river, she filled her pockets with stones, left her walking stick on the ground, and walked into the icy waters.

When she failed to return for lunch, Leonard ran across the fields to the river and found her stick lying upon the bank. After searching fruitlessly he rang the police. The body was found three weeks later by children, close to where she had drowned.

She was cremated in Brighton on 21 April and Leonard buried her ashes at the foot of one of the two great intertwining elms at Rodmell which the Woolfs called Leonard and Virginia.

Leonard's pain was too great to express. Outwardly he was self-controlled and calm, and insisted on being left alone. Quentin Bell, who saw him some days later, was horrified at his despair, 'stoic though he was'.[84] Only twice did he break down momentarily with Octavia Wilberforce while discussing Virginia's illness, and in front of Vanessa after returning from the cremation.

Leonard went on living at Rodmell, going to London to committee meetings, desperately filling his days with work to blot out the memory of his inability to save Virginia. Vanessa offered comfort but felt 'very useless'.[85] Vita predicted his suicide.

In April 1942, seeking change and in order to work more intensively, he moved back into London, living in three patched-up rooms in the bombed Mecklenburgh Square house. By October 1943 he could no longer bear the gloom and discomfort and took a lease on 24 Victoria Square. There he became friendly with his neighbour, Trekkie Parsons, whom he and Virginia had known and liked before the war. The friendship developed and, to quote Quentin Bell, Trekkie 'saved [him] from the depths of despair'.[86] She became his 'Dearest Tiger', and by 1944 had transformed his life from one of misery into happiness. She was much younger, a painter, married to the publisher Ian Parsons, who in turn became a close friend of Leonard. When John Lehmann ended his partnership with Leonard at the Hogarth Press in 1945, Parsons and his co-directors at Chatto & Windus, at Leonard's instigation, took Lehmann's place. It was an ideal arrangement for everyone.

Leonard led a busy life for the next twenty-five years, working, gardening, travelling abroad with Trekkie, his idealism and vitality undiminished until in April 1969 he suffered a stroke. He died on 14 August, aged 88.

Appendix

Mania, Madness and Creativity

Mental normality depends on a balance between the workings of our internal mental world and the real outside world; our fantastic ideas are constantly being modified and discarded in the light of reality. Madness develops when an individual becomes cut off from reality, isolated within himself, and loses touch with everyday feedback from the outside world. Ideas that to other people are absurd or dangerous, now come to seem 'true'. Self-control – a reflection of society's standards – disappears, and the madman, impulsive and unreasonable, lives and acts out his fantasies.

Virginia's episodes of manic depression were all preceded by weeks of increasing depression and fleeting signs of mania. Delusions and hallucinations appeared and warped her judgement. For a time she could conceal this but eventually she became obviously insane. During madness birds spoke to her in Greek, her dead mother materialised and harangued her, voices called her to 'do wild things'. She refused nourishment. Trusted companions like her husband Leonard and her sister Vanessa became enemies and were abused and assaulted; it seemed to her sister that Virginia had 'changed into a most unpleasant character'. A manic depressive always recovers from an attack, although it may last two or more years. As Virginia returned to sanity, delusions faded and she became her old self.

The onset of Virginia's depressions was invariably heralded by three symptoms: headache at the back of the head and neck, which was extremely painful, 'like enraged rats gnawing the nape of my neck',[1] and sometimes accompanied by 'flashes of light raying round my eyes';[2] sleeplessness; and racing thoughts; 'racing despair and exaltation – that long scale of unhappiness'.[3] Provided she went to bed, rested, stopped work and cancelled all engagements depression lasted only a few weeks; but if she attempted to keep going, symptoms rapidly worsened. The pain of headache then gave way to 'numbness'[4] and then, as breakdown neared, to visions and voices.

Depression is a universal reaction to loss and major reverses, but cyclothymic depression appears more often than not for no apparently discernible or justifiable reason. Its source is *biological*. A distressing event or physical illness that precedes or accompanies the cyclothymic depression is often blamed. It is not the *cause* although it may be responsible for potentiating the depression and may prolong and worsen the mental state to a dangerous degree.

Stressful and over-exciting occasions, in the absence of cyclothymic depression, could always upset and exhaust Virginia and send her to bed for several days. These moods were never serious and Virginia welcomed them at times: they had 'their advantages – one visits such remote strange places lying in bed'.[5] When she ran into difficulties writing *The Waves* she longed for a week in bed; 'My mind works in idleness. To do nothing in a profitable way'.[6]

Most people have no conception of the agony of pathological depression. The poet William Cowper was afflicted by 'such a dejection of spirits – day and night I was upon the rack, lying down in horrors and rising in despair', that he was convinced that 'none but they who have felt the same can have the least conception of it'.[7] Virginia Woolf, although she valued the experience of madness in providing self-knowledge and a source of creativity, was terrified by it, 'tremblingly afraid of my own insanity' and 'almost crippled when I came back to the world, unable to move a foot in terror'.[8]

Symptoms of depression can affect almost any system in the body, which frequently makes for confusion in diagnosis. The mood is one of gloom and pessimism, and anxiety is never far off. 'Such anguishes and despairs', Virginia experienced, 'never was anyone so tossed up and down by the body as I am'.[9] She was sure she was a failure, and she could see 'no pleasure in life whatsoever'.[10] Her mind felt 'a blank' and she would never again have the power of writing.[11] In a bad depression she would seize on some subject to worry about but no sooner was it dealt with by Leonard than a new one would take its place.

The loss of energy in cases of depression, both physical and mental, is striking. Virginia found it an effort to think logically; thoughts came slowly and concentration was difficult, reading and writing came to a halt. She felt clumsy and her movements uncoordinated. Her hand was stiff and she 'had the same stiffness in manipulating sentences'.[12] It was then that Virginia felt a perverse pleasure in bed, in being alone, her mind effortlessly filling with words and sentences and ideas for books. It was thus, while lying in bed recovering from the depression of 1929, that she conceived *A Room of One's Own*.

Insomnia is a characteristic of most depressions, although one small group of depressives (although not cyclothymes) sleep longer than usual. Normally when Virginia was stable she 'slept splendidly', but when depressed she would waken abruptly after three hours. Many depressives experience the horror of waking every morning between 2 and 3 a.m., sweating with fear. Scott Fitzgerald maintained that 'In a real dark night of the soul, it is always 3 o'clock in the morning.'[13] Cowper 'slept [his] usual 3 hours well

> and then awakened with ten times a stronger sense of my alienation from God than ever. Satan plied me close with horrible visions and more horrible voices. A numbness seized upon the extremities of my body and

> life seemed to retreat before it. My hands and feet became cold and stiff; a cold sweat stood upon my forehead.[14]

Virginia knew the same terror. 'All my spectres come out on a sleepless night.' She recorded an instance:

> Woke up perhaps at 3. Oh it's beginning it's coming – the horror – physically like a painful wave swelling about the heart – tossing me up. I'm unhappy unhappy! Down – God I wish I were dead. Pause. But why am I feeling this? Let me watch the wave rise. I watch. Vanessa. Children. Failure. Yes, I detect that. Failure. Failure. (The wave rises.) Oh they laughed at my taste in green paint! Wave crashes. I wish I were dead! I've only a few more years to live I hope. I can't face this horror any more – (this is the wave spreading out over me).

Sometimes she would doze off only to reawaken 'with a start. The wave again! The irrational pain; the sense of failure, generally some specific incident, as for example my taste in green paint or buying a new dress'.[15] When the new day arrived she was exhausted.

Depression brings about a progressive change of character. The philanthropist becomes a misanthrope, generosity turns into parsimony, calmness gives way to furious reaction, humour goes out the window. The previously confident gregarious individual has nothing to say, no ideas, no small talk, his mind emptied. When depressed, Virginia wanted to hide. 'I see nobody partly because I have nothing to say except Oh! shall I ever have anything to say except Oh!'[16] She felt anxious and 'very lonely'

> as though exposed on a high ledge in full light . . . very apprehensive. As if something cold and horrible – a roar of laughter at my expense – were about to happen. And I am powerless to ward it off: I have no protection and this anxiety and nothingness surround me with a vacuum . . . I want to burst into tears, but have nothing to cry for. Then a great restlessness seizes me.[17]

As the sense of alienation develops with depression, suspicion and paranoia begin to appear. The depressive becomes afraid of leaving home. A business trip, a holiday, away from home, even a visit to the shops can be a terrifying ordeal, a fearful strain. Virginia was seriously depressed in 1913 when Leonard, against his better inclination, took her to stay in the Holford Inn. Her anxiety was overwhelming and she lost control of her mind. She became more and more deluded, convinced she was an object of derision and that people were planning and plotting against her. The hotel staff recognised she was ill and behaved 'with the greatest kindness, sensitiveness and consideration but to no effect'.[18] Paranoia grew until even Leonard could no longer be wholly trusted. She was reluctant to eat and mealtimes turned into a nightmare for Leonard, for by this time she was probably hearing hallucinatory voices.

Depressives, are frequently reluctant to eat, and not simply because of loss of appetite. The depressed Cowper believed everyone hated him and that his food was poisoned. Robert Schumann had similar delusions and, like Virginia's cousin, starved himself to death. Virginia's reasons for not eating were not wholly dissimilar. She was convinced 'the voices I used to hear telling me to do all kinds of wild things . . . came from over-eating';[19] they had to be starved. Leonard was almost driven to breaking-point himself in 1913 trying to get Virginia to eat. 'If left to herself she . . would have gradually starved to death.'[20] Similar behaviour was developing in 1941, and by the time of her suicide she was extremely thin.

Although she enjoyed food and drink when well (her description of meals can be mouth-watering), she had, according to Leonard, 'a taboo against eating'. It was, he wrote, 'extraordinarily difficult ever to get her to eat enough to keep her strong and well'.[21] Leonard perhaps over-emphasised the problem, partly because he believed her mental stability depended on maintaining a 'good' weight, but also because Virginia became noticeably more anorexic when Leonard was worried and irritable and fussed over her food.

Sexual appetite is lost from the start. Virginia's physical libido, never very strong, rapidly disappeared. During the most passionate time of her affair with Vita Sackville-West, although she was disappointed not to receive a visit she was 'yet relieved at the same time'. Even during hypomania, when sexual appetites sometimes overflow, Virginia's sexual interest was as much intellectual as physical.

Depression is uniquely painful. Cowper saw it as 'the most terrible dismay of the soul',[22] and many a believer has compared his sufferings to the torments of Hell. Unlike a physical pain which, however unbearable, can be related to part of the body and, in a sense, isolated, the pain of depression involves the whole being. The depression *is* the pain. William Styron thought it like 'drowning or suffocating'.[23] Suicide may seem the only escape. Virginia 'did most emphatically attempt to end it all' in 1913.[24] Before her suicide in 1941 Virginia left a last note for Leonard saying, 'I can't go through another of those terrible times . . . I can't fight any longer. I know I am spoiling your life.'[25]

An alternative to suicide is to accept the pain, as Hector Berlioz did: 'One power was left to me – to suffer, to embrace madness.'[26] Cowper, in despair after having failed to kill himself, 'now began to look upon madness as though the only chance remaining. I had a strong foreboding that it would fare so with me, and I wished for it earnestly.'[27]

That was never Virginia's wish. She was terrified of madness and when normal took precautions against a recurrence by drinking milk and maintaining her weight – 'unless I weigh nine and a half stones I hear voices and see visions and can neither write nor sleep' – and retiring to bed and 'lying still directly my head aches'. Yet she recognised that insanity had its attractions: 'as an experience madness is terrific', she informed a friend. Like Charles Lamb after his recovery, she looked back on 'many hours of pure happiness . . . of having tasted all the grandeur and wildness of Fancy'.[28] She remembered 'lying in bed, mad, and seeing the sunlight quivering like gold water on the wall. I've heard the voice of the dead here. And felt, through it all, exquisitely happy.'[29]

Virginia's depressions were often ushered in by 'a dribbling little temperature', invariably diagnosed as influenza.[30] Influenza, or what passed for influenza, was seen as a potent cause of depression by psychiatrists, and Virginia's general practitioner repeatedly warned of its 'dangerous effects on the nervous system'.[31] Genuine influenza can leave its victims depressed, but Virginia's descriptions do not match up with true 'flu'. The raised temperature during cyclothymic depression, not at all uncommon, was caused by the depression and was not the cause of it.

At the beginning of the 1920s Virginia's depressions increased and a repeatedly raised temperature of 99 was investigated by specialists, who came up in turn with heart disease, trouble in the right lung, infection around the teeth (three of which were unnecessarily extracted) and 'pneumonia germs or 'flu'.

She was bothered by 'dropped beats' – of no real concern but alarming to someone depressed – and when she was exhausted her heart might begin to race 'like galloping horses got wild in my head'. Her back ached, limbs felt 'fidgety', and pain sometimes stabbed her chest.[32] There were moments when she felt on the point of death.

The cyclothymic depressions lasted usually between two and six weeks but they could be prolonged by stressful situations into many weeks. In 1936 Virginia was ill for most of the year as a result of a long period of strain, and she was depressed for nearly four months before her suicide. Minor short-lived depressions lifted abruptly, but more severe episodes often fluctuated up and down before finally resolving. Then followed a period of calm until the hypomanic phase occurred.

Hypomania is a lesser form of mania. Kay Jamison described her own experience as 'a light, lovely tincture of true mania . . . tiresome to my friends, perhaps; exhausting and exhilarating to me, definitely; but not disturbingly on the top'.[33] Life becomes more vivid, colourful, brighter, entrancing. Appetites increase. The mind bubbles and takes magical leaps over hitherto unclimbable mountains. When hypomanic Virginia would waken early, bursting with energy and zest, her mind full of ideas and plans for current and future work. She saw herself in a confident positive light. Gone was the fear of failure, envy of her sister, desire for children.

Books were her children and she saw them stretching like a magic carpet into the future. Naturally sociable when well, she now invited 'shoals of friends' for weekends and accepted every invitation to luncheon and dinner with her intimates, as well as to grander parties and social occasions where she was one of the chief centres of attraction. She lost her usual reserve and could be wickedly witty, weaving a cloud of fantasy around some embarrassed guest, sparkling 'with gaiety, delicate malice and gossip'. Fellow guests fell under her spell and, 'listening to her, forgot love affairs, stayed on and on into the small hours'.[34] Leonard always had cause to feel anxiety at such times, for with over-excitement and late hours exhaustion and depression were liable to follow. More than once she collapsed physically, usually after returning home.

These hypomanic spells were rarely severe and Leonard was usually able to exert a degree of control, urging her home from a late party, or to bed if at home. They were tremendously enjoyable, comparable but much superior to the effects of a pep pill such as Ecstasy. An understandable reluctance to give up the experience is why a number of cyclothymes refuse to accept treatment with lithium – which removes or diminishes mood swings.

When hypomania intensifies, the mind begins to turn too quickly for comfort. Grandiose, frankly absurd ideas pour forth which, if acted upon, can bring chaos and ruin. Insight and judgement are lost, and excitable monologues become less and less intelligible. Hilarity or irritability may be the predominant mood, so-called 'hilarious' and 'furious' forms of mania. Any opposition arouses violent anger and abuse, as Vanessa found in 1904 and Leonard discovered in 1915. Money is spent without thought and huge debts incurred, and sexual adventures begun. Virginia, when manic, was never driven in that direction, but her cyclothymic great-great-grandfather, the first James Stephen, spent time in a debtors' jail and died in poverty as a result of his 'furious' hypomania; and Virginia's cousin Jim Stephen when severely hypomanic, was moved to expose himself naked in windows and write pornographic verse and pursue women, including Virginia's half-sister.

At the height of the 1915 episode of mania Virginia's talk became 'wildly insane', and then 'completely incoherent, a mere jumble of dissociated words' and finally she fell into a coma, but conscious of her surroundings and of hallucinatory experiences.[35]

Mania is destructive but mild hypomania can be very productive; the hypomanic's business thrives, the scientist designs new research, paintings, music, books pour forth, fresh and original. But more than hypomania alone is needed for great originality or what may be called genius. That something is provided, paradoxically, by depression. It is the contradictory-sounding mixture of mania and depression, the so-called mixed state of manic depression, which can be a source of original ideas to a genius capable of making them 'real'.

Mixed manic depression – a mood of depression and self-blame mingles with rapid, vivid hallucinatory scenes; suicidal ideas exist alongside elation, and so on – is not uncommon, and perhaps particularly among cyclothymic artists. Robert Schumann, in the midst of exquisite suffering, heard glorious music which he later wrote down. John Ruskin saw 'horribly hideous forms' followed by wonderfully 'beautiful objects'.[36] A mad Virginia suffered 'every form and variety of nightmare and extravagant intensity of perception', from which 'in the light of reason' she constructed her stories.[37]

Mixed manic depression has two effects on creative cyclothymes. During the depressive process long-established patterns of thought and behaviour are shaken and sometimes broken down, old beliefs and habits are lost, and for a space a kind of mental vacuum exists. At the same time manic ideas swirl through the mind, thoughts which are perhaps foreign to that person in his normal state, and some of these may replace or combine with the original patterns and ideas. A way of thinking is changed and a solution to a seemingly impossible problem follows. The painter's perception of the world is transformed. Virginia Woolf discovered 'in one second

. . . how I could embody all my deposit of experience in a shape that fitted it'.[38] She was being truthful when she said, 'As an experience, madness is terrific'.[39]

Virginia was actually mad on three occasions only. Leonard said she had a major breakdown after her mother's death in 1895 but there is no evidence to support this. For most of her life Virginia was sane. A change of mood could alter her outlook, sometimes radically, but she was always able to reason and communicate. Only when she broke down totally did she lose touch with reality, and become cut off from Leonard. Manic depressive attacks resolve eventually, unless there physical complications like the beginnings of dementia or syphilis, or the cyclothyme's environment discourages change, and Virginia always returned to complete sanity. Many great men and women have suffered and gained from cyclothymia. The seeds of a great work of art or literature, or a scientific theory, may originate in madness but can germinate and flower only in the sunlight of sanity.

The incidence of cyclothymia in Western populations approaches five per cent, but only about a third develop symptoms of manic depression. It is more common among the upper than lower classes, one explanation being that the inherited creative drive of hypomania has helped each generation of cyclothymes to succeed and rise up the social ladder and so congregate near the top. Another less persuasive suggestion is that the strain of upward social mobility brings on manic depression.

Manic depression occurs equally among men and women, although depressive illness in general is twice as common in women. The usual age of onset is between the late teens and mid-twenties, but the first signs of cyclothymia may be overlooked, and several years elapse before any abnormal behaviour is noticed.

Without lithium treatment manic depression is liable to be followed by recurrences, although many years may elapse between attacks. Cyclothymic swings can occur once or twice a year or at longer intervals, every second year or more. Less usual is 'rapid cycling' – mood swings in quick succession over the course of the year – which occurs mainly in women (not in Virginia's case) and fails to respond to lithium.

With increasing age cyclothymia may worsen, but more from adversely changing circumstances and loss of hope than biological factors, and alcoholism and drug abuse are common complications. If much time is lost from work, many will lose their jobs, and the partner or spouse may lose patience and leave, and the ageing cyclothyme is liable to slide down the economic and social scale. The risk of suicide is high. Between 30 and 40 per cent attempt suicide at least once, and about one in five kill themselves.

The basic cause of cyclothymia remains unknown, but it has long been recognised that manic depression runs in families – 'something in the blood' as the old wives said – and it is now generally accepted that the disease has a genetic basis. The genes have not been located, but that is only a question of time. Manic depression will not occur in the absence of the responsible genes; yet their presence does not always result in clinical cyclothymia because of what geneticists call 'incomplete genetic penetration'.

Virginia Woolf's cyclothymic genes came through her father, Leslie Stephen, and his family can be traced back through four generations. The great-great-grandfather, James Stephen, came from Scotland, and at first prospered, but bouts of depression and hypomania caused him to ruin himself financially and to bring hardship to his wife and children. The great-grandfather worked alongside William Wilberforce to abolish the slave trade and became a force in Parliament. He may have been cyclothymic but he was always successful and never showed pronounced mental instability. Virginia's father and grandfather were both outstanding men who broke down several times with severe depression. Both had enormous drive and the ability to work with great intensity for long periods. All Virginia's full siblings were prone to depression and a first cousin, Jim Stephen, developed manic depression and died in an asylum in his early thirties.

The effect of cyclothymic genes is to set up a predisposition to depression and mania. Outside influences – such as emotional stress, brain injury or infections – have to be involved for clinical cyclothymia to be triggered. The complex brain mechanisms concerned are little understood, but it is known that mood changes correspond to alterations in the concentration of certain chemical neurotransmitters at neuronal terminals or synapses; hydroxy-tryptamine (serotonin) levels are low in depression and high in mania. But other neurotransmitters must also be involved, and the interactions result in variations of nervous inhibition and excitation.

Cyclothymia usually first develops against a background of anxiety rather than any specific upsetting event. Virginia became anxious and highly strung after the death of her mother, Julia, and again when her half-sister Stella, who had taken her mother's place, died two years later, but it was another year before cyclothymia commenced. Once established, her mood swung up and down with predictable regularity in line with the changing seasons. The late winter or early spring months between January and March were associated with depression (there was a comparatively minor and short-lived replay in the autumn); the early summer months with hypomania.

These changes are believed to be influenced by the amount of and intensity of light, together perhaps with the hormone, melatonin, and changes in the sleep/wake cycle. There are those (mostly women) who suffer from Seasonal Affective Disorder (SAD), becoming depressed in the winter months and elated in summer, but they differ from cyclothymes in that when depressed they eat compulsively and sleep long and deeply; SAD is probably a separate disease.

Individual patterns of cyclothymia tend not to change, but the depth and height of swings depends on how stressful life is. If the cyclothyme is emotionally disturbed at the time a swing is due, biological and psychological forces join up to potentiate the mood change.

When Virginia led a quiet life, cyclothymic swings were minimal. When her life became rackety and stressful they were liable to be dangerously intense. Her first breakdown followed her father's death in February 1904, a vulnerable time, and the cyclothymic depression was reinforced by grief and 'confusion' into madness. After recovering she lived quietly with the family, but when Vanessa married and had her first child, and Virginia began a flirtation with her husband, cyclothymic swings grew turbulent. The 1913 breakdown followed the strains of marriage and the New Year cyclothymic depression.

The strains and stresses in Virginia's life can be readily traced in the variability of her mood swings. Depressions brought about by events occurring outside expected cyclothymic times – and which therefore lacked biological force – had little intensity or persistence. All her major breakdowns were set off by powerful emotions, particularly grief and anger, combining with the cyclothymia.

The intensity of any emotional reaction is linked to temperament; the more highly strung and insecure the cyclothyme the greater the reaction – although outward signs do not always mirror the distress felt. Some authorities maintain that manic depressives are anxiety prone and over-sensitive, always craving affection and approval.[39] It was largely true for Virginia Woolf, and her dependence on one or two people made her particularly vulnerable to their loss or threatened loss. But many other types of personality exist among manic depressives and they cannot all be fitted into one compartment. Perhaps the most important quality for the cyclothyme's survival is the will to lead a purposeful life, however ravaged by cyclothymia, and to maintain a firm supportive relationship.

Every cyclothyme needs constant help from understanding companions. Many cyclothymes instinctively seek out an ideal person – early on Virginia acknowledged her need for a 'maternal protector' – with whom they can develop a protective relationship. Cyclothymes such as Ruskin and Van Gogh, who failed to establish one, drifted inexorably into chronic mental illness.

A close lasting relationship with a cyclothyme is never easy. A partner has to be perceptive, have a character strong enough to dominate the cyclothyme at critical times, take charge when hypomania threatens to run out of control, and become mother to a child in deep depression. There is little resistance when the mood is one of despair, but hypomania brings argument and discord. The inconsistent behaviour tests love to the full and many marriages and relationships break up under the strain.

The Woolfs' marriage was never threatened. The 1913 breakdown, ghastly as it was, resulted in the resolution of many of Virginia's fears and strengthening of their relationship. Virginia's trust in Leonard was complete, and however depressed she might be she never doubted his loyalty. He was always her 'strong linchpin'. In turn, Leonard confirmed his need for and admiration of Virginia and willingly took on the role of 'maternal protector'. Virginia's relatives criticised him for being rigid, humourless and puritanical; her brother-in-law Clive Bell openly said that Leonard was making her lose her looks and sense of fun. It is true that Leonard did limit her social engagements and force her to leave a party before midnight, and insist she lead a quiet life, but by doing so he gave her the stability she needed for her writing. Virginia recognised that and 'adored' him and willingly accepted his domination. Her health and work became Leonard's primary concerns, taking precedence over his own interests. Although he wrote and published much throughout their marriage, there was never any hint of rivalry between husband and wife.

In time their marriage grew in depth and resilience. The child/parent-like relationship of the first half gradually gave way to a more adult partnership. Leonard readily acknowledged his need for Virginia in the later years as he became depressed and insecure. Only in the final year or two did Leonard lose sight of Virginia and fail to notice, until too late, the unmistakable signs of madness.

There were other maternal protectors: her sister Vanessa, and a number of women at different times, but they paled beside Leonard. She could have had no better guardian and protector.

Without Leonard she would probably have written none of her great innovative novels.

Virginia had no other protection. Neither of the Woolfs had a religious faith; Virginia had been brought up by determinedly agnostic parents, and Leonard was openly hostile to Christianity and organised religion. The Labour Party and, until 1935, the League of Nations, represented his faith but, while Virginia called herself a socialist, she was not really interested in political issues, and merely followed and supported Leonard. Feminism, and the related subject of pacifism, were her ideals and in her latter years she worked hard for them; but they could provide no shelter from manic depression.

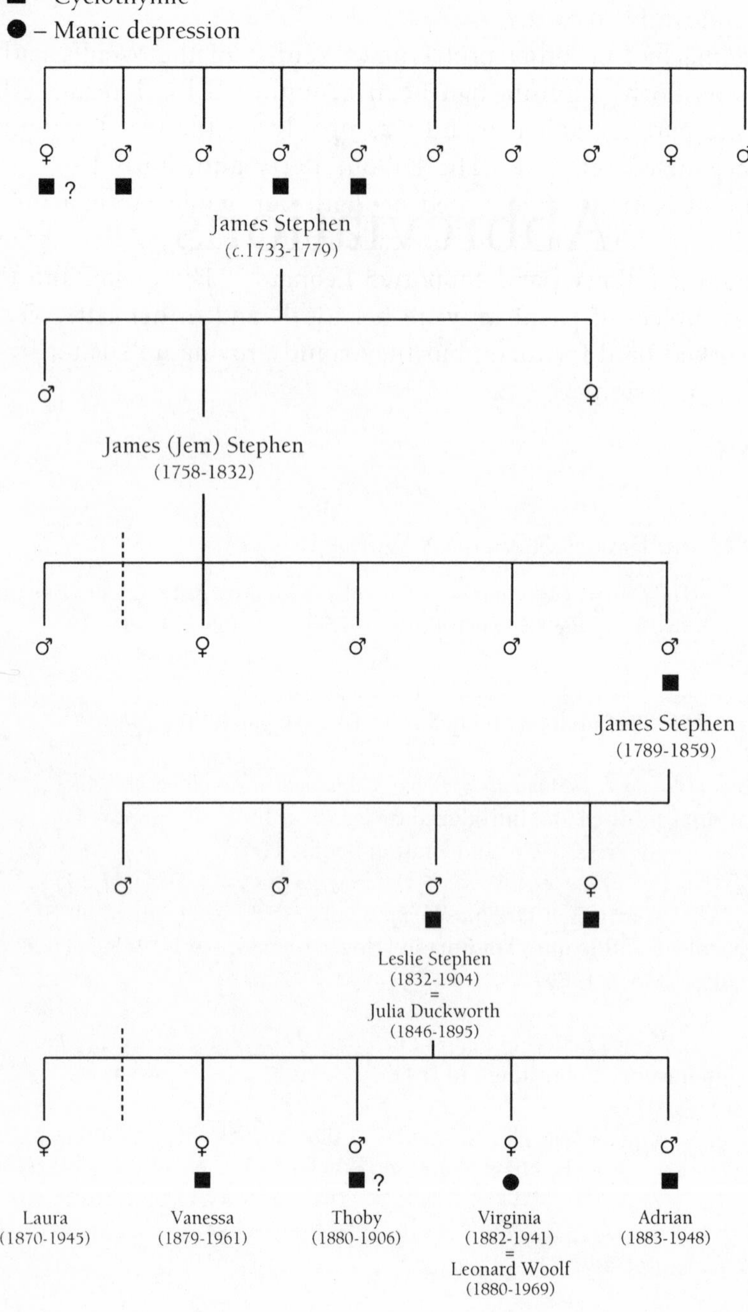
■ – Cyclothymic
● – Manic depression
♀ ♂ ♂ ♂ ♂ ♂ ♂ ♂ ♀ ♂
■ ? ■ ■ ■
James Stephen
(c.1733-1779)
♂ ♀
James (Jem) Stephen
(1758-1832)
♂ ♀ ♂ ♂ ♂
■
James Stephen
(1789-1859)
♂ ♂ ♂ ♀
■ ■
Leslie Stephen
(1832-1904)
=
Julia Duckworth
(1846-1895)
♀ ♀ ♂ ♀ ♂
■ ■ ? ● ■
Laura
(1870-1945)
Vanessa
(1879-1961)
Thoby
(1880-1906)
Virginia
(1882-1941)
=
Leonard Woolf
(1880-1969)
Adrian
(1883-1948)

Abbreviations

LETTERS AND DIARIES OF VIRGINIA WOOLF

Diary *The Diary of Virginia Woolf* 5 vols. edited by Anne Olivier Bell and Andrew McNeillie (Hogarth Press, 1976–82 / Penguin Books, 1988)

Early Journals *Virginia Woolf A Passionate Apprentice: The Early Journals, 1897–1909* edited by Mitchell A. Leaska (Hogarth Press, 1990)

Moments of Being *Moments of Being: Unpublished Autobiographical Writings* edited and introduced by Jeanne Schulkind (Sussex, The University Press, 1976, and Grafton Books, 1985).

Letters *The Letters of Virginia Woolf* 6 vols., 1975-1984, edited by Nigel Nicolson and Joanne Trautmann (Hogarth Press, vol 1 1975, vol 4 1978, vols 2, 3, 5, 6 1984)

Marler *Selected Letters of Vanessa Bell* edited by Regina Marler (Bloomsbury Publishing Ltd, 1993)

Nicolson *Vita and Harold: The Letters of Vita Sackville-West and Harold Nicolson* edited by Nigel Nicolson (Weidenfeld & Nicolson, 1992)

Spotts *Letters of Leonard Woolf* edited by Frederic Spotts (Weidenfeld & Nicolson, 1989)

DeSalvo & Leaska *The Letters of Vita Sackville-West to Virginia Woolf* edited by Louise DeSalvo and Mitchell A. Leaska (Virago Press, 1992)

QUOTED WORKS BY LEONARD WOOLF

L W *Autobiography* *An Autobiography* vol. 1, 1880–1911; vol. 2, 1911–1969 (Oxford University Press, 1980)

Principia Politica *Principia Politica: A Study of Communal Psychology* (Hogarth Press, 1953)

Wise Virgins *The Wise Virgins: A Story of Words, Opinions and a Few Emotions* (Edward Arnold, 1914)

Notes

PREFACE

1 23/4/01, *Letters* I, p.40
2 VW to CB, 4/9/10, *Letters* I, p.433
3 4/9/27, *Diary*, III, p.153

CHAPTER 1

1 *see* Bell II, p.14
2 *see* Annan, p.103
3 *Moments of Being*, p.93
4 4/5/28, *Diary* III, p.182
5 *Mausoleum Book*, p.61
6 *Lancet* obituary July 1887, p.204
7 *Moments of Being*, p.98
8 *Mausoleum Book*, p.26
9 *see* Martin, p.407–8
10 *Moments of Being*, p.94
11 *Mausoleum Book*, p.60
12 I *assume* VW was recalling her mother's words when she was writing 'Professions for Women', (p.150)
13 *Notes from Sick Rooms*, p.1
14 *Moments of Being*, p.98
15 Ibid 359
16 *Moments of Being*, p.100
17 *Notes from Sick Rooms*, p.4

CHAPTER 2

1 *see* Annan, p.43
2 *Moments of Being*, p.146
3 *Mausoleum Book*, pp.12–17
4 *see* Gérin, p.156
5 *Mausoleum Book*, p.19
6 *see* Gérin, p.159
7 *see* Gérin, p.177
8 *see* Gérin, p.183
9 *see* Gérin, p.187
10 *Mausoleum Book*, p.53
11 *see* Annan, p.81

CHAPTER 3

1 *Mausoleum Book*, p.83
2 *Mausoleum Book*, p.44
3 *Mausoleum Book*, p.83

4 *Mausoleum Book*, p.59
5 *see* Love, p.119
6 *see* Annan, p.97
7 *see* King, p.26
8 *Mausoleum Book*, p.80
9 *Mausoleum Book*, p.93
10 *see* Annan, p.83
11 *see* Annan, p.86
12 3/12/23 *Diary* II, p.276
13 *Moments of Being*, p.45
14 *Mausoleum Book*, p.96

CHAPTER 4

1 *Moments of Being*, p.198
2 *Moments of Being*, p.87
3 9/1/15, *Diary* I, p.13
4 *Moments of Being*, p.91
5 LS to JS, 20/2/83, *see* King, p.47
6 *see* A. Garnett, p.107
7 LS to JS, 13/4/84, *see* King, p.34
8 VW to CB, 20/4/08, *Letters* I, p.326
9 *Moments of Being*, p.103
10 *Moments of Being*, p.87
11 *Moments of Being*, p.80
12 *The Waves*, p.104
13 *Moments of Being*, p.81
14 Ibid.
15 Ibid.
16 *Moments of Being*, p.49
17 *Moments of Being*, p.50
18 Mrs Ramsay's belief in *To the Lighthouse* (p.46)
19 *Moments of Being*, p.51
20 Jim Stephen was eventually sent to St Andrew's Mental Hospital in Northamptonshire, where he starved himself to death, *see* Caramagno, pp.l01–3
21 *Moments of Being*, p.77
22 Wilberforce to Elizabeth Robins, 23/12/40, *see* Dunn, p.296
23 *Moments of Being*, p.185
24 *Moments of Being*, p.193
25 Ibid.
26 VW to VB, 21/7/11, *Letters* I, p.469

CHAPTER 5

1 *Moments of Being*, p.103
2 *Mausoleum Book*, p.xxvi
3 *Moments of Being*, p.112
4 *Moments of Being*, p.116
5 7/4/1897, *Early Journals*, p.67
6 10/4/1897, *Early Journals*, p.68
7 28/4/1897, *Early Journals*, p.77
8 9/5/1897, *Early Journals*, p.83
9 *Moments of Being*, p.137
10 1/1/1898, *Early Journals*, p.134
11 VD to VB, 6/7/42, *see* King, p.67
12 *Moments of Being*, p.112
13 *Moments of Being*, p.149
14 Menstruation began in October 1896, according to Stella's diary (*see* King, p.57). Virginia and Vanessa, always spent at least the first day of a period in bed. 25/10/17, *Diary* I, p.66
15 *Moments of Being*, p.158
16 Ibid.
17 *Moments of Being*, p.159
18 15/4/08, VW to CB, *Letters* I, p.324
19 28/11/28, *Diary* III, p.208
20 VW to VD, Oct/Nov 1902, Letters I, p.61
21 VW to VD, 30/4/03, Letters I, p.75

2 VW to VD, 7/7/03, *Letters* I, p.85
3 VW to VD, 30/6/03, *Letters* I, p.82
4 VW to VD, Oct/Nov 1902, *Letters* I, p.57
5 VW to VD, 4/3/04, *Letters* I, p.130
6 VW to VD, 31/3/04, *Letters* I, p.136.
7 VW to VD, 28/2/04, *Letters* I, p.130
8 VW to VD, 4/3/04, *Letters* I, p.134
9 VW to Emma Vaughan, 25/4/04, *Letters* I, p.138
0 Ibid.
1 VW to VD, 6/5/04, *Letters* I, p.139
2 VW to VD, 22/9/04, *Letters* I, p.142, *see* Bell I, p.90
3 VW to VD, 22/9/04, *Letters* I, p.142

CHAPTER 6

1 *Letters* I, (Nicolson) p.xv
2 *Moments of Being*, pp.204–205
3 *Moments of Being*, p.205
4 Lytton Strachey, quoted from Holroyd, p.60
5 *Moments of Being*, p.209
6 *Moments of Being*, p.208
7 LS to LW, Jan 1905, Spotts, p.75
8 VW to VD, 18/12/06, *Letters* I, p.266
9 VW to VD, 10/12/06, *Letters* I, p.259
0 VW to VD, 31/12/06, *Letters* I, p.274
1 Ibid.
12 VW to VD, 30/12/06, *Letters* I, p.273
13 VW to VD, 3/6/07, *Letters* I, p.297
14 VB to VW, 30/7/07, *Letters* I, p.51
15 VB to Dora Carrington, 25/1/32, p.371
16 *Diary II*, 17/10/24, p.316
17 *The Voyage Out*, p.206
18 VW to VB, 31/12/18, *Letters* II, p.310
19 VW to VD, 13/5/08, *Letters* I, p.331
20 VW to CB, May 1908; *Letters* I, p.333
21 *Diary* III, 6/1/25, p.4
22 (Christopher Isherwood) *see* Noble, p.217
23 VW to CB, May 1908, *Letters* I, p.333
24 VW to CB, 6/5/08, *Letters* I, p.329
25 VW to CB, 9/8/08, *Letters* I, p.344
26 VW to CB, 7/2/09, *Letters* I, p.382
27 VW to Gwen Raverat, 22/3/25, *Letters* III, p.172
28 VW to VB, 28/7/10, *Letters* I, p.430
29 VW to CB, 4/9/10, *Letters* I, p.433

CHAPTER 7

1 VB 'Memoir', *see* Spalding, p.94
2 VB 'Memoir', *see* Dunn, p.147
3 VW to VB, 8/6/11, *Letters* I, p.466
4 *see* Tomalin, p.35
5 VW to Molly MacCarthy,

March 1912, *Letters* I, p.492
6 VW to LW, 1/5/12, *Letters* I, p.496

CHAPTER 8

1 LW *Autobiog.* I, p.18
2 Spotts, p.7
3 LW *Autobiog.* I, p.14
4 Bella Woolf to LW, 4/5/01, Spotts, p.16
5 *see* Holroyd, p.83
6 LW *Autobiog* I, p.93
7 Ibid.
8 LW *Autobiog.* I, p.282
9 LW *Autobiog.* II, p.6
10 LS to LW 1907, Spotts, p.131
11 LS to James Strachey, 15/6/11, *see* Holroyd, p.233
12 LW *Autobiog* II, p.14
13 LW to LS, 12/12/06, Spotts, p.122
14 Spotts, p.139
15 LS to LW, 19/2/09, Spotts, p.147
16 Ibid.
17 LW to LS, 4/9/09, Spotts, p.149
18 Ibid.
19 LW to John Lehmann, 18/9/43, Spotts, p.345
20 LW to LS, 19/5/07, Spotts, p.128
21 LW *Autobiog.* I, p.230
22 Bella Woolf to LW 27/7/09, Spotts, p.172
23 LW to VW, 29/4/12, Spotts, p.172
24 VW to LS, 5/3/12, *Letters* I, p.491
25 VB to VW, 2/6/12, *Letters* I, p.117
26 VW to VVD, 24/6/12, *Letters* I, p.505
27 *Moments of Being*, p.205
28 VW to LW, 1/5/12, *Letters* I, p.496
29 Ibid.
30 LW to VW, 29/4/12, Spotts, p.172
31 VW to ES, 2/8/30, *Letters* IV, p.194
32 VW to LW, 1/5/12, *Letters* I, p.496
33 VW to ES, 2/8/30, *Letters* IV, p.194
34 *Diary* III, 3/9/28, p.194
35 Marie Woolf to LW, 7/8/12, Spotts, p.178
36 LW *Autobiog.* II, p.55
37 Savage's opinions are taken from his writings on 'Insanity and Marriage, *J. Mental Sci* 57, 97–112, (1911); 'The Factors of Insanity', *Lancet*, 26/10/07, 1138–1140; 'Discussion on Insanity and Marriage', *BMJ*, 22/10/10, 1242–1243
38 LW *Autobiog.* II, p.115
39 LW *Autobiog.* II, p.56
40 VW to Janet Case, 13/8/12, *Letters* II, p.1

CHAPTER 9

1 VW to LW, Nov 1912, *Letters* II, p.12
2 Gerald Brenan to Rosemary Dinnage, 1967, Spotts p.162
3 VW to Ka Cox, 4/9/12, *Letters* II, p.6
4 VB to CB. 27/12/12, *see* Marler, p.131
5 VSW to HN, 17/8/26, Nicolson, p.158

6 *Wise Virgins*, p.52
7 VB to VW, 26/1/13, *see* Dunn, p.190
8 LW *Autobiog.* II, p.56
9 VW to VD, 11/4/13, *Letters* II, p.22
10 VW to Ethel Sands, 9/2/27, *Letters* III, p.329
11 15/9/27, *Diary* III, p.14
12 5/9/26, *Diary* III, p.106
13 *Principia Politica*, p.108
14 LW *Autobiog.* II p.105
15 VB to RF, 26/7/13, *see* Bell II, p.12
16 LW to VW, 8/4/13, Spotts, p.182
17 VW to LW, 4/8/13, *Letters* II, p.34
18 VB to LW, 28/8/13, *see* Marler, p.141
19 LW *Autobiog.* II, p.116
20 VW to LW, 4/12/13, *Letters* II, p.35
21 VW to LW, 8/3/14, *Letters* II, p.40
22 LW to VW, 13/3/14, Spotts, p.205
23 *see* Bell II, p.19
24 VW to VSW, 23/9/25, *Letters* III, p.214
25 27/1/15, *Diary* I, p.29
26 17/1/15, *Diary* I, p.20
27 24/1/15, *Diary* I, p.27
28 VW to LS, 26/2/15, *Letters* II, p.61
29 Ibid.
30 VW to ES, 1/7/30, *Letters* IV, p.183
31 VB to RF, 25/6/15, *see* Bell II, p.26

Chapter 10

1 9/1/24, *Diary* II, p.282
2 VW to ES, 22/6/30, *Letters* IV, p.179
3 VW to ES, 16/10/30, *Letters* IV, p.230
4 Ibid.
5 Christina Rossetti, 'Goblin Market'
6 *Diary* II, 26/1/20, p.13
7 *Moments of Being*, p.81
8 *Diary* III, 14/6/25, p.29
9 VW to LW, 31/10/17, *Letters* II, p.193
10 Clarissa Dalloway's choice in *Mrs Dalloway* (p.29)
11 LW *Autobiog.* II, p.53
12 21/12/24, *Diary* II, p.324
13 31/1/15, *Diary* I, p.31
14 VW to VB, 30/7/16, *Letters* II, p.107
15 VW to VB, 8/5/27, *Letters* III, p.369
16 VB to RF, 16/10/16, *see* Marler, p.200
17 VB to LS, 24/10/16, *see* Bell II, p.23
18 LS to VB, 25/10/16, *see* Bell II, p.23
19 VW to VB, 27/2/19, *Letters* II, p.335
20 9/6/19, *Diary* I, p.278
21 3/7/19, *Diary* I, p.285
22 LW *Autobiog.* II, p.209
23 *Diary* II,15/2/20, p.20
24 18/3/21, *Diary* II, p.101
25 1/11/24, *Diary* II, p.320
26 VW to OM, Feb 1924, *Letters* III, p.90
27 VW to Madge Vaughan, 9 May, *Letters* I, p.395

28 VW to VB, 22/5/17, *Letters* II, p.155
29 VW to Ethel Sands, 31/5/25, *Letters* III, p.187

CHAPTER 11

1 8/8/21, *Diary* II, p.125
2 22/1/22, *Diary* II, p.156
3 VW to VD, 23/1/23, *Letters* III, p.8
4 Maurice Craig 'Discussion of Early Treatment of Mental Disorders', *Lancet*, 7/11/25, p.967
5 VW to VB, 29/1/18, *Letters* II, p.213
6 22/10/27, *Diary* III, p.161
7 VW to ES, 14/11/30, *Letters* IV, p.253
8 Maurice Craig, Ibid.
9 LW *Autobiog.* II, p.114
10 Maurice Craig's obituary, *Lancet*, 12/1/35, p.87
11 *Mrs Dalloway*, p.87
12 *Diary* II, 25/10/20, p.72
13 *Diary* II, 17/3/23, p.238
14 VW to VB, 20/2/22, *Letters* II, p.504
15 *Diary* II, 11/6/22, p.176
16 *Diary* II, 28/6/23, p.250
17 *Diary* II, 2/1/23, p.221
18 *Diary* II, 28/6/23, p.250
19 Ibid.
20 *Diary* II, 15/10/23, p.270
21 *Diary* II, 3/1/24, p.281
22 *Diary* II, 9/1/24, p.282
23 *Mrs Dalloway*, p.5

CHAPTER 12

1 15/12/22, *Diary* II, p.216
2 5/7/24, *Diary* II, p.306
3 19/2/23, *Diary* II, p.234
4 5/7/24, *Diary* II, p.306
5 VW to Jacques Raverat, 24/1/25, *Letters* III, p.154
6 VW to VSW, 16/11/25, *Letters* III, p.221
7 VW to David Garnett, 4/1/25, *Letters* III, p.153
8 5/7/24, *Diary* II, p.306
9 VW to Jacques Raverat, 26/12/24, *Letters* III, p.149
10 VW to VSW, 26/1/26, *Letters* III, p.231
11 LW *Autobiog.* II, p.268
12 15/9/24, *Diary* II, p.313
13 A theory LW developed through the character of Harry in *The Wise Virgins* (p.57)
14 VSW to VW, 16/7/24, DeSalvo & Leaska, p.53
15 VW to VSW, 19/8/24, *Letters* III, p.125
16 15/9/24, *Diary* II, p.313
17 17/10/24, *Diary* II, p.316
18 8/4/25, *Diary* III, p.6
19 Ibid.
21 VSW to VW, 26/5/25, DeSalvo & Leaska, p.65
22 30/7/25, *Diary* III, p.37
23 5/9/25, *Diary* III, p.38
24 VW to VSW, 7/9/25, *Letters* III, p.204
25 'On Being Ill', p.196
26 VW to VSW 13/10/25, *Letters* III, p.217
27 27/11/25, *Diary* III, p.46
28 VSW to VW, 23/10/25, DeSalvo & Leaska, p.80
29 7/12/25, *Diary* III, p.48
30 Ibid.

31 VW to VSW, 9/12/25, *Letters* III, p.227
32 23/2/26, *Diary* III, p.59
33 21/12/25, *Diary* III, p.51
34 Ibid.
35 19/1/26, *Diary* III, p.57
36 21/12/25, *Diary* III, p.51
37 23/11/26, *Diary* III, p.116
38 VSW to VW, 1/1/26, DeSalvo & Leaska, p.87
39 VW to VB, 13/6/26, *Letters* III, p.273
40 VSW to HN, 7/11/26, Nicolson, p.168
41 5/9/26, *Diary* III, p.106
42 28/9/26, *Diary* III, p.111
43 Ibid.
44 8/2/26, *Diary* III, p.57
45 18/4/26, *Diary* III, p.75
46 25/5/26, *Diary* III, p.87
47 4/9/27, *Diary* III, p.153
48 VSW to HN, 23/11/26, Nicolson, p.174
49 VSW to HN, 30/11/26, Nicolson, p.175
50 HN to VSW, 17/12/26, Nicolson, p.176
51 VSW to HN, 21/12/26, Nicolson, p.178
52 23/1/27, *Diary* III, p.123
53 18/4/26, *Diary* III, p.75
54 25/5/26, *Diary* III, p.87
55 23/7/27, *Diary* III, p.147
56 4/7/27, *Diary* III, p.144
57 23/7/27, *Diary* III, p.147
58 VW to VSW, 14/6/27, *Letters* III, p.391
59 VW to Eddy Sackville-West, 22/10/28, *Letters* III, p.548
60 22/3/28, *Diary* III, p.177
61 *Portrait of a Marriage*, Nicolson, p.186
62 VW to VSW, 9/10/27, *Letters* III, p.427
63 VSW to VW, 11/10/27, DeSalvo & Leaska, p.252
64 31/5/28 *Diary* III, p.183
65 *see* Glendenning, p.201
66 VW to VSW, 9/10/27 , *Letters* III, p.427
67 VW to VSW, 13/10/27, *Letters* III, p.429
68 22/9/28, *Diary* III, p.197
69 VW to LW, 28/9/28, *Letters* III, p.538
70 VW to LW, 25/9/28, *Letters* III, p.534
71 *see* Glendenning, p.201
72 VSW to HN, Nicolson, 17/8/26, p.158
73 Glendenning, p.180
74 Ibid., p.196
75 25/11/29, *Diary* III, p.267
76 7/7/28, *Diary* III, p.187
77 VW to VSW, 28/1/29, *Letters* IV, p.8
78 LW to VB, 28/1/29, Spotts, p.235
79 VSW to VW, 6/2/29, DeSalvo & Leaska, p.321
80 13/4/29, *Diary* III, p.220
81 28/3/29, *Diary* III, p.218
82 10/8/29, *Diary* III, p.240
83 5/8/29, *Diary* III, p.238
84 VW to VSW, 25/7/31, *Letters* IV, p.362
85 VSW to HN, 8/11/49, Nicolson, p.391
86 18/6/27, *Diary* III, p.138
87 7/2/31, *Diary* IV, p.10
88 30/9/26, *Diary* III, p.113
89 7/2/31, *Diary* IV, p.10

90 11/10/29, *Diary* III, p.253
91 28/9/29, *Diary* III, p.111
92 16/9/29, *Diary* III, p.253
93 VB to VW, 15/10/31, *see* Marler, p.367
94 ES to VW, 23/10/31, (Nicolson) *Letters* IV, p.395
95 17/10/31, *Diary* IV, p.49
96 VW to Ben Nicolson, 1/11/31, *Letters* IV, p.400
97 VSW to William Plomer, 6/12/31, *Letters* IV, p.411
98 VW to ES, 16/7/30, *Letters* IV, p.187
99 VW to VSW, 5/5/30, *Letters* IV, p.162
100 VW to ES, 3/9/30, *Letters* IV, p.207
101 2/6/31, *Diary* IV, p.29

CHAPTER 13

1 3/2/32, *Diary* IV, p.70
2 25/11/21, *Diary* II, p.144
3 2/8/24, *Diary* II, p.307
4 LW *Autobiog.* p.315
5 *see* Lehmann, p.75
6 9/5/26, *Diary* III, p.80
7 LW *Autobiog.* II, p.256
8 *see* Holroyd, p.481
9 'On Being Ill', p.196
10 *Principia Politica*, p.68
11 *Principia Politica*, p.65
12 VW to ES, 19/12/31, *Letters* IV, p.415
13 25/12/31, *Diary* IV, p.55
14 27/12/31, *Diary* IV, p.55
15 22/1/32, *Diary* IV, p.64
16 12/3/32, *Diary* IV, p.81
17 Ibid.
18 24/3/32, *Diary* IV, p.85
19 25/6/35, *Diary* IV, p.326
20 25/5/32, *Diary* IV, p.102
21 VW to ES, 26/5/32, *Letters* V, p.66
22 5/8/32, *Diary* IV, p.120
23 10/11/32, *Diary* IV, p.130

CHAPTER 14

1 15/1/33, *Diary* IV, p.142
2 *Political Quarterly* in Spotts, p.379
3 VW to VD, 18/4/35, *Letters* V, p.384
4 *see* Bell II, p.189
5 LW *Autobiog.* II, p.327
6 LW *Autobiog.* II, p.369
7 LW *Autobiog.* II, p.368
8 Bell II, p.258
9 *Three Guineas*, p.123
10 28/4/35, *Diary* IV, p.307
11 2/7/34, *Diary* IV, p.223
12 VW to ES, 18/5/31, *Letters* IV, p.332
13 17/9/35, *Diary* IV, p.342
14 29/4/33, *Diary* IV, p.153
15 VW to M. Llewellyn Davies, 28/4/35, *Letters* V, p.388
16 9/5/35, *Diary* IV, p.310
17 VB to CB, 26/5/35, *see* Dunn, p.231
18 1/6/35, *Diary* IV, p.318
19 5/6/35, *Diary* IV, p.319
20 VW to OM, 4/10/35, *Letters* V, p.428
21 4/9/35, *Diary* IV, p.337
22 2/11/32, *Diary* IV, p.129
23 15/10/35, *Diary* IV, p.346
24 27/10/35, *Diary* IV, p.348
25 16/1/36, *Diary* V, p.8
26 11/3/36, *Diary* V, p.15
27 13/3/36, *Diary* V, p.16

28 VW to VB, 1/10/38, *Letters* VI, p.275
29 24/3/36, *Diary* V, p.20
30 3/11/36, *Diary* V, p.28
31 VW to ES, 4/9/36, *Letters* VI, p.70
32 3/11/36, *Diary* VI, p.71
33 3/11/36, *Diary* V, p.28
34 5/11/36, *Diary* V, p.30
35 LW *Autobiog.* II, p.301
36 LW *Autobiog.* II, p.299
37 *see* letter from VW to VB, 22/7/36, *Letters* VI, p.57
38 VW to LW, 14/7/36, *Letters* VI, p.54
39 VW to ES, 26/8/36, *Letters* VI, p.67
40 24/11/36, *Diary* V, p.35
41 LW to Julian Bell, 5/7/36, Spotts, p.407
42 LW to Julian Bell, 15/11/36, Spotts, p.409
43 VW to ES, 24/2/37, *Letters* VI, p.109
44 VW to ES, 28/6/37, *Letters* VI, p.141
45 19/7/37, *Diary* V, p.102
46 VW to Molly MacCarthy, 16/1/38, *Letters* VI, p.208
47 18/12/37, *Diary* V, p.121
48 12/12/38, *Diary* V, p.191
49 B. Webb, *Diary*, p.443
50 23/10/31 *Diary* IV, p.51
51 22/10/37, *Diary* V, p.115
52 VB to VSW, 2/4/41, *see* Marler, p.475
53 VW to VB, 17/8/37, *Letters* VI, p.158
54 11/8/37, *Diary* V, p.106
55 VW to VB, 3/2/38, *Letters* VI, p.211
56 VB to VW, 4/2/38, *see* Bell II, p.203
57 12/10/37, *Diary* V, p.112
58 *Three Guineas*, p.9
59 VW to ES, 7/6/38, *Letters* VI, p.234
60 *see* Bell II, p.258
61 12/10/37, *Diary* V, p.112
62 4/2/38, *Diary* V, p.127
63 *see* Bell II, p.205
64 12/4/38, *Diary* V, p.133
65 VW to ES , 11/9/38, *see* Nicolson's note, *Letters* VI, p.270
66 VW to ES, 7/6/38, *Letters* VI, p.234
67 VB to Julian, 10/10/36, *see* Marler, p.422
68 6/7/39, *Diary* V, p.324
69 LW *Autobiog.* II, p.376
70 Ibid.

Chapter 15

1 3/9/39, *Diary* V, p.233
2 VW to ES,. 12/9/39, *Letters* VI, p.358
3 7/10/39, *Diary* V, p.241
4 3/9/39, *Diary* V, p.233
5 2/12/39, *Diary* V, p.248
6 9/12/39, *Diary* V, p.250
7 VW to VSW, 3/12/39, *Letters* VI, p.373
8 VW to ES, 1/2/40, *Letters* VI, p.380
9 19/1/40, *Diary* V, p.257
10 VW to ES, 1/2/40, *Letters* VI, p.380
11 2/2/40, *Diary* V, p.262
12 8/2/40, *Diary* VI, p.264
13 VW to ES, 19/3/40, *Letters* VI, p.386

14 7/3/40, *Diary* V, p.270
15 20/3/40, *Diary* V, p.271
16 Ibid.
17 25/4/40, *Diary* V, p.281
18 LW *Autobiog.* II, p.409
19 13/5/40, *Diary* V, p.283
20 Ibid.
21 20/5/40, *Diary* V, p.258
22 15/5/40, *Diary* V, p.284
23 7/6/40, *Diary* V, p.292
24 15/5/40 *Diary* V, p.284
25 VW to VD, 8/9/40, *Letters* VI, p.428
26 15/5/40, *Diary* V, p.284
27 12/7/40, *Diary* V, p.301
28 16/8/40, *Diary* V, p.311
29 VW to Ben Nicolson, 24/8/40, *Letters* VI, p.421
30 31/8/34, *Diary* V, p.313
31 26/7/40, *Diary* V, p.306
32 VW to Sybil Colefax, 14/8/40, *Letters* VI, p.415
33 VW to ES, 11/9/40, *Letters* VI (and Nicolson's note), p.431
34 28/7/40, *Diary* V, p.306
35 VW to VSW, 30/8/40, *Letters* VI, p.424
36 2/9/40, *Diary* V, p.314
37 5/9/40, *Diary* V, p.315
38 20/10/40, *Diary* V, p.330
39 VW to ES, 11/9/40, *Letters* VI, p.429
40 VW to ES, 12/9/40, *Letters* VI, p.430
41 VW to ES, 14/11/40, *Letters* VI, p.443
42 5/11/40, *Diary* V, p.336
43 VW to VSW, 15/11/40, *Letters* VI, p.445
44 LS to Carrington, *see* Bell II, p.80
45 14/9/40, *Diary* V, p.319
46 12/10/40, *Diary* V, p.328
47 29/9/40, *Diary* V, p.325
48 1/11/40, *Diary* V, p.334
49 16/12/40, *Diary* V, p.343
50 19/12/40, *Diary* V, p.344
51 VW to ES, 6/12/40, *Letters* VI, p.449
52 16/12/40, *Diary* V, p.343
53 6/12/40, *Diary* V, p.342
54 LW *Autobiog.* II, p.420
55 VW to ES, 12/1/41, *Letters* VI, p.459
56 Ibid.
57 Wilberforce to Elizabeth Robins, 28/2/41, *see* Jalland, p.173
58 29/11/40, *Diary* V, p.342
59 16/12/40, *Diary* V, p.343
60 24/12/40, *Diary* V, p.346
61 22/12/40, *Diary* V, p.345
62 15/1/41, *Diary* V, p.352
63 VW to ES, 1/2/41, *Letters* VI, p.465
64 26/2/41, *Diary* V, p.356
65 8/3/41, *Diary* V, p.357
66 9/1/41, *Diary* V, p.351
67 Ibid.
68 26/1/41, *Diary* V, p.354
69 VW described the three phases to ES, 1/7/30, *Letters* IV, p.183
70 VW to ES, 1/3/41, *Letters* VI, p.474
71 LW to M. Llewellyn Davies, 1/9/41, Spotts, p.254
72 Wilberforce to Elizabeth Robins, Dec 40, *see* Jalland, p.167
73 VW to Wilberforce, 31/12/40, *Letters* VI, p.456
74 Wilberforce to Elizabeth

Robins, 31/1/41, p.172
75 VW to VSW, 19/1/41, *Letters* VI, p.461
76 VW to Wilberforce, 4/3/41, *Letters* VI, p.476
77 Wilberforce to Elizabeth Robins, 22/3/41, *see* Jalland, p.179
78 VW told Lehmann the novel was 'too silly and trivial' to publish. VW to John Lehmann, 27/3/41, *Letters* VI, p.486
79 LW *Autobiog.* II, p.434
80 Ibid.
81 Wilberforce to Elizabeth Robins, 26/3/41, *see* Jalland, p.181
82 VW to VB, 23/3/41, *Letters* VI, p.485
83 VW to LW, 18/3/41, *Letters* VI, p.481 This is the letter left for LW on the sitting-room table, which he found on 28 March – *see* Nicolson notes 481, 486
84 *see* Bell, *Elders and Betters*, p.126
85 VB to VSW, 22/4/41, *see* Marler, p.476
86 *see* Bell, *Elders and Betters*, p.126

Appendix

1 VW to OM, 9/10/36, *Letters* VI, p.76
2 28/5/31, *Diary* IV, p.27
3 4/1/36, *Diary* V, p.4
4 VW to ES, 1/7/30, *Letters* IV, p.183
5 VW to ES, 8/8/21, *Letters* IV, p.183
6 16/2/30, *Diary* III, p.287
7 *see Letters and Prose Writings of William Cowper*, vol. I, edited by James King and Charles Ryskamp (Oxford University Press)
8 VW to ES, 16/10/30, *Letters* IV, p.230
9 11/2/28, *Diary* III, p.174
10 Ibid.
11 Ibid.
12 20/1/19, *Diary* I, p.233
13 *see* Scott Fitzgerald, *The Crack-Up* (1936)
14 *see* William Cowper, *Letters and Prose Writings*, vol I
15 *Diary* III, 15/9/26, p.110
16 *Diary* V, 1/3/37, p.63
17 Ibid.
18 LW *Autobiog.* vol 2, p.109
19 VW to VD. 22/9/04, *Letters* I, p.142
20 LW *Autobiog.* II, p.116
21 Ibid.
22 William Cowper (*see* above)
23 Styron, p.17
24 VW to Gerald Brenan, 25/12/22, *Letters* II
25 VW to LW, 18/3/41, *Letters* VI
26 Hector Berlioz, *The Memoirs*, Trans. David Cairns, Panther, 1974
27 William Cowper (see above)
28 Charles Lamb to S. T. Coleridge, *Letters*, 9/6/96
29 *Diary* II, 9/1/24, p.283
30 VW to Molly MacCarthy, 9/2/26, *Letters* III, p.272
31 VW to ES, 27/2/30, *Letters* IV, p.144
32 *Diary* II, 8/8/21, p.125

33 *see* Jamison, *An Unquiet Mind*
34 Isherwood, *see* Noble, p.217
35 LW *Autobiog.* II, p.124
36 Bragman, Louis, J. *Amer. J. Psychiatry* 1137-59, 91, 1935, The Case of John Ruskin, p1151
37 VW to ES, 16/10.30, *Letters* IV, p.230
38 Ibid.
39 VW to ES, 22/6/30, *Letters* IV, p.179
40 *Rado. B., Int. J. Psychoanalysis*, 9 p.420, 1928

Bibliography

Abse, Joan *John Ruskin, The Passionate Moralist* (Quartet Books, 1980)

Annan, Noel *Leslie Stephen* (University of Chicago Press, London, 1986)

Bell, Quentin *Virginia Woolf: A Biography* vols. 1 and 2 (Hogarth Press, 1972)
— *Elders and Betters* (John Murray, 1995)

Caramagno, T. C. *The Flight of the Mind: Virginia Woolf's Art and Manic-Depressive Illness* (University of California Press, 1992)

Chissell, Joan *Schumann* (J. M. Dent & Sons, 1967)

Cowper, William *Letters and Prose Writings* vol 1 Edited James King and Charles Ryskamp (Oxford University Press 1981)

DeSalvo, Louise *Virginia Woolf, The Impact of Childhood Sexual Abuse on her Life and Work* (The Woman's Press, 1989)

Dunn, Jane *A Very Close Conspiracy: Vanessa Bell and Virginia Woolf* (Jonathan Cape, 1990)

Garnett, Angelica *Deceived with Kindness: A Bloomsbury Childhood* (Chatto & Windus, 1995)

Garnett, David *Great Friends: Portraits of Seventeen Writers* (Macmillan, 1979)

Gérin, Winifred *Anne Thackeray Ritchie: A Biography* (Oxford University Press, 1981)

Glendenning, Victoria *Vita: The Life of Vita Sackville-West* (Penguin Books, 1983)

Gordon, Lyndall *Virginia Woolf: A Writer's Life* (Oxford University Press, 1984)

Holroyd, Michael *Lytton Strachey* (Chatto & Windus, 1994)

Jalland, Pat *Octavia Wilberfoce, The Autobiography of a Pioneer* (Cassell, 1989)

Jamieson, Kay Redfield *An Unquiet Mind* (Free Press, 1993, Picador, 1995)
Touched with Fire: Manic-Depressive Illness and the Artistic Temperament (Free Press, 1994)

King, James *Virginia Woolf* (Penguin Books Ltd, 1994)

Leaska, Mitchell A. *The Novels of Virginia Woolf: From Beginning to End* (Weidenfeld & Nicolson / The John Jay Press, 1977)

Lee, Hermoine *Virginia Woolf* (Chatto & Windus, 1996)

Lehmann, John *Virginia Woolf and Her World* (Thames & Hudson, 1975)

Love, Jean O. *Virginia Woolf. Sources of Madness and Art* (University of California Press, 1973)

Martin, Robert Bernard *Tennyson: The Unquiet Heart* (Clarendon Press, 1980)

Nicolson, Nigel *Portrait of a Marriage* (Weidenfeld & Nicolson, 1992)

Noble, Joan Russell (ed.) *Recollections of Virginia Woolf* (Wm Morrow & Co/ Cardinal, 1972)

Ostwald, Peter F. *Schumann: Music and Madness* (Victor Gollancz, 1985)

Rose, Phyllis *Woman of Letters, A Life of Virginia Woolf* (Routledge & Kegan Paul, 1978 / OUP–Pandora, 1986)

Showalter, Elaine *Female Malady: Women, Madness and English Culture* (Virago Press, 1987)

Skidelsky, Robert *John Maynard Keynes*, vol. 1 (Macmillan, 1983)

Spalding, Frances *Vanessa Bell* (Weidenfeld & Nicolson, 1983; Orion (Phoenix), 1994)

Stephen, James *The Memoirs of James Stephen: Written by Himself for the Use of His Children,* edited by Merle M. Bevington (Hogarth Press, 1954)

Stephen, Leslie Sir *The Mausoleum Book* Introduction by Alan Bell

(OUP–Clarendon Press, 1977)

Mrs Leslie Stephen, (Julia) *Notes from Sick Rooms Notes from Sick Rooms*: (Puckerbrook Press, 1880).

Styron, William *Darkness Visible: A Memoir of Madness* (Jonathan Cape, 1991)

Tomalin, Claire *Katherine Mansfield: A Secret Life* (Viking, 1987 / Penguin Books, 1988)

Trombley, Stephen *All That Summer She Was Mad: Virginia Woolf and Her Doctors* (Junction Books, 1981)

Wagner-Martin, Linda *Sylvia Plath: A Biography* (Chatto & Windus, 1988 / Cardinal, 1990)

Webb, Beatrice B W Diary The Diary of Beatrice Webb vol. 4, 1924–1943, edited by Norman and Jeanne MacKenzie (London School of Economics / Virago Press, 1985)

Quoted Works by Virginia Woolf

Mrs Dalloway Definitive Collected Edition (Hogarth Press, 1990)

Orlando (Grafton Books, 1987)

'On Being Ill' in *Collected Essays* vol. 4 (Chatto & Windus, 1969)

'Professions for Women' in *The Death of a Moth* (Hogarth Press, 1942)

The Voyage Out (Granada, 1982)

The Waves (Hogarth Press, 1990)

'Thoughts on Peace in an Air Raid' in *The Death of the Moth* (Hogarth Press, 1942)

Three Guineas Introduced by Hermione Lee (Hogarth Press, 1986)

To the Lighthouse (Hogarth Press, 1990)

Index

Abbreviations used:

VW – Virginia Woolf
LW – Leonard Woolf
LS – Leslie Stephen
VB – Vanessa Bell
VSW – Vita Sackville-West
DNB – Dictionary of National Biography